EMOTIONAL INTELLIGENCE
training

ATD Workshop Series

EMOTIONAL INTELLIGENCE
training

KARL MULLE

PRESS

Alexandria, Virginia

ATD Press is an internationally renowned source of insightful and practical information on talent development, workplace learning, and professional development.

ATD Press
1640 King Street
Alexandria, VA 22314

Ordering information for print edition: Books published by ATD Press can be purchased by visiting ATD's website at td.org/books or by calling 800.628.2783 or 703.683.8100.

Library of Congress Control Number: 2016948930 (print edition only)

ISBN-10: 1-60728-098-1
ISBN-13: 978-1-60728-098-9
e-ISBN: 978-1-60728-101-6

ATD Press Editorial Staff:
Director: Kristine Luecker
Manager: Christian Green
Community of Practice Manager, Learning & Development: Amanda Smith

Trainers Publishing House (TPH) Staff:
Publisher: Cat Russo
Project, Editorial, and Production Management: Jacqueline Edlund-Braun
TPH Copyeditor: Tora Estep
Cover and Text Design: Ana Ilieva Foreman/Design
Composition: Kristin Goble, PerfecType, Nashville, TN, and Debra Deysher, Double D Media, Reading, PA

Cover Art: Shutterstock
Presentation Slide and Handout Art: Fotolia
Printed by Data Reproductions Corporation, Auburn Hills, MI, www.datarepro.com

The ATD Workshop Series

Whether you are a professional trainer who needs to pull together a new training program next week, or someone who does a bit of training as a part of your job, you'll find the ATD Workshop Series is a timesaver.

Topics deliver key learning on today's most pressing business needs, including training for change management, coaching, communication skills, customer service, emotional intelligence, facilitation, leadership, new employee orientation, new supervisors, presentation skills, project management, and time management. The series is designed for busy training and HR professionals, consultants, and managers who need to deliver training quickly to optimize performance now.

Each ATD Workshop book provides all the content and trainer's tools you need to create and deliver compelling training guaranteed to

- **enhance** learner engagement
- **deepen** learner understanding
- **increase** learning application.

Each book in the series offers innovative and engaging programs designed by leading experts and grounded in design and delivery best practices and theory. It is like having an expert trainer helping you with each step in the workshop process. The straightforward, practical instructions help you prepare and deliver the workshops quickly and effectively. Flexible timing options allow you to choose from half-day, one-day, and two-day workshop formats, or to create your own, using the tips and strategies presented for customizing the workshops to fit your unique business environment. Each ATD Workshop book also comes with guidance on leveraging learning technologies to maximize workshop design and delivery efficiency and access to all the training materials you will need, including activities, handouts, tools, assessments, and presentation slides.

Contents

Foreword

In 2002, we launched the ASTD Trainer's WorkShop Series—a collection of books authored by practitioners that focused on the design and delivery of training on popular soft-skills topics. The creation of this series was a departure for us. These workshops-in-a-book were created to help internal trainers expedite their program delivery by using appropriate and exceptionally designed content that could be adapted and repurposed.

These topics, dealing with issues ranging from customer service to leadership to manager skills, continue to be important training programs offered in companies and organizations of all sizes and across the globe. The ASTD Trainer's WorkShop Series has helped more than 60,000 trainers and occasional trainers deliver top-notch programs that meet business needs and help drive performance.

And while many things about the delivery of soft-skills training have not changed in the last decade, there have been advances in technology and its use in training. So, when we began talking about how to refresh this popular series, we knew we needed to incorporate technology and new topics. We also wanted to make sure that the new series was cohesively designed and had input from author-practitioners who are, after all, the heart and soul of this series.

In this series, we are pleased to feature the work of outstanding trainers and innovators in the field of talent development. Inside *Emotional Intelligence Training* by Karl Mulle, and each of the titles in the series, you'll find innovative content and fresh program agendas to simplify your delivery of key training topics. You'll also find consistency among titles, with each presented in a contemporary manner, designed by peers, and reflecting the preferences of training professionals who conduct workshops.

We hope that you find tremendous value in the ATD Workshop Series.

Tony Bingham
President & CEO
Association for Talent Development (ATD)
August 2016

Preface

When I was first approached to put together this workshop series I said: "Sure! How hard can it be?" After all, my colleague Jeff Feldman and I had already coauthored a book on emotional intelligence that was published by ASTD Press in 2008. I had designed and delivered numerous half-day, full-day, and two-day workshops on the topic. Then I started putting pen to paper.

I realized very quickly that it is one thing to personally absorb a certain amount of knowledge in this field, interpret that knowledge, and then translate it into a series of very organic learning experiences. It is quite another thing to explain to other people *how to do it* in a written format that is sometimes referred to as a *training manual* or *workshop guide.*

For me to say "I teach this piece first, and this takes 10 minutes. And then I move into this section for 15 minutes, and then we do this activity, and here is how I would debrief it, and so on" is to add a level of structure to the learning experience that only approximates what really happens. In addition, numerous pictures, models, concepts, and even stories get passed around from one trainer to the next and become the pool of information that we collectively share with only one real goal—*that people learn.*

I have done my best to give credit where credit is due and to provide step-by-step instructions about how to teach this material. The important thing is that if you are going to use the slides and handouts and learning activities with accompanying instructions to facilitate a workshop, then I hope that you will ingest the content and deliver it in your own personal style.

The first time I ever taught a course, I was extremely nervous. A professor friend of mine gave me some surprising advice: "Throw away your first 100 clients." I was shocked. Then he said: "I don't mean literally. But it takes time to grow into your style. You have learned a lot, but when you are in the actual training environment, it is just you and your participants. At the end of the day what you are really doing is reaching into your heart, and pulling out the truth that is in you at that moment, and then offering it to others. What they do with it is up to them." I think this is good advice. Do not become too invested in the success or failure of your techniques. Learn and grow yourself as you help others to learn and grow as well.

Please consider these outlines and structures to be *guidelines* that help you find your special place in the world of emotional intelligence training. I am always amazed when companies and organizations opt for six-sigma training and then eliminate other training programs because of "overlap." The reason given is always that it would be an inefficient use of time and money for employees to learn the same material *twice*. It amuses me, because I have taught the same material hundreds of times, and each time I learn something new. I hope you have the same rewarding experience as you present this material wherever you have the opportunity.

Karl Mulle, MACP
Bloomington, Minnesota
August 2016

Introduction

How to Use This Book

What's in This Chapter

- Why emotional intelligence training is important
- What you need to know about training
- Estimates of time required
- A broad view of what the book includes

Why Is Developing Your Emotional Intelligence Important?

Perhaps answering the question "What is emotional intelligence?" will help us to understand why developing your emotional intelligence is important. Emotional intelligence has been defined as *using your emotions intelligently to gain the performance you wish to see within yourself and to achieve interpersonal effectiveness with others.* The definition itself provides us with the reason. So if I desire to achieve my goals in life and have effective relationships, then developing my emotional intelligence is important.

But how do we know that the definition isn't self-serving? According to Daniel Goleman (1998), who has conducted studies in more than 200 large companies: "The research shows that for jobs of all kinds, *emotional intelligence is twice as important* an ingredient of outstanding performance as ability and technical skill combined. The higher you go in the organization, the more important these qualities are for success. When it comes to leadership, they are almost everything."

In many ways, our simple definition doesn't say enough. Emotional intelligence works more like a construct, a comprehensive model that is used to understand how cognitions and emotions impact both personal and interpersonal behaviors. If you are emotionally intelligent, then you are self-aware, you know yourself well, you know your strengths, and you are clear about what you need to develop. You manage impulsive, unpleasant, and disruptive emotions that often lead to unwanted behaviors. You also know how to tap into self-motivating emotions such as confidence, passion, enthusiasm, desire, happiness, and anticipation. You understand other people, how to influence people, how to lead people through times of change, how to handle conflict, and how to build high-performance teams.

Emotional intelligence, then, is the *X-factor* that separates those who are successful at managing their emotional energy and navigating through life from those who find themselves in emotional wreckage, derailed, and sometimes even disqualified from the path to success. It is important to develop because it separates those who know themselves well and take personal responsibility for their actions from those who lack self-awareness and repeat the same mistakes. It separates those who can manage their emotions and motivate themselves from those who are overwhelmed by their emotions and let their emotional impulses control their behaviors. It separates those who are good at connecting with others and creating positive relationships from those who seem insensitive and uncaring. Finally, it is important to develop because it separates those who build rapport, have influence, and collaborate effectively with others from those who are demanding, lack empathy, and are therefore difficult to work with.

Developing emotional intelligence is a lifelong journey. The workshop agendas, activities, and resources in this book are designed to help your workforce better understand themselves and others so that they can build rapport, lead change, handle conflict, and collaborate effectively.

What Do I Need to Know About Training?

The ATD Workshop Series is designed to be adaptable for many levels of both training facilitation and topic expertise. Circle the answers in this quick assessment that most closely align with your state of expertise.

QUICK ASSESSMENT: HOW EXPERT DO I NEED TO BE?			
Question	**Authority**	**Developing Expertise**	**Novice**
What is your level of expertise as a facilitator?	• More than 5 years of experience • Consistently receive awesome evaluations • Lead highly interactive sessions with strong participant engagement	• From 1 to 5 years of experience • Catch myself talking too much • May feel drained after training • Participants sometimes sit back and listen instead of engage	• Less than 1 year of experience • No idea what to do to be successful • Eager to develop a facilitative style

QUICK ASSESSMENT: HOW EXPERT DO I NEED TO BE?			
Question	**Authority**	**Developing Expertise**	**Novice**
How proficient are you with the topic?	• Well versed • Have taken courses • Read books/ authored articles • Created training materials • Am sought out by peers on this topic • It is my passion	• On my way • Have taken courses • Read books • Created workshop materials • Would benefit from the book's support tools	• I can spell it! • Had a course in school • Received feedback from respected colleagues indicating I have a natural inclination for this topic (but feel a bit like an imposter)

Two-fold novice: Your best bet is to stick closely to the materials as they are designed. Spend extra time with the content to learn as much as possible about it. Read the examples and sample stories, and plan examples of your own to share. Also, closely read Chapter 8 on training delivery, and consider practicing with a colleague before delivering the program. Take comfort in the tested materials you are holding and confidence in your ability to apply them!

Developing your expertise in one or both areas: Logical choices for you may include using the outline and materials, and then including material you have developed that is relevant to the topic *and* your participants' workplace needs. Or, take the core content of the materials and revise the learning techniques into interactive approaches you have used with success in the past. Play to your strengths and develop your growth areas using the resources in this volume that complement your existing skills.

Authority twice over: Feel free to adapt the agendas and materials as you see fit and use any materials that you have already developed, or simply incorporate training activities, handouts, and so forth from this volume into your own agenda. Enjoy the benefits of ready-to-use processes and support tools and have fun tailoring them to your preferences and organizational needs.

How Much Time Will Preparation Take?

Putting together and facilitating a training workshop, even when the agendas, activities, tools, and assessments are created for you, can be time consuming. For planning purposes, estimate about four days of preparation time for a two-day course.

What Are the Important Features of the Book?

Section I includes the various workshop designs (from half day to two days) with agendas and thumbnails from presentation slides as well as a chapter on customizing the workshop for your circumstances. The chapters included are

- Chapter 1. Half-Day Workshop (3 to 4 hours program time) + Agenda + PPT (thumbnails)
- Chapter 2. One-Day Workshop (7.5 hours program time) + Agenda + PPT (thumbnails)
- Chapter 3. Two-Day Workshop (15 hours program time) + Agenda + PPT (thumbnails)
- Chapter 4. Customizing the Emotional Intelligence Workshops.

The workshop chapters include advice, instructions, workshop-at-a-glance tables, as well as full program agendas.

Section II is standard from book to book in the ATD Workshop Series as a way to provide a consistent foundation of training principles. This section's chapters follow the ADDIE model—the classic instructional design model named after its steps (analysis, design, development, implementation, and evaluation). The chapters are based on best practices and crafted with input from experienced training practitioners. They are meant to help you get up to speed as quickly as possible. Each chapter includes several additional recurring features to help you understand the concepts and ideas presented. The Bare Minimum gives you the bare bones of what you need to know about the topic. Key Points summarize the most important points of each chapter. What to Do Next guides you to your next action steps. And, finally, the Additional Resources and References sections at the end of each chapter give you options for further reading to broaden your understanding of training design and delivery. Section II chapters include

- Chapter 5. Identifying Needs for Emotional Intelligence Training
- Chapter 6. Understanding the Foundations of Training Design
- Chapter 7. Leveraging Technology to Maximize and Support Design and Delivery
- Chapter 8. Delivering Your Emotional Intelligence Workshop: Be a Great Facilitator
- Chapter 9. Evaluating Workshop Results.

Section III covers information about post-workshop learning:

- Chapter 10. The Follow-Up Coach

Section IV includes thumbnail versions of all the supporting documents for reference and online guidance for accessing the documents online:

- Chapter 11. Learning Activities
- Chapter 12. Assessments
- Chapter 13. Handouts
- Chapter 14. Online Supporting Documents and Downloads.

The book includes everything you need to prepare for and deliver your workshop:

- **Agendas,** the heart of the series, are laid out in three columns for ease of delivery. The first column shows the timing, the second gives the presentation slide number and image for quick reference, and the third gives instructions and facilitation notes. These are designed to be straightforward, simple agendas that you can take into the training room and use to stay on track. They include cues on the learning activities, notes about tools or handouts to include, and other important delivery tips.

- **Learning activities,** which are more detailed than the agendas, cover the objectives of the activity, the time and materials required, the steps involved, variations on the activity in some cases, and wrap-up or debriefing questions or comments.

- **Assessments, handouts, and tools** are the training materials you will provide to learners to support the training program. These can include scorecards for games, instructions, reference materials, samples, self-assessments, and so forth.

- **Presentation media** (PowerPoint slides) are deliberately designed to be simple so that you can customize them for your company and context. They are provided for your convenience. Chapter 7 discusses different forms of technology that you can incorporate into your program, including different types of presentation media.

All the program materials are available for download, customization, and duplication. See Chapter 14 for instructions on how to access the materials.

How Are the Agendas Laid Out?

The following agenda is a sample from the two-day workshop.

Day One: (9:00 a.m. to 4:30 p.m.)

TIMING	SLIDES	ACTIVITIES/NOTES/CONSIDERATIONS
Before the Workshop (at least 60 minutes)		**Workshop Setup** Arrive one hour before the start to ensure the room is set up, equipment works, and materials are arranged for the participants. This gives you time to make them feel truly welcomed. Chatting with them builds a trusting relationship and opens them up for learning.
9:00 a.m. (10 min)	Slide 1 **ATD** Workshop Emotional Intelligence The New Science of Leadership Two-Day Workshop: Day One	**Welcome and Introduction to Emotional Intelligence** Welcome participants and introduce yourself. Let participants know that in this workshop they will explore the topic of emotional intelligence (EI) as it relates to *leadership effectiveness*. Because EI is such a broad topic (and time in this workshop is limited), set the stage for the program by asking participants to introduce themselves to the group and share one learning goal that they have for the workshop. Use this as an opportunity to set expectations for the workshop and to discuss learning objectives. If a participant's learning goal does not align well with the learning objectives for the workshop, write it down as a "sidebar" on a sheet of flipchart paper and let the participant know that you will address these concepts during the Q&A portion of the workshop if time permits. Revisit this list at the end of the program.

TIMING	SLIDES	ACTIVITIES/NOTES/CONSIDERATIONS
9:10 a.m. (5 min)	Slide 2 Learning Objectives: Day One • Understand the four-domain model of emotional intelligence and the 18 competencies that support the domains • Explore the connection between emotional intelligence and leadership • Describe the difference between resonant and dissonant leadership • Define six styles of leadership and how they relate to resonant leadership • Identify which competencies you need to develop to effectively lead others • Learn basic tools for developing competencies that support the visionary leadership style • Learn basic tools for developing competencies that support the coaching leadership style	**Learning Objectives** • **Handout 39: Two-Day Workshop Learning Objectives: The New Science of Leadership** Lay out the basic flow of the workshop. Rather than explaining each objective, explain how each objective will be covered. "I will spend some time talking about. . . . And then we will have a small group discussion . . ." Reference participant learning goals as appropriate.

How Do I Use This Book?

If you've ever read a "Choose Your Own Adventure" book, you will recognize that this book follows a similar principle. Think back to the self-assessment at the beginning of this introduction:

- If you chose *authority*, you can get right to work preparing one of the workshops in Section I. Use Section II as a reference.

- If you chose *developing expertise*, read Section II in depth and skim the topic content.

- If you chose *novice at training and the topic,* then spend some serious time familiarizing yourself with both Sections I and II of this volume as well as the topic content.

Once you have a general sense of the material, assemble your workshop. Select the appropriate agenda and then modify the times and training activities as needed and desired. Assemble the materials and familiarize yourself with the topic, the activities, and the presentation media.

Key Points

- The workshops in this book are designed to be effective at all levels of trainer expertise.

- Good training requires an investment of time.

- The book contains everything you need to create a workshop, including agendas, learning activities, presentation media, assessments, handouts, and tools.

What to Do Next

- Review the agendas presented in Section I and select the best fit for your requirements, time constraints, and budget.

- Based on your level of expertise, skim or read in-depth the chapters in Section II.

- Consider what kind of follow-up learning activities you will want to include with the workshop by reviewing Section III.

Additional Resources

Biech, E. (2008). *10 Steps to Successful Training.* Alexandria, VA: ASTD Press.

Biech, E., ed. (2014). *ASTD Handbook: The Definitive Reference for Training & Development,* 2nd edition. Alexandria, VA: ASTD Press.

Emerson, T., and M. Stewart. (2011). *The Learning and Development Book.* Alexandria, VA: ASTD Press.

Goleman, D. (1998). *Working With Emotional Intelligence.* New York: Bloomsbury.

McCain, D.V. (2015). *Facilitation Basics,* 2nd edition. Alexandria, VA: ATD Press.

Russell, L. (1999). *The Accelerated Learning Fieldbook.* San Francisco: Jossey-Bass/Pfeiffer.

Stolovitch, H.D., and E.J. Keeps. (2011). *Telling Ain't Training,* 2nd edition. Alexandria, VA: ASTD Press.

SECTION I
The Workshops

Chapter 1

Half-Day Emotional Intelligence Workshop: The New Science of Success

What's in This Chapter

- Objectives of the half-day Emotional Intelligence Workshop
- Summary chart for the flow of content and activities
- Half-day program agenda

Do your workshop participants have the goal of increasing their emotional intelligence? Are they getting feedback from coaches, supervisors, or mentors that they need to work on their emotional intelligence? The phrase is often used on development plans or in feedback conversations with varying degrees of understanding about what it actually means on both sides of the conversation—manager and employee. The reason emotional intelligence can be confusing and misunderstood is that it is not a simple behavior that can be easily defined in a competency dictionary. More accurately, it is a set of 18 or more competencies that relate to four or more domains of effectiveness depending on which model is referenced. Most people need help to be able to understand what emotional intelligence is and how to develop more of it. That is where this workshop comes in.

The half-day, one-day, and two-day formats in this series are framed around Daniel Goleman's four domains of emotional intelligence: self-awareness, self-management, social awareness, and relationship management. To figure out which agenda is the right fit for your participants and your organization, start with this question: How many domains can realistically be addressed within the given timeframe? One challenge with designing and delivering a half-day workshop is that the time constraints force you to either explore several topics in less depth or choose a smaller set of topics to explore more thoroughly. Another challenge is trying to cover enough content while still providing opportunities for participants to practice and apply what they are learning. My belief is that it is better to select a more focused set of topics so that you can offer participants the opportunity to learn applicable skills. For that reason, this half-day format has been designed around two of Goleman's domains—self-awareness and self-management—to focus on the new science of *success*.

Any workshop, regardless of length, benefits from incorporating the principles of activity-based training. This workshop design presents activities that engage participants in relevant and meaningful learning experiences, small group discussion, and skills practice. Be sure to allow time for discussion and reflection to increase learning and retention.

Half-Day Workshop Objectives: The New Science of Success

By the end of the half-day workshop, participants will be able to

- Learn about the anatomy of an emotion and how emotions and thoughts work together to influence behaviors
- Understand the link between emotional intelligence and success in life
- Discern the difference between automatic limbic decisions and intentional, conscious decisions
- Discover when their automatic processes serve them well, and when these processes need to be better managed
- Practice agile thinking, increasing self-awareness and intentional thinking
- Leverage due diligence and intuition to make effective decisions
- Develop cognitive and behavioral strategies to *manage emotions intelligently*.

Half-Day Workshop Overview

TOPICS	TIMING
Welcome and Introduction to Emotional Intelligence	5 minutes
Learning Objectives	5 minutes
The Anatomy of an Emotion	5 minutes
Learning Activity 1: When Emotions Get the Best of Us	10 minutes
The Anatomy of an Emotion, Take Two	10 minutes
Two Brain Systems That Control Your Attention	10 minutes
Learning Activity 2: System 1 vs. System 2 Thinking	20 minutes
Agile Thinking: Awareness Plus Intentionality	10 minutes
BREAK	**15 minutes**
Emotions, Thoughts, and Behaviors	10 minutes
Learning Activity 3: Three Behavioral Principles	5 minutes
Learning Activity 4: Behavior Strategies	10 minutes*
Cognitive Strategies	10 minutes
Learning Activity 5: Emotional Triggers Exercise	15 minutes
EQuip Yourself for Success: Manage Expectations	10 minutes
Learning Activity 6: EQuip Yourself for Success: Managing Expectations Discussion	10 minutes
EQuip Yourself for Success: Choose Your Battles	5 minutes
Learning Activity 7: EQuip Yourself for Success: Practice Asking System 2 Questions	10 minutes
Learning Activity 8: EQuip Yourself for Success: Reframe	10 minutes
Q&A	10 minutes
Learning Activity 9: EQuip Yourself for Success: Action Plan	10 minutes
Wrap-Up	5 minutes
TOTAL	**210 minutes (3.5 hours)**

*Or 20 minutes, depending on activity variation chosen. If video clip variation is chosen, an additional 10 minutes will need to be added or made up elsewhere in the agenda timing.

Half-Day Workshop Agenda

You can use the agenda on the following pages as a quick-reference, bird's-eye view to the workshop while you are facilitating. The learning activity pages in Chapter 11 provide the details that support the workshop design, so be sure to have those pages available during your facilitation, as well as a reference set of handouts.

TIMING	SLIDES	ACTIVITIES/NOTES/CONSIDERATIONS
Before the Workshop (at least 60 minutes)		**Workshop Setup** Arrive one hour before the start to ensure the room is set up, equipment works, and materials are arranged for the participants. This gives you time to make them feel truly welcomed. Chatting with them builds a trusting relationship and opens them up for learning.
9:00 a.m. (5 min)	Slide 1 **ATD** Workshop Emotional Intelligence The New Science of Leadership Two-Day Workshop: Day One	**Welcome and Introduction to Emotional Intelligence** Welcome participants and introduce yourself. Let participants know that in this workshop they will explore the topic of emotional intelligence (EI) as it relates to *success*. Because EI is such a broad topic (and time in this workshop is limited), set the stage for the program by asking participants to introduce themselves to the group and share one learning goal that they have for the workshop. Use this as an opportunity to set expectations for the workshop and to discuss learning objectives. If a participant's learning goal does not align well with the learning objectives for the workshop, write it down as a "sidebar" on a sheet of flipchart paper and let the participant know that you will address these concepts during the Q&A portion of the workshop if time permits. Revisit this list at the end of the program.
9:05 a.m. (5 min)	Slide 2 Half-Day Workshop Objectives • Learn about the anatomy of an emotion and how emotions and thoughts work together to influence behaviors • Understand the link between emotional intelligence and success in life • Discern the difference between automatic, limbic decisions and intentional, conscious decisions • Discover when your automatic processes serve you well, and when they need to be better managed • Practice agile thinking, increasing self-awareness and intentional thinking • Leverage diligence and intuition to make effective decisions • Develop cognitive and behavioral strategies to *manage emotions intelligently*	**Learning Objectives** • **Handout 1: Half-Day Workshop Learning Objectives: The New Science of Success** Use the handout and slide to lay out the basic flow of the workshop. Briefly explain how each objective will be covered. Let them know that you will spend some time talking about the ideas and concepts, and then they will have a chance for small group discussion and activities to explore the concepts further.

TIMING	SLIDES	ACTIVITIES/NOTES/CONSIDERATIONS
9:10 a.m. (5 min)	Slide 3 The Anatomy of an Emotion *Once upon a time, I was walking in the forest. . . and I came upon a Big, Bad, ...*	**Learning Content/Lecture** **The Anatomy of an Emotion** • **Handout 2: The Anatomy of an Emotion** Use this handout and set of slides to grab your participants' attention with a quick primer on why emotional intelligence is so important. Begin with a strong statement about how we are wired to experience events and situations *emotionally* before we experience those same events and situations *rationally*. Then explain the anatomy of an emotion using Slides 3 and 4, which serve as a foundation for the course and will help you transition your participants to the first learning activity. I usually stick fairly close to a "script" for this section. Slide 3 presents what I refer to as "the original story of your emotions." Say: Once upon a time you were walking in a forest and you came upon something dangerous—such as a big bear. Your eye saw the bear and immediately sent a message down to your adrenal glands. Your adrenal glands pumped adrenaline into your system, your heart beat faster, your breathing quickened, your palms got sweaty, your muscles tensed up, and you were prepared for fight or flight. NOTE: Both Slides 3 and 4 are animated (if you have licensed the custom version of the slides). Click through the animation at the appropriate portion of the script. If you are using the ready-to-use pdf version of the slide deck, simply point out the portion of the slide as you run through the script. (Slide 1 of 2)

TIMING	SLIDES	ACTIVITIES/NOTES/CONSIDERATIONS
	Slide 4

The Anatomy of an Emotion

An emotion is a signal
to take _____Action_____

That's why it is called an
E-MOTION | Move directly into Slide 4 and say:

Your response was actually an *emotional* response triggering your brain to move you toward taking action. That's essentially what all emotions are—signals to take *action*. That's why it is called e–*motion*.

This second slide makes the point that emotions are *signals*. I often share the analogy of a smoke detector here. The detector signals that there is a fire to pay attention to. Similarly, emotions signal that there is a situation that requires your attention.

After these two introductory slides, flow right into Learning Activity 1.

(Slide 2 of 2) |
| 9:15 a.m.

(10 min) | Slide 5

When Emotions Get the Best of Us

Think of a real-life example in which your emotions took control of your behaviors and caused you to do something that you later regretted. Turn to the person next to you and answer the following:

1. What was the situation?
2. What were you feeling?
3. What did you do?
4. What were the consequences? | **Learning Activity 1: When Emotions Get the Best of Us**

• **Handout 3: When Emotions Get the Best of Us**

This small group activity will help participants connect with the reason we all need this workshop. It will lead them to identify a past experience that they will revisit during the application phase of the workshop.

Use this slide and the instructions in the learning activity to conduct the discussion. There is no need to debrief this activity, except to mention that you will revisit these stories later in the workshop. |

TIMING	SLIDES	ACTIVITIES/NOTES/CONSIDERATIONS
9:25 a.m. (10 min)	Slide 6 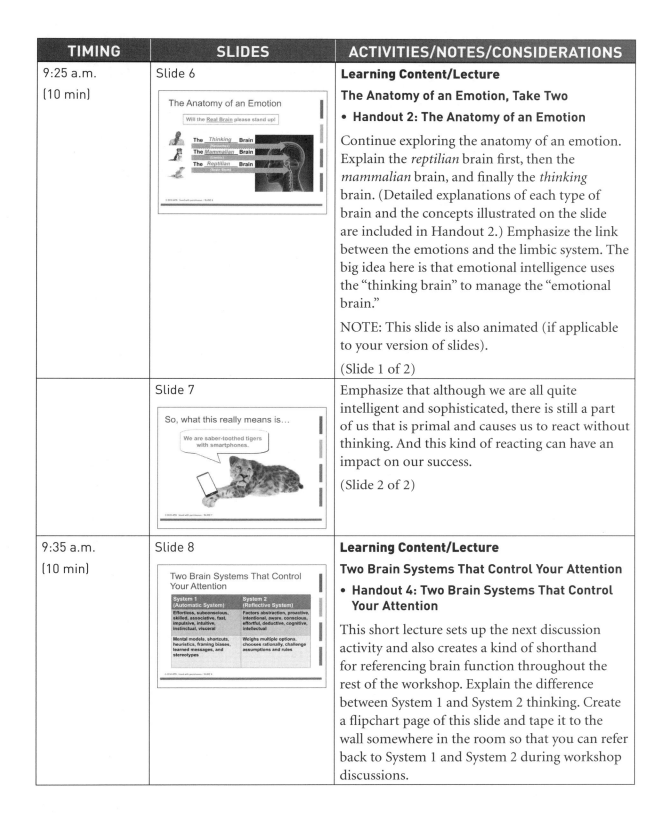	**Learning Content/Lecture** **The Anatomy of an Emotion, Take Two** • **Handout 2: The Anatomy of an Emotion** Continue exploring the anatomy of an emotion. Explain the *reptilian* brain first, then the *mammalian* brain, and finally the *thinking* brain. (Detailed explanations of each type of brain and the concepts illustrated on the slide are included in Handout 2.) Emphasize the link between the emotions and the limbic system. The big idea here is that emotional intelligence uses the "thinking brain" to manage the "emotional brain." NOTE: This slide is also animated (if applicable to your version of slides). (Slide 1 of 2)
	Slide 7	Emphasize that although we are all quite intelligent and sophisticated, there is still a part of us that is primal and causes us to react without thinking. And this kind of reacting can have an impact on our success. (Slide 2 of 2)
9:35 a.m. (10 min)	Slide 8	**Learning Content/Lecture** **Two Brain Systems That Control Your Attention** • **Handout 4: Two Brain Systems That Control Your Attention** This short lecture sets up the next discussion activity and also creates a kind of shorthand for referencing brain function throughout the rest of the workshop. Explain the difference between System 1 and System 2 thinking. Create a flipchart page of this slide and tape it to the wall somewhere in the room so that you can refer back to System 1 and System 2 during workshop discussions.

TIMING	SLIDES	ACTIVITIES/NOTES/CONSIDERATIONS
9:45 a.m. (20 min)	Slide 9 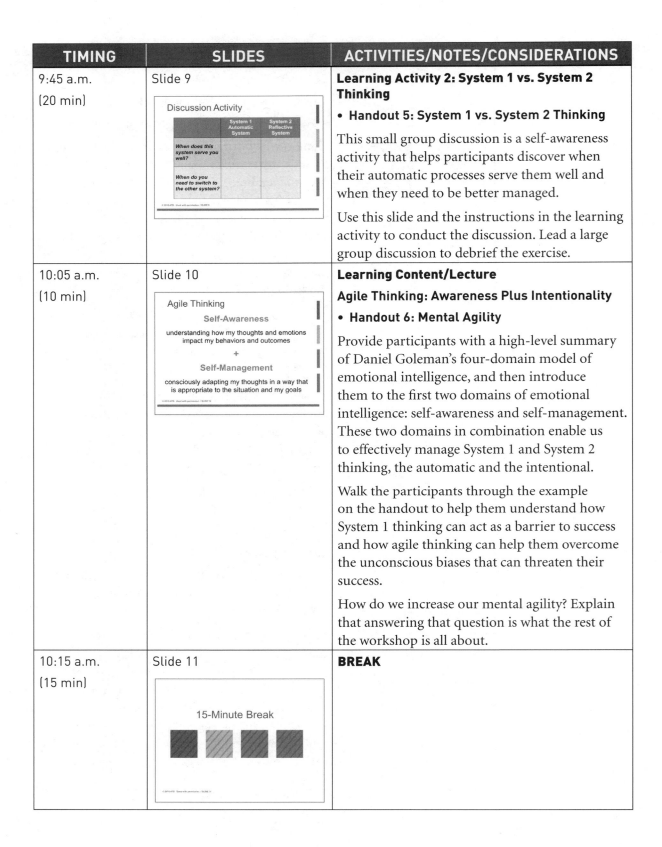	**Learning Activity 2: System 1 vs. System 2 Thinking** • **Handout 5: System 1 vs. System 2 Thinking** This small group discussion is a self-awareness activity that helps participants discover when their automatic processes serve them well and when they need to be better managed. Use this slide and the instructions in the learning activity to conduct the discussion. Lead a large group discussion to debrief the exercise.
10:05 a.m. (10 min)	Slide 10	**Learning Content/Lecture** **Agile Thinking: Awareness Plus Intentionality** • **Handout 6: Mental Agility** Provide participants with a high-level summary of Daniel Goleman's four-domain model of emotional intelligence, and then introduce them to the first two domains of emotional intelligence: self-awareness and self-management. These two domains in combination enable us to effectively manage System 1 and System 2 thinking, the automatic and the intentional. Walk the participants through the example on the handout to help them understand how System 1 thinking can act as a barrier to success and how agile thinking can help them overcome the unconscious biases that can threaten their success. How do we increase our mental agility? Explain that answering that question is what the rest of the workshop is all about.
10:15 a.m. (15 min)	Slide 11	**BREAK**

TIMING	SLIDES	ACTIVITIES/NOTES/CONSIDERATIONS
10:30 a.m. (10 min)	Slide 12 Emotions, Thoughts, and Behaviors A Holistic Model reinforce → Thoughts → influence Emotions Emotions reinforce ↖ Behaviors ↩ influence	**Learning Content/Lecture** **Emotions, Thoughts, and Behaviors** • **Handout 7: Emotions, Thoughts, and Behaviors** Use this handout and slide to help participants develop cognitive and behavioral strategies to *manage emotions intelligently*. Be sure to emphasize the key learning point here: People manage their emotions by managing either their *cognitions* or their *behaviors*. NOTE: This slide is animated (if applicable to your version of slides).
10:40 a.m. (5 min)	Slide 13 Emotions, Thoughts, and Behaviors **Three Behavioral Principles** • **Principle 1:** Emotions and behaviors do not like to operate in ways that are incongruent with one another. • **Principle 2:** Behaviors can lead emotions just as emotions can lead behaviors. • **Principle 3:** It is often easier to control behaviors than emotions.	**Learning Activity 3: Three Behavioral Principles** • **Handout 8: Behavioral Strategies for Managing Your Emotions** Use the slide and handout to briefly overview the three behavioral principles to help manage emotions. The activity will get the participants out of their seats and discovering the importance of congruence between emotions and behavior. Follow the instructions in the learning activity to conduct and debrief the activity. Learning Activity 3 will roll right into Learning Activity 4.
10:45 a.m. (10 min) (or 20 min if you choose the video clip option)	Slide 14 Behavioral Strategies Discussion	**Learning Activity 4: Behavior Strategies** This activity will help participants understand and experience the physiology behind behaviors and emotions. You can choose one of two options for this activity. You will need to adjust timing, depending on which variation you choose. Use the instructions in the learning activity to conduct this activity.

TIMING	SLIDES	ACTIVITIES/NOTES/CONSIDERATIONS
10:55 a.m. (10 min)	Slide 15 Emotions, Thoughts, and Behaviors The ABCs of Life Activating event Belief or self-talk Consequential emotional response Dispute your thinking	**Learning Content/Lecture** **Cognitive Strategies** • **Handout 9: Cognitive Strategies and the ABCs of Life** Use this slide and handout to discuss how to use cognitive strategies to manage emotions. Briefly present Ellis' ABCs of Life model to the participants, emphasizing his basic thesis: Your feelings follow your beliefs; what you believe about your world determines how you feel. NOTE: This slide is animated (if applicable to your version of slides).
11:05 a.m. (15 min)	Slide 16 Emotional Triggers Exercise 	A	B	C	D	 Emotional Trigger	Underlying Belief or Value	Impact When Triggered	What Can I Do? (cognitive or behavioral strategies) Example: Being unfairly judged or treated.	**Learning Activity 5: Emotional Triggers Exercise** • **Handout 10: Emotional Triggers Exercise** This activity revisits the examples the participants identified earlier that described a time when their emotions got the best of them. Or they are free to come up with a different example to use here if they desire. They will use this story to practice System 2 thinking to manage their thoughts. You may want to work through the chart with the participants using the example given on the slide to get them started. Use this slide and the instructions in the learning activity to conduct and debrief the activity.

TIMING	SLIDES	ACTIVITIES/NOTES/CONSIDERATIONS
11:20 a.m. (10 min)	Slide 17 EQuip Yourself for Success 1. Manage Your Expectations **Expectations** **Reality**	**Learning Content/Lecture** **EQuip Yourself for Success: Manage Expectations** • **Handout 11: EQuip Yourself for Success: Manage Expectations** Explain that any slide or handout in the workshop that begins with the phrase "EQuip Yourself for Success" will share an application point. In the next section of the workshop they will explore four application points for managing emotions by managing thoughts: 1. Manage expectations 2. Choose your battles 3. Practice asking System 2 questions 4. Reframe. To discuss this slide, begin with the idea that one of the principal sources of emotional conflict and resentment in the workplace is the mismatch between what we expect and what we actually get from the people we depend on to deliver results. The two parallel lines represent this mismatch with *Expectations* above the top line and *Reality* below the bottom line. The arrow between the two represents how expectations often fall short of reality. Then reemphasize the idea that the principal source of emotional conflict and resentment in the workplace is the *mismatch* between what we expect and what we actually get from the people we depend on to deliver results. This content will set up the next learning activity, which gives participants a chance to practice a managing expectations conversation. NOTE: This slide is animated (if you have licensed the custom version of the slides). If you are using the ready-to-use pdf version of the slides, point out the portion of the slide as you discuss it.

TIMING	SLIDES	ACTIVITIES/NOTES/CONSIDERATIONS
11:30 a.m. (10 min)	Slide 18 EQuip Yourself for Success Managing Expectations Discussion • What do you expect of yourself? • What do you expect of me? • What do I expect of myself? • What do I expect of you?	**Learning Activity 6: EQuip Yourself for Success: Managing Expectations Discussion** • **Handout 12: EQuip Yourself for Success: Manage Expectations Discussion** This application activity is designed to engage System 2 thinking to avoid System 1's tendency to get upset when expectations are not clearly defined. The takeaway for participants who have a difficult time with this activity is that they actually need to conduct these kinds of conversations in real life. Use this slide and the instructions in the learning activity to conduct and debrief the activity.
11:40 a.m. (5 min)	Slide 19 EQuip Yourself for Success 2. Choose Your Battles 5¢ 10¢ 9–9–9 RULE	**Learning Content/Lecture** **EQuip Yourself for Success: Choose Your Battles** • **Handout 13: EQuip Yourself for Success: Choose Your Battles** This second application of cognitive strategies is designed to engage System 2 thinking to avoid System 1's tendency to spend emotional energy on unworthy battles. Introduce this slide by explaining that the events and experiences of life belong on a continuum somewhere between "nickle and dime stuff" and the saber-toothed tigers of life. Explain the 9-9-9 Rule and its powerful questions on the handout.
11:45 a.m. (10 min)	Slide 20 EQuip Yourself for Success 3. Practice Asking System 2 Questions System 1 Questions / System 2 Questions Example: Why are you so difficult? / What can I do to support you?	**Learning Activity 7: EQuip Yourself for Success: Practice Asking System 2 Questions** • **Handout 14: EQuip Yourself for Success: Practice Asking System 2 Questions** The third application of cognitive strategies is designed to engage System 2 thinking to avoid System 1's tendency to ask critical judging questions instead of listening and learning questions. Use this slide and the instructions in the learning activity to conduct and debrief the activity.

TIMING	SLIDES	ACTIVITIES/NOTES/CONSIDERATIONS
11:55 a.m. (10 min)	Slide 21 EQuip Yourself for Success 4. Reframe	**Learning Activity 8: EQuip Yourself for Success: Reframe** • **Handout 15: EQuip Yourself for Success: The Power of Reframes** The fourth application of cognitive strategies is designed to engage System 2 thinking to avoid System 1's tendency to stereotype people or jump to negative conclusions about people. Use this slide and the instructions in the learning activity to conduct and debrief the activity.
12:05 p.m. (10 min)	Slide 22 Q & A	**Q&A** There are three parts to facilitating the Q&A. First, let participants know the workshop is not over yet. Say: "Before I give you time to work on your action plan, what questions do you have about today's workshop?" Second, wait a full 7 seconds to give people time to reflect and process. Third, if there is time after you have addressed their questions, revisit any learning goals that participants discussed at the beginning of the workshop (and recorded on the flipchart) that were not covered by the program. Refer participants to the one-day or two-day program, if appropriate.
12:15 p.m. (10 min)	Slide 23 Action Plan ☑ IDEA ☑ PLAN ☑ ACTION ☑ SUCCESS	**Learning Activity 9: EQuip Yourself for Success: Action Plan** • **Handout 16: EQuip Yourself for Success: Action Plan** This activity is designed to create alignment between the workshop content and the participants' development plans. Give participants 10 minutes to reflect on lessons learned and to fill out the action plan as outlined in Handout 16.

TIMING	SLIDES	ACTIVITIES/NOTES/CONSIDERATIONS
12:25 p.m. (5 min) Ends at 12:30 p.m.	Slide 24 Wrap-Up Key Learning Points	**Wrap-Up** • **Assessment 1: Workshop Evaluation** Close workshop on a positive note. Distribute the workshop evaluations. As they are completing the evaluations, ask them to think about the most valuable idea or strategy they learned today. When you have all the evaluations, ask everyone to form a circle. Start by sharing something that *you* learned today. Then toss a soft throwing object such as a Koosh ball to one participant and ask him or her to share a key learning point. Continue tossing the ball around the circle until everyone who is willing to share has shared. Be available to answer any questions participants may still have about the workshop content. Share plans for follow-up coaching, if applicable (see Chapter 10 for ideas to follow up the training with support and activities). Thank participants for their contributions and wish them well.

What to Do Next

- Determine the schedule for training workshops; reserve location and catering you may wish to provide.

- Identify and invite participants.

- Inform participants about any pre-work, if applicable, that you want completed before the workshop begins.

- Review the workshop objectives, activities, and handouts to plan the content you will use.

- Prepare copies of the participant materials and any activity-related materials you may need. Refer to Chapter 14 for information about how to access and use the supplemental materials provided for this workshop.

- Gather tactile items, such as Koosh balls, crayons, magnets, Play-Doh, or others, that you wish to place on the tables for tactile learners. See Chapter 8 for other ideas to enhance the learning environment of your workshop.

- Prepare yourself both emotionally and physically. Confirm that you have addressed scheduling and personal concerns so that you can be fully present to facilitate the workshop.

References

Ellis, A. (1988). *How to Stubbornly Refuse to Make Yourself Miserable About Anything.* Secaucus, NJ: Carol Publishing.

Ellis, A. (1997). *How to Control Your Anger Before It Controls You.* Secaucus, NJ: Carol Publishing.

Goleman D. (1995). *Emotional Intelligence: Why It Can Matter More Than IQ.* New York: Bantam.

Goleman, D. (1998). *Working With Emotional Intelligence.* New York: Bantam.

Kahneman, D. (2011). *Thinking Fast and Slow.* New York: Farrar, Straus, and Giroux.

Chapter 2

One-Day Emotional Intelligence Workshop: The New Science of Relationships

What's in This Chapter

- Objectives of the one-day Emotional Intelligence Workshop
- Summary chart for the flow of content and activities
- One-day program agenda

There are several approaches you can take to designing and delivering a one-day workshop on emotional intelligence. Broadly speaking, emotional intelligence is a set of 18 or more competencies that relate to Goleman's (1998) four emotional intelligence domains: self-awareness, self-management, social awareness, and relationship management.

The half-day, one-day, and two-day agendas in this book use these four domains as their foundation. To figure out which agenda is the right fit for your participants and your organization, start with this question: How many domains can realistically be addressed within the given timeframe? If the goal is a general overview, then elements of the half-day and one-day workshops as outlined in Chapters 1 and 2 can be combined to create a more introductory workshop. The domains lend themselves nicely to a one-day program that focuses on *self* in the morning and *others* in the afternoon. In my experience, however, a more general one-day session tends to leave participants wanting to dive deeper into the relationship domains. For that reason I have chosen to focus the one-day format on *relationship effectiveness*.

Any workshop, regardless of length, benefits from incorporating the principles of active training. This workshop design presents activities that engage participants in relevant and meaningful learning experiences, small group discussion, and skills practice. Be sure to allow time for discussion and reflection to increase learning and retention.

One-Day Workshop Objectives: The New Science of Relationships

By the end of the one-day workshop, participants will be able to

- Learn about the anatomy of an emotion and how emotions and thoughts work together to influence behaviors
- Explore the four-domain model of emotional intelligence
- Define *emotional intelligence* as a set of competencies that can be learned
- Explore the competencies related to social awareness and relationship effectiveness
- Practice how to build rapport and demonstrate empathy
- Manage defensiveness and develop collaborative intention
- Understand discretionary emotional energy and explore the conditions that increase employee engagement
- Increase influence by mapping out and evaluating personal influence networks
- Develop strategies for increasing teamwork and collaboration among team members with different emotional triggers
- Increase confidence in managing conflict and difficult emotional conversations.

One-Day Workshop Overview

TOPICS	TIMING
Welcome and Introduction to Emotional Intelligence	10 minutes
Learning Objectives	5 minutes
The Anatomy of an Emotion	20 minutes
Learning Activity 10: The E-Motion Chart	20 minutes
Emotional Intelligence Defined	5 minutes
Learning Activity 11: Self-Awareness Competencies	5 minutes

TOPICS	TIMING
Learning Activity 12: Self-Management Competencies	10 minutes
BREAK	**15 minutes**
Learning Activity 13: Social Awareness Competencies	5 minutes
Learning Activity 14: Relationship Management Competencies	10 minutes
Learning Activity 15: The Emotional Competency of Empathy	10 minutes
Effective Listening	5 minutes
Learning Activity 16: Effective Listening Exercise	30 minutes
Creating a Collaborative Environment	10 minutes
Learning Activity 17: Collaborative Intention Self-Assessment	5 minutes
Learning Activity 18: Empathy and Feeling Blockers	15 minutes
LUNCH	**60 Minutes**
The Competencies of Inspiration and Influence	5 minutes
Learning Activity 19: Discretionary Emotional Energy	25 minutes
EQuip Yourself for Success: Build the Relationship Before You Need It	5 minutes
Learning Activity 20: Map Your Personal Influence Network	10 minutes
Learning Activity 21: Evaluate Your Personal Influence Network	15 minutes
EQuip Yourself for Success: Practice Personality Talk	15 minutes
BREAK	**15 minutes**
Learning Activity 22: Personality Talk	45 minutes
Learning Activity 23: Teaming and Collaboration Action Plan	10 minutes
EQuip Yourself for Success: Understand Two Messages and Build Communication Rapport	1 minute
Learning Activity 24: The Two Messages	4 minutes
Learning Activity 25: Building Rapport	10 minutes
The Competency of Conflict Management	20 minutes
Learning Activity 26: Practice XYZ Talk	15 minutes
Q&A	5 minutes
Learning Activity 27: EQuip Yourself for Success: Action Plan	5 minutes
Wrap-Up	5 minutes
TOTAL	**450 minutes (7.5 hours)**

One-Day Workshop Agenda

You can use the agenda on the following pages as a quick-reference, bird's-eye view to the workshop while you are facilitating. The learning activity pages in Chapter 11 provide the details that support the workshop design, so be sure to have those pages available during your facilitation, as well as a reference set of handouts.

TIMING	SLIDES	ACTIVITIES/NOTES/CONSIDERATIONS
Before the Workshop (at least 60 minutes)		**Workshop Setup** Arrive one hour before the start to ensure the room is set up, equipment works, and materials are arranged for the participants. This gives you time to make them feel truly welcomed. Chatting with them builds a trusting relationship and opens them up for learning.
9:00 a.m. (10 min)	Slide 1 ATD Workshop Emotional Intelligence The New Science of Relationships One-Day Workshop	**Welcome and Introduction to Emotional Intelligence** Welcome participants and introduce yourself. Let participants know that in this workshop they will explore the topic of emotional intelligence (EI) as it relates to *relationship effectiveness*. Because EI is such a broad topic (and time in this workshop is limited), set the stage for the program by asking participants to introduce themselves to the group and share one learning goal that they have for the workshop. Use this as an opportunity to set expectations for the workshop and to discuss learning objectives. If a participant's learning goal does not align well with the learning objectives for the workshop, write it down as a "sidebar" on a sheet of flipchart paper and let the participant know that you will address these concepts during the Q&A portion of the workshop if time permits. Revisit this list at the end of the program.
9:10 a.m. (5 min)	Slide 2 One-Day Workshop Objectives • Learn how emotions and thoughts influence behaviors • Explore the four-domain model of emotional intelligence (EI) • Define EI as a set of competencies that can be learned • Explore social awareness and relationship effectiveness • Practice how to build rapport and demonstrate empathy • Manage defensiveness and develop collaborative intention • Understand discretionary emotional energy; increase engagement • Develop strategies for increasing teamwork and collaboration • Increase influence by evaluating personal influence networks • Increase confidence in managing conflict and emotional conversations	**Learning Objectives** • **Handout 17: One-Day Workshop Learning Objectives: The New Science of Relationships** Use this handout and slide to lay out the basic flow of the workshop. Briefly explain how each objective will be covered. Let them know that you will spend some time talking about the ideas and concepts, and then they will have a chance for small group discussion and activities to explore the concepts further.

TIMING	SLIDES	ACTIVITIES/NOTES/CONSIDERATIONS
9:15 a.m. (20 min)	Slide 3 The Anatomy of an Emotion Once upon a time, I was walking in the forest. . . and I came upon a Big, Bad, ----- © 2016 ATD. Used with permission. / SLIDE 1	**Learning Content/Lecture** • **Handout 18: The Anatomy of an Emotion** Use this handout and set of slides to grab your participants' attention with a quick primer on why emotional intelligence is so important. Begin with a strong statement about how we are wired to experience events and situations *emotionally* before we experience those same events and situations *rationally*. Then explain the anatomy of an emotion using Slides 3 and 4, which serve as a foundation for the course and help you transition your participants to the first learning activity. I usually stick fairly close to a "script" for this section. Slide 3 presents what I refer to as "the original story of your emotions." Say: > Once upon a time you were walking in a forest and you came upon something dangerous—such as a big bear. Your eye saw the bear and immediately sent a message down to your adrenal glands. Your adrenal glands pumped adrenaline into your system, your heart beat faster, your breathing quickened, your palms got sweaty, your muscles tensed up, and you were prepared for fight or flight. NOTE: Both Slides 3 and 4 are animated (if you have licensed the custom version of the slides). Click through the animation at the appropriate portion of the script. If you are using the ready-to-use pdf version of the slide deck, simply point out the portion of the slide as you run through the script. (Slide 1 of 4)

TIMING	SLIDES	ACTIVITIES/NOTES/CONSIDERATIONS
	Slide 4 The Anatomy of an Emotion **An emotion is a signal** to take _____ Action **That's why it is called an** E–MOTION	Move directly into Slide 4 and say: Your response was actually an *emotional* response triggering your brain to move you toward taking action. That's essentially what all emotions are—signals to take *action*. That's why it is called e–*motion*. (Slide 2 of 4)
	Slide 5 The Anatomy of an Emotion Will the Real Brain please stand up! The *Thinking* Brain (Neocortex) The *Mammalian* Brain (Limbic) The *Reptilian* Brain (Brain Stem)	Continue exploring the anatomy of an emotion. Explain the *reptilian* brain first, then the *mammalian* brain, and finally the *thinking* brain. (Detailed explanations of each type of brain and the concepts illustrated on the slide are included in Handout 18.) Emphasize the link between emotions and the limbic system. The big idea here is that emotional intelligence uses the "thinking brain" to manage the "emotional brain." NOTE: This slide is also animated (if applicable to your version of slides). (Slide 3 of 4)
	Slide 6 So, what this really means is… We are saber-toothed tigers with smartphones.	Emphasize that although we are all quite intelligent and sophisticated, there is still a part of us that is primal and causes us to react without thinking. And this kind of reacting can have an impact on our success. (Slide 4 of 4)
9:35 a.m. (20 min)	Slide 7 The E-Motion Chart The Emotion / +/– / Signal to Hear / When the Emotion Controls Me Anger/Defensiveness Anxiety/Fear Guilt/Shame Depression/Burnout	**Learning Activity 10: The E-Motion Chart** • **Handout 19: The E-Motion Chart** This small group activity focuses participants on discussing the signals that emotions send them. They will come to understand that emotions are to be embraced as a kind of biofeedback that enables them to better navigate life. Use this slide and the instructions in the learning activity to conduct the discussion and debrief the activity. Be prepared to supplement group responses if the participants miss any key insights.

TIMING	SLIDES	ACTIVITIES/NOTES/CONSIDERATIONS
9:55 a.m. (5 min)	**Slide 8** "The rules of work are changing. We are being judged by a new yardstick: not just by how smart we are, or by our training and expertise, but also by how well we handle ourselves and each other." — Daniel Goleman *Working With Emotional Intelligence*	**Learning Content/Lecture** **Emotional Intelligence Defined** **• Handout 20: Emotional Intelligence Defined** This group of slides introduces participants to Daniel Goleman's four-domain model of emotional intelligence. Share his quote, which highlights that EI is all about how we manage ourselves and our relationships. (Slide 1 of 4)
	Slide 9 Emotional Intelligence Defined Emotional intelligence is… Using your emotions *intelligently,* to gain the performance you wish to see within yourself, and *to achieve interpersonal effectiveness with others.* —Jeff Feldman and Karl Mulle *Put Emotional Intelligence to Work*	Share another definition to deepen their understanding of emotional intelligence. (Slide 2 of 4)
	Slide 10 Emotional Intelligence Defined Emotional intelligence at work is the capacity for… • Self-Awareness—recognizing your feelings and behaviors • Self-Management—managing your feelings and behaviors, and staying motivated in spite of setbacks and obstacles • Social Awareness—understanding what others feel • Relationship Management—building rapport and collaborating with others	This definition is further broken down into four categories of human behavior that Goleman calls the four domains of emotional intelligence. Delineate these four categories and then show participants the four-domain model on the next slide. (Slide 3 of 4)
	Slide 11 The Four-Domain Model 		Personal Competence	Social Competence
Recognition	Self-Awareness	Social Awareness
Regulation	Self-Management	Relationship Management		Show participants this visual graphic of the four-domain model and then briefly recap: There are behaviors that ultimately help us manage our emotional/limbic impulses, and these behaviors fall into four categories that we recognize as the four-domain model of emotional intelligence. Before advancing to the next slide, explain to participants that each of the domains is further broken down into a set of competency behaviors. This is good news: If we can define something behaviorally, then we can develop it. (Slide 4 of 4)

TIMING	SLIDES	ACTIVITIES/NOTES/CONSIDERATIONS
10:00 a.m. (5 min)	Slide 12 18 Competencies **Self-Awareness** • **Emotional Self-Awareness:** Reading one's own emotions and recognizing their impact • **Accurate Self-Assessment:** Knowing one's strengths and limits • **Self-Confidence:** A sound sense of one's self-worth and capabilities.	**Learning Activity 11: Self-Awareness Competencies** • **Handout 21: Self-Awareness Competencies** Briefly describe the competencies of *self-awareness* and give participants 5 minutes in small groups to discuss the situational importance of these competencies in the workplace. Use this slide and the instructions in the learning activity to conduct the discussion. You will not need to debrief this exercise.
10:05 a.m. (10 min)	Slide 13 18 Competencies **Self-Management** • **Emotional Self-Control:** Keeping disruptive emotions and impulses under control • **Transparency:** Displaying honesty and integrity; trustworthiness • **Adaptability:** Flexibility in adapting to changing situations or overcoming obstacles • **Achievement or Self-Motivation:** Drive to improve performance to meet inner standards of excellence • **Initiative:** Readiness to act and seize opportunities • **Optimism:** Seeing the upside in events	**Learning Activity 12: Self-Management Competencies** • **Handout 22: Self-Management Competencies** Briefly describe the competencies of *self-management* and give participants 10 minutes in discussion groups to discuss the situational importance of these competencies in the workplace. Use this slide and the instructions in the learning activity to conduct the discussion. You will not need to debrief this exercise.
10:15 a.m. (15 min)	Slide 14 15-Minute Break	**BREAK**
10:30 a.m. (5 min)	Slide 15 18 Competencies **Social Awareness** • **Empathy:** Sensing others' emotions, understanding their perspectives, and taking active interest in their concerns • **Organizational Awareness:** Reading the currents, decision networks, and politics at the organizational level • **Service:** Recognizing and meeting follower, client, or customer needs	**Learning Activity 13: Social Awareness Competencies** • **Handout 23: Social Awareness Competencies** Briefly describe the competencies of *social awareness* and give participants 5 minutes in discussion groups to discuss the situational importance of these competencies in the workplace. Use this slide and the instructions in the learning activity to conduct the discussion. You will not need to debrief this exercise.

TIMING	SLIDES	ACTIVITIES/NOTES/CONSIDERATIONS
10:35 a.m. (10 min)	Slide 16 18 Competencies **Relationship Management** • **Inspirational Leadership:** Guiding and motivating with a compelling vision • **Influence:** Wielding a range of tactics for persuasion • **Developing Others:** Bolstering others' abilities through feedback and guidance • **Change Catalyst:** Initiating, managing, and leading in a new direction • **Conflict Management:** Resolving disagreements • **Teamwork and Collaboration:** Cooperation and team building	**Learning Activity 14: Relationship Management Competencies** • **Handout 24: Relationship Management Competencies** Briefly describe the competencies of *relationship management* and give participants 10 minutes in discussion groups to discuss the situational importance of these competencies in the workplace. Use this slide and the instructions in the learning activity to conduct the discussion. To debrief this exercise, explain that for the first half of the day, the workshop focuses almost entirely on *self-awareness* and *self-management* and then the second half focuses on *social awareness* and *relationship management.*
10:45 a.m. (10 min)	Slide 17 The Competency of Empathy **Your Understanding** Your view of the situation, your perspective, your intention, your needs and feelings, your behaviors **Their Understanding** Their view of the situation, their perspectives, their intentions, their needs and feelings, their behaviors Understanding Gap On whose side of the gap do you start to build the bridge?	**Learning Activity 15: The Emotional Competency of Empathy** • **Handout 25: The Emotional Competency of Empathy** This demonstration activity will help participants explore the emotional competency of empathy, which is the foundation of all relationship effectiveness. Choose two participants to demonstrate what it really means to develop empathy. Use this slide and the instructions in the learning activity to conduct the discussion. Rather than debrief this activity, simply use it as a transition to the next section on effective listening.
10:55 a.m. (5 min)	Slide 18 Effective Listening Listening is... Ensuring that what left your mind is what arrived in my heart and mind without distortion. —John Powell [paraphrased]	**Learning Content/Lecture** • **Handout 26: Effective Listening** Read the quote from John Powell and then ask: "So how do we do it?" (Slide 1 of 2)

TIMING	SLIDES	ACTIVITIES/NOTES/CONSIDERATIONS
	Slide 19 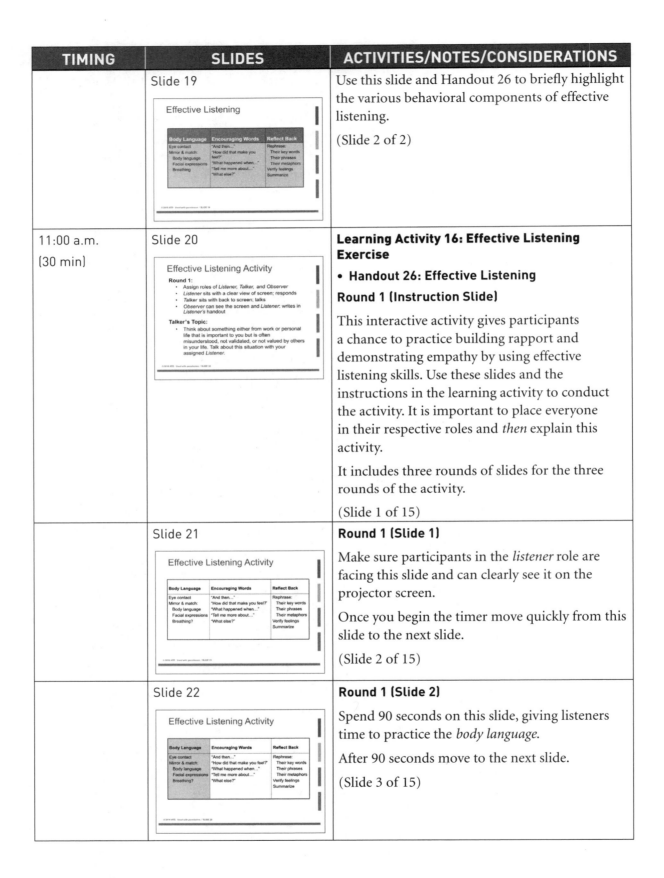	Use this slide and Handout 26 to briefly highlight the various behavioral components of effective listening. (Slide 2 of 2)
11:00 a.m. (30 min)	Slide 20	**Learning Activity 16: Effective Listening Exercise** • **Handout 26: Effective Listening** **Round 1 (Instruction Slide)** This interactive activity gives participants a chance to practice building rapport and demonstrating empathy by using effective listening skills. Use these slides and the instructions in the learning activity to conduct the activity. It is important to place everyone in their respective roles and *then* explain this activity. It includes three rounds of slides for the three rounds of the activity. (Slide 1 of 15)
	Slide 21	**Round 1 (Slide 1)** Make sure participants in the *listener* role are facing this slide and can clearly see it on the projector screen. Once you begin the timer move quickly from this slide to the next slide. (Slide 2 of 15)
	Slide 22	**Round 1 (Slide 2)** Spend 90 seconds on this slide, giving listeners time to practice the *body language*. After 90 seconds move to the next slide. (Slide 3 of 15)

TIMING	SLIDES	ACTIVITIES/NOTES/CONSIDERATIONS
	Slide 23 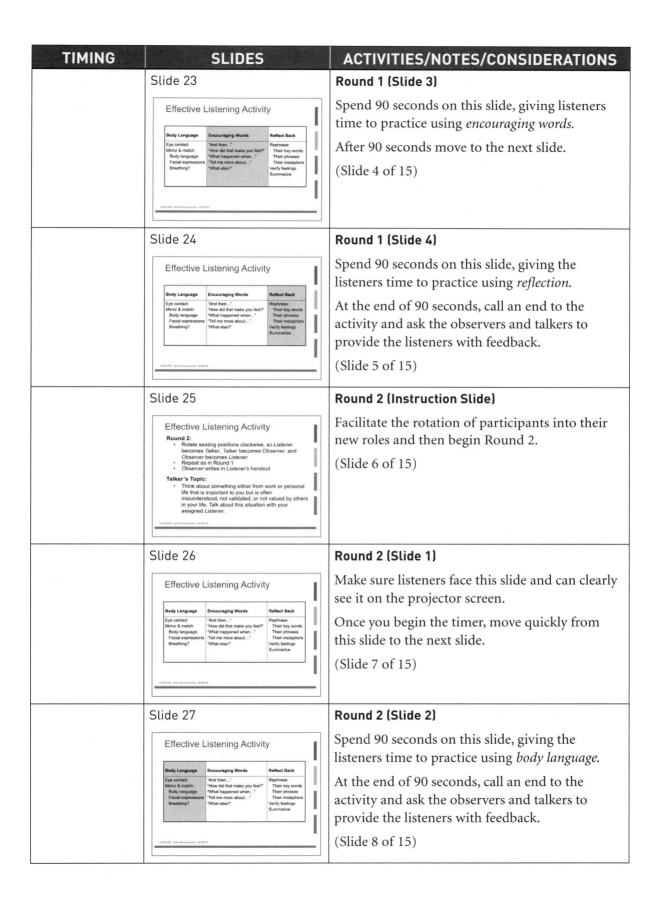	**Round 1 (Slide 3)** Spend 90 seconds on this slide, giving listeners time to practice using *encouraging words*. After 90 seconds move to the next slide. (Slide 4 of 15)
	Slide 24	**Round 1 (Slide 4)** Spend 90 seconds on this slide, giving the listeners time to practice using *reflection*. At the end of 90 seconds, call an end to the activity and ask the observers and talkers to provide the listeners with feedback. (Slide 5 of 15)
	Slide 25	**Round 2 (Instruction Slide)** Facilitate the rotation of participants into their new roles and then begin Round 2. (Slide 6 of 15)
	Slide 26	**Round 2 (Slide 1)** Make sure listeners face this slide and can clearly see it on the projector screen. Once you begin the timer, move quickly from this slide to the next slide. (Slide 7 of 15)
	Slide 27	**Round 2 (Slide 2)** Spend 90 seconds on this slide, giving the listeners time to practice using *body language*. At the end of 90 seconds, call an end to the activity and ask the observers and talkers to provide the listeners with feedback. (Slide 8 of 15)

TIMING	SLIDES	ACTIVITIES/NOTES/CONSIDERATIONS
	Slide 28 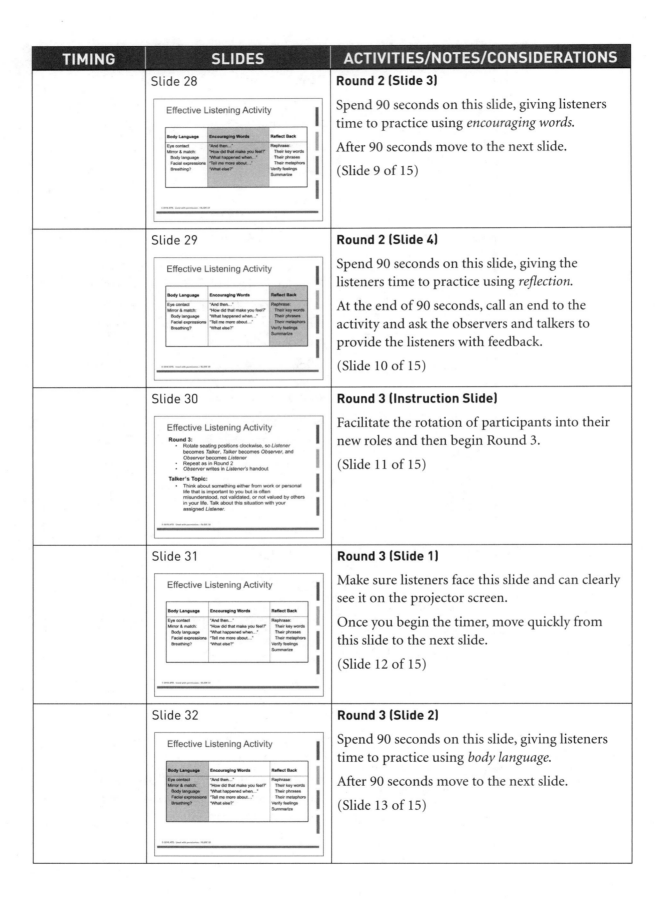	**Round 2 (Slide 3)** Spend 90 seconds on this slide, giving listeners time to practice using *encouraging words*. After 90 seconds move to the next slide. (Slide 9 of 15)
	Slide 29	**Round 2 (Slide 4)** Spend 90 seconds on this slide, giving the listeners time to practice using *reflection*. At the end of 90 seconds, call an end to the activity and ask the observers and talkers to provide the listeners with feedback. (Slide 10 of 15)
	Slide 30	**Round 3 (Instruction Slide)** Facilitate the rotation of participants into their new roles and then begin Round 3. (Slide 11 of 15)
	Slide 31	**Round 3 (Slide 1)** Make sure listeners face this slide and can clearly see it on the projector screen. Once you begin the timer, move quickly from this slide to the next slide. (Slide 12 of 15)
	Slide 32	**Round 3 (Slide 2)** Spend 90 seconds on this slide, giving listeners time to practice using *body language*. After 90 seconds move to the next slide. (Slide 13 of 15)

TIMING	SLIDES	ACTIVITIES/NOTES/CONSIDERATIONS
	Slide 33 Effective Listening Activity *(slide image)*	**Round 3 (Slide 3)** Spend 90 seconds on this slide, giving listeners time to practice using *encouraging words*. After 90 seconds move to the next slide. (Slide 14 of 15)
	Slide 34 Effective Listening Activity *(slide image)*	**Round 3 (Slide 4)** Spend 90 seconds on this slide, giving the listeners time to practice using *reflection*. At the end of 90 seconds, call an end to the activity and ask the observers and talkers to provide the listeners with feedback. (Slide 15 of 15)
11:30 a.m. (10 min)	Slide 35 Creating a Collaborative Environment *(slide image)*	**Learning Content/Lecture** **Creating a Collaborative Environment** • **Handout 27: Collaborative Intention** Use Handout 27 to explain the concept of *collaborative intention*.
11:40 a.m. (5 min)	Slide 36 Collaborative Intention *(slide image)*	**Learning Activity 17: Collaborative Intention Self-Assessment** • **Assessment 2: Collaborative Intention Self-Assessment** Ask participants to think about a current project that they are working on with other team members. With this specific project in mind, ask each participant to complete his or her collaborative intention self-assessment. Use this slide and the instructions in the learning activity to conduct the activity. This is intended as a reflective activity, not a discussion. The results are personal, and the assessment is designed to give participants a kind of reality check to ensure that their actual intentions and behaviors align well with how they say they value collaboration.

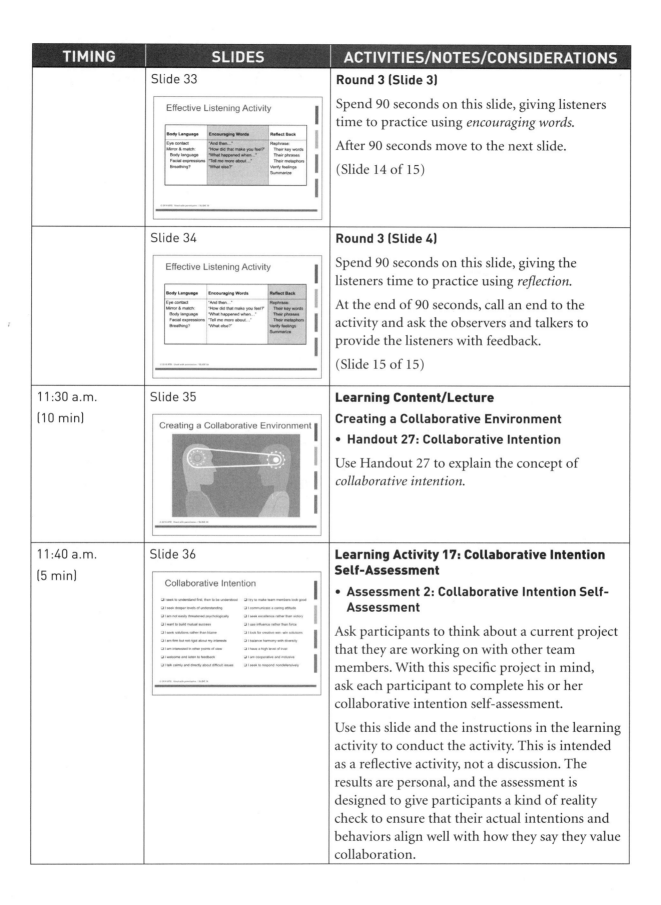

TIMING	SLIDES	ACTIVITIES/NOTES/CONSIDERATIONS
11:45 a.m. (15 min)	Slide 37 Empathy and Feeling Blockers **Judging Responses** **Invalidating Responses** ❑ Criticizing ❑ Diverting ❑ Name-calling ❑ Logical Argument ❑ Diagnosing ❑ Reassuring ❑ Praising Evaluatively **Sending Solutions** ❑ Ordering ❑ Threatening ❑ Moralizing ❑ Excessive or Inappropriate Questioning ❑ Advising	**Learning Activity 18: Empathy and Feeling Blockers** • **Handout 28: Empathy and Feeling Blockers Checklist** Briefly explain the concept of *feeling blockers* and then give each table group a set of feeling blockers to discuss. If time is tight you may need to shorten the number of feeling blockers that you give each group. Refer participants to the handout as a tool they can use when they return to their workplaces.
12:00 p.m. (60 min)	Slide 38 Lunch	**LUNCH**
1:00 p.m. (5 min)	Slide 39 The Competencies of Inspiration and Influence **Discretionary Emotional Energy** $$Q \times A = E$$	**Learning Content/Lecture** **The Competencies of Inspiration and Influence** • **Handout 29: Discretionary Emotional Energy** Briefly overview the equation $Q \times A = E$ developed by Jack Welch as well as the concept of *discretionary emotional energy*. Then move directly into Learning Activity 19.
1:05 p.m. (25 min)	Slide 40 The Competencies of Inspiration and Influence **Discussion Activity** • What engenders discretionary emotional energy? • What destroys it?	**Learning Activity 19: Discretionary Emotional Energy** • **Handout 29: Discretionary Emotional Energy** This discussion activity helps participants to understand discretionary emotional energy and explore the conditions that increase employee engagement. Use this slide and the instructions in the learning activity to conduct and debrief the discussion.

TIMING	SLIDES	ACTIVITIES/NOTES/CONSIDERATIONS
1:30 p.m. (5 min)	Slide 41 EQuip Yourself for Success ① Build the Relationship Before You Need It	**Learning Content/Lecture** **EQuip Yourself for Success: Build the Relationship Before You Need It** • **Handout 30: EQuip Yourself for Success: Map Your Personal Influence Network** Explain to participants that you are going to explore three applications that are particularly important for increasing the emotional competencies of influence, teamwork, and collaboration. Say: "The first application is build the relationship before you need it." Then move on to the next slide. (Slide 1 of 2)
	Slide 42 EQuip Yourself for Success Build the Relationship Before You Need It	Introduce the importance of cultivating a broad network of relationships with the people inside and outside your company whose support you need to carry out your initiatives. (Slide 2 of 2)
1:35 p.m. (10 min)	Slide 43 Map Your Personal Influence Network • Who do you go to get work done? • Outside of work, who do you talk to about work on a regular basis? • Who is an important source of career information, help, and advice? • Who comes to you for information, help, and advice? • Which business units do you interact with on a regular basis? • What employee groups do you associate with on a regular basis?	**Learning Activity 20: Map Your Personal Influence Network** • **Handout 30: EQuip Yourself for Success: Map Your Personal Influence Network** Give participants 7 minutes to map out their personal influence network. Use this slide and the instructions in the learning activity to complete this learning activity.
1:45 p.m. (15 min)	Slide 44 Evaluate Your Network 1. Would network maps other people you know look the same (low score) as your network or would they branch out and extend your network (high score)? 2. Do the people in your network have a wide variety of backgrounds and perspectives? 3. Does your network include "go-to people" (connectors)? Are you a "go-to person"? 4. Do you cultivate both strong and weak bonds? 5. Do you use your network to help you influence others? Gather information? Broaden your view? 6. Are you proactive and thoughtful about building your network?	**Learning Activity 21: Evaluate Your Personal Influence Network** • **Handout 31: EQuip Yourself for Success: Evaluate Your Personal Influence Network** Give participants 5 minutes to evaluate their networks and then 10 minutes to discuss their maps in groups of two or three. Use this slide and the instructions in the learning activity to complete and debrief this learning activity.

TIMING	SLIDES	ACTIVITIES/NOTES/CONSIDERATIONS
2:00 p.m. (15 min)	**Slide 45** EQuip Yourself for Success 1 Build the Relationship Before You Need It 2 Practice Personality Talk	**Learning Content/Lecture** **Practice Personality Talk** • **Handout 32: EQuip Yourself for Success: Practice Personality Talk** Introduce the second application, practice personality talk, and then move directly to the next slide. (Slide 1 of 4)
	Slide 46 Personality 101: Understanding Temperament Types **Fast Paced** **Decisive** **Need for information is low** **Steady, methodical pace** **Pensive, reflective** **Need for information is high**	Use this slide to introduce participants to the *vertical* continuum of the personality model. (Slide 2 of 4)
	Slide 47 Personality 101: Understanding Priority Types **People Priority** **Task Priority** Relationally driven / Self-contained Emotional revealers / Emotional concealers People are primary / Getting job done is primary Getting job done is secondary to relationship / Effect on people is secondary	Introduce participants to the *horizontal* continuum of the personality model. (Slide 3 of 4)
	Slide 48 Personality 101: All Together Fast Paced **Influencing Style** / **Driven Style** Entertaining, visionary, highly influential, enthusiastic, histrionic, want people to look at them and listen to them, craves recognition / Efficient, highly organized, decisive, assertive, excellent task masters, very responsible for the work People Priority / Task Priority **Affiliative Style** / **Analytical Style** Slower pace because they don't want to rock the boat, very sensitive and considerate of other people's feelings, people pleasers, empathizers / Slower pace, examine details, make decisions slowly and deliberately, they want precision, accuracy, lots of information Steady, Methodial Pace	Then use this slide to put all four quadrants of the personality model together for the participants. Explain the following personality concepts: • Everyone possesses aspects of all four styles, but we tend to specialize in one or two styles. • There is no right or wrong style. • All styles are equally important. Teams need a diversity of all styles in order to be effective. • Different personality styles have different emotional needs. • In the world of emotional intelligence and relationship effectiveness, we can make better emotional connections with people when we understand their personality styles and their corresponding emotional needs.

TIMING	SLIDES	ACTIVITIES/NOTES/CONSIDERATIONS
		This is just a brief introduction to the topic. Let participants know that they will be discussing these needs and how to respond to them after the break. (Slide 4 of 4)
2:15 p.m. (15 min)	Slide 49 15-Minute Break	**BREAK**
2:30 p.m. (45 min)	Slide 50 Developing the Competency of Teamwork **For the style you are discussing, answer the following:** 1. What do you appreciate about this style? 2. What are the primary concerns of this style? What do people with this style like or need? 3. What do others do that upsets people with this style? What behaviors do you do that could push this person's buttons? 4. How would you want to approach this person? What body language and tone of voice should you use? What might you say to someone with this style to be more effective? What kinds of questions would you ask? What are the communication dos and don'ts for this style?	**Learning Activity 22: Personality Talk** • **Handout 33: Develop the Competency of Teamwork** Divide participants into four groups and give each group one of the four quadrant styles to discuss. Use this slide and the instructions in the learning activity to complete and debrief the activity. As part of the debrief, refer participants to the chart on the second page of the handout, which provides a valuable framework for working successfully with different personality styles.
3:15 p.m. (10 min)	Slide 51 Developing the Competency of Teamwork **Action Plan** ☑ IDEA ☑ PLAN ☑ ACTION ☑ SUCCESS	**Learning Activity 23: Teaming and Collaboration Action Plan** • **Handout 34: Teaming and Collaboration Action Plan** This reflection activity will help participants develop an action plan for improving a working relationship with someone based on the personality talk model. Give participants 7 minutes to reflect and complete the action plan on Handout 34. Use this slide and the instructions in the learning activity to complete this learning activity.

TIMING	SLIDES	ACTIVITIES/NOTES/CONSIDERATIONS
3:25 p.m. (1 min)	Slide 52 EQuip Yourself for Success 1 Build the Relationship Before You Need It 2 Practice Personality Talk 3 Understand the Two Messages and How to Build Rapport	**Learning Content/Lecture** **EQuip Yourself for Success: Understand Two Messages and Build Communication Rapport** • **Handout 35: EQuip Yourself for Success: The Two Messages and Communication Rapport** Introduce the third application: understand the two messages and how to build rapport and then move to the next slide.
3:26 p.m. (4 min)	Slide 53 The Two Messages True or False? Communication is... ■ Words (7%) ■ Tone (38%) ■ Nonverbal (55%)	**Learning Activity 24: The Two Messages** • **Handout 35: EQuip Yourself for Success: The Two Messages and Communication Rapport** In this demonstration activity, choose one volunteer to demonstrate the critical link between congruent communication and the emotional competencies of influence and inspiration. Use this slide and the instructions in the learning activity to complete this learning activity. (Slide 1 of 2)
	Slide 54 The Two Messages The Two Messages You Send Every Time You Talk: The _Content_ Message The _Feeling_ Message *If you want to be successful with people, you need to send them positive feeling messages.*	Explain that we send two messages every time we speak. One message is the *content* message, which says these are the words I want you to hear. The other message is the *feeling* message, which says this is how I really feel about you. We communicate this feeling message with our body language and tone of voice. If we want to be successful in communication, we need to send people positive feeling messages. NOTE: This slide is animated (if you have licensed the custom version of the slides). Click through the animation at the appropriate portion of the script. If you are using the ready-to-use pdf version of the slide deck, simply point out the portion of the slide as you run through the script. (Slide 2 of 2)

TIMING	SLIDES	ACTIVITIES/NOTES/CONSIDERATIONS
3:30 p.m. (10 min)	Slide 55 Building Rapport Let's practice... • "Can I help you?" • "Yes ... but..." • "Yes ... and ..." • "Why ... you ...?" vs. "What can I...?" or "How can I...?" • "When ... if ... then ..." • Common Interests • Metaphorical language • Sensory language • Mirroring	**Learning Activity 25: Building Rapport** • **Handout 35: EQuip Yourself for Success: The Two Messages and Communication Rapport** Now it's your participants' turn to practice. For this activity participants will stand up in circles of 5 or 6 participants per group to practice managing messages for better communication rapport. Use this slide and the instructions in the learning activity to complete and debrief the activity.
3:40 p.m. (20 min)	Slide 56 The Competency of Conflict Management Let me introduce you to two people: Person A Person B Who has a problem?	**Learning Content/Lecture** **The Competency of Conflict Management** • **Handout 36: The Competency of Conflict Management** Share that the rest of the day will be spent on exploring the emotional competency of conflict management. This section includes nine learning content slides and then a learning activity. You will explore the three steps of conflict management with participants to increase their confidence in managing conflict and difficult emotional conversations, but first introduce them to the conflict example between Person A and Person B. You can invent any conflict scenario between A and B. Here is just one example: Person A is sharing an idea at a team meeting when he or she is interrupted by Person B. Person A is upset, and Person B is oblivious. (Slide 1 of 9)

TIMING	SLIDES	ACTIVITIES/NOTES/CONSIDERATIONS
	Slide 57 **Rules of Engagement** 1. The person who is _upset_ _owns_ the problem. 2. The person who _owns_ the problem, _solves_ the problem. 3. Person _A_ needs to initiate _conflict_ _resolution_.	Use this slide to revisit the original idea of the day—that an emotion is a signal to spur us to action. In your example, the *signal* resides in the body of Person A, so Person A needs to initiate conflict resolution. Be sure to discuss the consequences of Person A reacting aggressively (either with hostile or passive aggression) rather than initiating conflict resolution. NOTE: This slide is animated (if you have licensed the custom version of the slides), which will allow you to "fill in" the blanks as you walk through the slide. If you are using the ready-to-use pdf version of the slide deck, simply point out the portion of the slide as you talk about it. (Slide 2 of 9)
	Slide 58 **Steps to Manage Conflict** **1** **Focus on Feelings First**—manage your own emotions, especially anger, irritation, and defensiveness	Introduce the first step in conflict management: manage your own emotions, especially anger, irritation, and defensiveness. Emotional self-management is necessary to avoid defensiveness. Remind participants that their goal is to conduct a conflict resolution conversation, not to vent feelings. (Slide 3 of 9)
	Slide 59 **Emotional Self-Management** ANGER **is a feeling that makes your mouth work faster than your MIND.** —*Evan Eser*	Read aloud the quote on this slide to help participants understand the role anger can play in conflict management. NOTE: This slide is animated (if you have licensed the custom version of the slides). (Slide 4 of 9)

TIMING	SLIDES	ACTIVITIES/NOTES/CONSIDERATIONS
	Slide 60 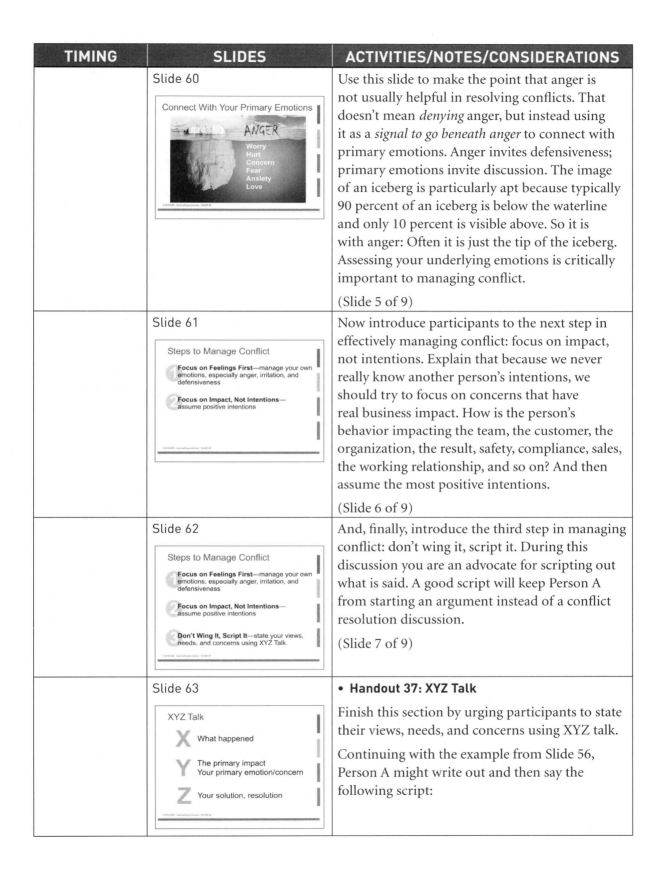	Use this slide to make the point that anger is not usually helpful in resolving conflicts. That doesn't mean *denying* anger, but instead using it as a *signal to go beneath anger* to connect with primary emotions. Anger invites defensiveness; primary emotions invite discussion. The image of an iceberg is particularly apt because typically 90 percent of an iceberg is below the waterline and only 10 percent is visible above. So it is with anger: Often it is just the tip of the iceberg. Assessing your underlying emotions is critically important to managing conflict. (Slide 5 of 9)
	Slide 61	Now introduce participants to the next step in effectively managing conflict: focus on impact, not intentions. Explain that because we never really know another person's intentions, we should try to focus on concerns that have real business impact. How is the person's behavior impacting the team, the customer, the organization, the result, safety, compliance, sales, the working relationship, and so on? And then assume the most positive intentions. (Slide 6 of 9)
	Slide 62	And, finally, introduce the third step in managing conflict: don't wing it, script it. During this discussion you are an advocate for scripting out what is said. A good script will keep Person A from starting an argument instead of a conflict resolution discussion. (Slide 7 of 9)
	Slide 63	• **Handout 37: XYZ Talk** Finish this section by urging participants to state their views, needs, and concerns using XYZ talk. Continuing with the example from Slide 56, Person A might write out and then say the following script:

TIMING	SLIDES	ACTIVITIES/NOTES/CONSIDERATIONS
		X: "When I didn't get to finish what I was saying at the team meeting yesterday"
		Y: "I became concerned that we are not addressing an important safety issue as we move forward with this decision," or "I became concerned that we are not addressing an important customer need." (Use language that addresses concern about the real business impact.)
		Z: "And I would like to revisit the conversation with you so we can address the issue."
		(Slide 8 of 9)
	Slide 64	Share that in any conflict conversation, we can only control our side of the dialogue. Even if the other person is hostile, we can still diffuse emotions and focus on conflict resolution by using ZYX talk.
	The Response: ZYX Talk Z "You would like…" Y "Because you felt…" X "When…happened…"	(Slide 9 of 9)
4:00 p.m. (15 min)	Slide 65	**Learning Activity 26: Practice XYZ Talk**
	Practice XYZ Talk **Script it out** X What happened Y The primary impact / Your primary emotion/concern Z Your solution, resolution	**• Handout 37: XYZ Talk**
		Tell your participants they will now practice using XYZ talk with a partner. Give them 5 minutes to complete the XYZ script in Handout 37 and then have them share their scenarios and scripts with their partners.
		Use this slide and the instructions in the learning activity to complete this exercise.
4:15 p.m. (5 min)	Slide 66	**Q&A**
	Q & A	There are three parts to facilitating the Q&A:
		First, let participants know the workshop is *not* over yet. Say: "Before I give you time to work on your action plan, what questions do you have about today's workshop?"
		Second, wait a full 7 seconds to give people time to reflect and process.

TIMING	SLIDES	ACTIVITIES/NOTES/CONSIDERATIONS
		Third, if there is time after you have addressed their questions, revisit any learning goals that participants discussed at the beginning of the workshop (and recorded on the flipchart) that were not covered by the program. Refer participants to the half-day or two-day program, if appropriate.
4:20 p.m. (5 min)	Slide 67 Action Plan ☑ IDEA ☑ PLAN ☑ ACTION ☑ SUCCESS	**Learning Activity 27: EQuip Yourself for Success: Action Plan** • **Handout 38: EQuip Yourself for Success: Action Plan** This activity is designed to create alignment between the workshop content and the individual participant's development plan. Give participants 5 minutes to reflect on lessons learned and to fill out the action plan as outlined in Handout 38.
4:25 p.m. (5 min) Ends at 4:30 p.m.	Slide 68 Wrap-Up Key Learning Points	**Wrap-Up** • **Assessment 1: Workshop Evaluation** Close the workshop on a positive note. Distribute the workshop evaluations. As they are completing the evaluations, ask them to think about the most valuable idea or strategy they learned today. When you have all the evaluations, ask everyone to form a circle. Start by sharing something that *you* learned today. Then toss a soft throwing object such as a Koosh ball to one participant and ask him or her to share a key learning point. Continue tossing the ball around the circle until everyone who is willing to share has shared. Be available to answer any questions participants may still have about the workshop content. Share plans for follow-up coaching, if applicable (see Chapter 10 for ideas to follow up the training with support and activities). Thank participants for their contributions and wish them well.

What to Do Next

- Determine the schedule for training workshops; reserve location and catering you may wish to provide.

- Identify and invite participants.

- Inform participants about any pre-work, if applicable, that you want completed before the workshop begins.

- Review the workshop objectives, activities, and handouts to plan the content you will use.

- Prepare copies of the participant materials and any activity-related materials you may need. Refer to Chapter 14 for information about how to access and use the supplemental materials provided for this workshop.

- Gather tactile items, such as Koosh balls, crayons, magnets, Play-Doh, or others, that you wish to place on the tables for tactile learners. See Chapter 8 for other ideas to enhance the learning environment of your workshop.

- Prepare yourself both emotionally and physically. Confirm that you have addressed scheduling and personal concerns so that you can be fully present to facilitate the workshop.

References

Bolton, R. (1979). *People Skills: How to Assert Yourself, Listen to Others, and Resolve Conflicts.* New York: Simon & Schuster.

Covey, S. R. (1989). *The 7 Habits of Highly Effective People.* New York: Simon & Schuster.

Feldman, J., and K. Mulle. (2007). *Put Intelligence to Work: EQuip Yourself for Success.* Alexandria, VA: ASTD Press.

Goleman, D. (1995). *Emotional Intelligence: Why It Can Matter More Than IQ.* New York: Bantam.

Goleman, D. (1998). *Working With Emotional Intelligence.* New York: Bantam.

Chapter 3

Two-Day Emotional Intelligence Workshop: The New Science of Leadership

What's in This Chapter

- Objectives of the two-day Emotional Intelligence Workshop

- Summary chart for the flow of content and activities

- Two-day program agenda

In the half-day workshop, we link emotional intelligence to success because so much of our success in life has to do with self-awareness and self-management, and because in a half day, it would be difficult to cover more than the first two domains of the emotional intelligence four-domain model. In the full-day workshop, we link emotional intelligence to relationship management, focusing on topics such as empathy, influence, personality, and conflict.

In this two-day workshop, then, we link emotional intelligence to *leadership*. The link between emotional intelligence and leadership begins with the concept of resonance, an emotional connection that happens between two or more people when they exert positive influence on one another. Drawing on research with more than 3,000 executives, Daniel Goleman and his colleagues (2002) outlined six distinct styles of leadership: four that encourage *resonance* (visionary, coaching, affiliative, democratic) and two that focus on demanding compliance or performance and that can promote *dissonance* (pacesetting, commanding). The two-day agenda focuses on the four styles of leadership that are particularly effective at promoting resonance in relationships. Participants in this workshop learn how to develop each of these four styles by strengthening the emotional competencies that support each style. Each style requires about a half day of workshop time, so the two-day format is perfect for facilitating emotional intelligence through the lens of leadership.

Any workshop, regardless of length, benefits from incorporating the principles of active training. This workshop design presents activities that engage participants in relevant and meaningful learning experiences, small group discussion, and skills practice. Be sure to allow time for discussion and reflection to increase learning and retention.

Two-Day Workshop Objectives: The New Science of Leadership

By the end of Day One of the two-day workshop, participants will be able to

- Understand the four-domain model of emotional intelligence and the 18 competencies that support the four domains
- Explore the connection between emotional intelligence and leadership
- Describe the difference between resonant and dissonant leadership
- Define six styles of leadership and how they relate to resonant leadership
- Identify which competencies they need to develop to effectively lead others
- Learn basic tools for developing the emotional competencies that support the *visionary* leadership style
- Learn basic tools for developing the emotional competencies that support the *coaching* leadership style.

By the end of Day Two of the two-day workshop, participants will be able to

- Explore a model for deciding how to apply leadership styles to different situations
- Learn basic tools for developing the emotional competencies that support the *affiliative* leadership style
- Manage unconscious bias and create a culture that respects diversity and inclusion
- Develop strategies for creating a motivating and engaged culture

- Learn basic tools for developing the emotional competencies that support the *democratic* leadership style
- Identify strategies for win–win collaboration and team decision-making.

Two-Day Workshop Overview

Day-One Overview

TOPICS	TIMING
Welcome and Introduction to Emotional Intelligence	10 minutes
Learning Objectives	5 minutes
The Anatomy of an Emotion	15 minutes
Emotional Intelligence Defined	5 minutes
Learning Activity 28: Emotional Intelligence Self-Assessment	10 minutes
Emotional Intelligence and Leadership	1 minute
Learning Activity 29: Emotional Contagion	2 minutes
Resonant Leadership	1 minute
Learning Activity 30: A Person Who Has Made a Difference in My Life	8 minutes
Dissonant Leadership	1 minute
Learning Activity 31: Resonant vs. Dissonant Leadership	7 minutes
Learning Activity 32: Goleman's Six Styles of Leadership	10 minutes
BREAK	**15 minutes**
Learning Activity 33: My Leadership Style	20 minutes
Learning Activity 34: Leadership Style Action Plan	10 minutes
Transition to Application: The Big Idea	1 minute
Learning Activity 35: The Indispensable Competency of Empathy	14 minutes
The Visionary Competencies	**1 minute**
The Competency of Self-Awareness	4 minutes
Learning Activity 36: Managing Defensiveness	10 minutes
Vision and Self-Awareness	5 minutes
Learning Activity 37: Keep Your Eye on the Grand Marshmallow	10 minutes
Learning Activity 38: The Riddle: The Competency of Self-Confidence	5 minutes
Learning Activity 39: Practice Relational Thinking	10 minutes
LUNCH	**60 minutes**
The Competency of Change Catalyst	10 minutes
Learning Activity 40: Visionary Style and Managing Transition	10 minutes
Learning Activity 41: Communicating Your Vision	30 minutes
The Coaching Competencies	**1 minute**
Asking Great Questions	4 minutes

TOPICS	TIMING
Learning Activity 42: Judger–Learner Questions	10 minutes
GROW Coaching Model Questions	5 minutes
Plus-Delta Model	5 minutes
BREAK	**15 minutes**
Learning Activity 43: Coaching Dialogue	40 minutes
Learning Activity 44: The Competency of Developing Others	7 minutes
Coaching Culture	3 minutes
Learning Activity 45: The Hot/Cold Game	30 minutes
Effective Feedback	10 minutes
Learning Activity 46: SBI Practice	20 minutes
Learning Activity 47: Coaching Action Plan and Closing	10 minutes
TOTAL	**450 minutes (7.5 hours)**

Day-Two Overview

TOPICS	TIMING
Learning Activity 48: Welcome and Lessons Learned	10 minutes
Learning Objectives: Day Two	5 minutes
Two Coaching Behaviors	15 minutes
Learning Activity 49: Discussion of the Meta-Model for Working Effectively With Others	30 minutes
The Affiliative Competencies	**5 minutes**
Learning Activity 50: The Tallest Freestanding Dot Tower	15 minutes
Learning Activity 51: The Elements of Effective Team Process	10 minutes
BREAK	**15 minutes**
Learning Activity 52: The Uniqueness–Belonging Model	20 minutes
Creating an Inclusive Culture	10 minutes
Aligning Strengths	5 minutes
Learning Activity 53: Motivation 3.0	40 minutes
LUNCH	**60 minutes**
Using Employee Engagement Surveys	20 minutes
The Democratic Competencies	**5 minutes**
Learning Activity 54: The Competency of Influence	15 minutes
Learning Activity 55: The Six Principles of Influence	15 minutes
The Competency of Conflict Management	5 minutes
Learning Activity 56: Case Studies in Conflict	25 minutes
Four Steps of Conflict Management	5 minutes
BREAK	**15 minutes**
Step 1: Attack the Problem, Not the Person	5 minutes

TOPICS	TIMING
Learning Activity 57: Step 1 Practice: Identify and Collaborate	5 minutes
Step 2: Figure Out Everyone's Interests and Expectations	10 minutes
Learning Activity 58: Step 2 Practice: Inputs, Outputs, and Managing the Process	15 minutes
Be Clear About Your Own Goals and Priorities	5 minutes
Step 3: Brainstorm Win–Win Options	5 minutes
Learning Activity 59: Step 3 Practice: Brainstorm	20 minutes
Step 4: Insist on Using Fair Procedures or Principles	5 minutes
Learning Activity 60: Step 4 Practice: Rock, Paper, Scissors	5 minutes
Learning Activity 61: Step 4 Practice: Decision Matrix Exercise	10 minutes
Q&A	5 minutes
Learning Activity 62: EQuip Yourself for Success: Action Plan	10 minutes
Wrap-Up	5 minutes
TOTAL	**450 minute (7.5 hours)**

Two-Day Workshop Agenda: Day One

With all that you are focused on when facilitating a workshop, it can be useful to have a quick-reference, bird's-eye view of the workshop. This agenda is intended for that purpose. The learning activities pages in Chapter 11 provide the details that support the workshop activities and group discussions. Chapters 12 and 13 will provide the assessments and handouts needed to facilitate the workshop.

Day One: (9:00 a.m. to 4:30 p.m.)

TIMING	SLIDES	ACTIVITIES/NOTES/CONSIDERATIONS
Before the Workshop (at least 60 minutes)		**Workshop Setup** Arrive one hour before the start to ensure the room is set up, equipment works, and materials are arranged for the participants. This gives you time to make them feel truly welcomed. Chatting with them builds a trusting relationship and opens them up for learning.

TIMING	SLIDES	ACTIVITIES/NOTES/CONSIDERATIONS
9:00 a.m. (10 min)	Slide 1 **ATD** Workshop Emotional Intelligence The New Science of Leadership Two-Day Workshop: Day One	**Welcome and Introduction to Emotional Intelligence** Welcome participants and introduce yourself. Let participants know that in this workshop they will explore the topic of emotional intelligence (EI) as it relates to *leadership effectiveness*. Because EI is such a broad topic (and time in this workshop is limited), set the stage for the program by asking participants to introduce themselves to the group and share one learning goal that they have for the workshop. Use this as an opportunity to set expectations for the workshop and to discuss learning objectives. If a participant's learning goal does not align well with the learning objectives for the workshop, write it down as a "sidebar" on a sheet of flipchart paper and let the participant know that you will address these concepts during the Q&A portion of the workshop if time permits. Revisit this list at the end of the program.
9:10 a.m. (5 min)	Slide 2 Learning Objectives: Day One • Understand the four-domain model of emotional intelligence and the 18 competencies that support the domains • Explore the connection between emotional intelligence and leadership • Describe the difference between resonant and dissonant leadership • Define six styles of leadership and how they relate to resonant leadership • Identify which competencies you need to develop to effectively lead others • Learn basic tools for developing competencies that support the visionary leadership style • Learn basic tools for developing competencies that support the coaching leadership style	**Learning Objectives** • **Handout 39: Two-Day Workshop Learning Objectives: The New Science of Leadership** Lay out the basic flow of the workshop. Rather than explaining each objective, explain how each objective will be covered. "I will spend some time talking about. . . . And then we will have a small group discussion . . ." Reference participant learning goals as appropriate.

TIMING	SLIDES	ACTIVITIES/NOTES/CONSIDERATIONS
9:15 a.m. (15 min)	Slide 3 The Anatomy of an Emotion Once upon a time, I was walking in the forest. . . and I came upon a Big, Bad, -----	**Learning Content/Lecture** • **Handout 40: The Anatomy of an Emotion** Use this handout and set of slides to grab your participants' attention with a quick primer on why emotional intelligence is so important. Begin with a strong statement about how we are wired to experience events and situations *emotionally* before we experience those same events and situations *rationally*. Then explain the anatomy of an emotion using Slides 3 and 4, which serve as a foundation for the workshop and help you transition your participants to the first learning activity. I usually stick fairly close to a "script" for this section. Slide 3 presents what I refer to as "the original story of your emotions." Say: > Once upon a time you were walking in a forest and you came upon something dangerous—such as a big bear. Your eye saw the bear and immediately sent a message down to your adrenal glands. Your adrenal glands pumped adrenaline into your system, your heart beat faster, your breathing quickened, your palms got sweaty, your muscles tensed up, and you were prepared for fight or flight. NOTE: Both Slides 3 and 4 are animated (if you have licensed the custom version of the slides). Click through the animation at the appropriate portion of the script. If you are using the ready-to-use pdf version of the slide deck, simply point out the portion of the slide as you run through the script. (Slide 1 of 4)

TIMING	SLIDES	ACTIVITIES/NOTES/CONSIDERATIONS
	Slide 4 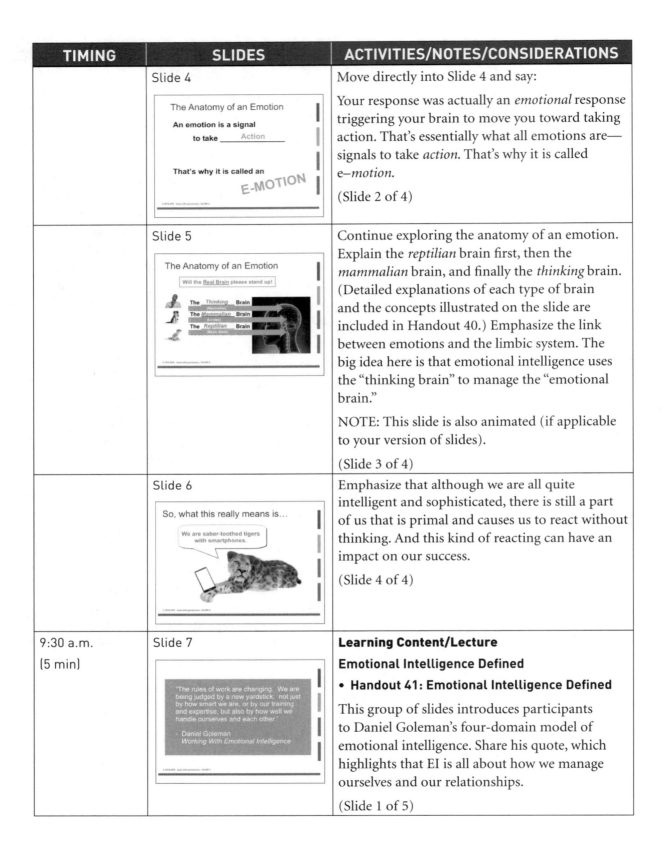 The Anatomy of an Emotion An emotion is a signal to take _____ Action That's why it is called an E-MOTION	Move directly into Slide 4 and say: Your response was actually an *emotional* response triggering your brain to move you toward taking action. That's essentially what all emotions are—signals to take *action*. That's why it is called e–*motion*. (Slide 2 of 4)
	Slide 5 The Anatomy of an Emotion Will the Real Brain please stand up! The _Thinking_ Brain [Neocortex] The _Mammalian_ Brain [Limbic] The _Reptilian_ Brain [Brain Stem]	Continue exploring the anatomy of an emotion. Explain the *reptilian* brain first, then the *mammalian* brain, and finally the *thinking* brain. (Detailed explanations of each type of brain and the concepts illustrated on the slide are included in Handout 40.) Emphasize the link between emotions and the limbic system. The big idea here is that emotional intelligence uses the "thinking brain" to manage the "emotional brain." NOTE: This slide is also animated (if applicable to your version of slides). (Slide 3 of 4)
	Slide 6 So, what this really means is… We are saber-toothed tigers with smartphones.	Emphasize that although we are all quite intelligent and sophisticated, there is still a part of us that is primal and causes us to react without thinking. And this kind of reacting can have an impact on our success. (Slide 4 of 4)
9:30 a.m. (5 min)	Slide 7 "The rules of work are changing. We are being judged by a new yardstick: not just by how smart we are, or by our training and expertise, but also by how well we handle ourselves and each other." - Daniel Goleman *Working With Emotional Intelligence*	**Learning Content/Lecture** **Emotional Intelligence Defined** • **Handout 41: Emotional Intelligence Defined** This group of slides introduces participants to Daniel Goleman's four-domain model of emotional intelligence. Share his quote, which highlights that EI is all about how we manage ourselves and our relationships. (Slide 1 of 5)

TIMING	SLIDES	ACTIVITIES/NOTES/CONSIDERATIONS
	Slide 8 **Emotional Intelligence Defined** Emotional intelligence is… Using your emotions *intelligently,* to gain the performance you wish to see within yourself, and *to achieve interpersonal effectiveness with others.* —Jeff Feldman and Karl Mulle *Put Emotional Intelligence to Work*	Share another definition to deepen their understanding of emotional understanding. (Slide 2 of 5)
	Slide 9 **Emotional Intelligence Defined** Emotional intelligence at work is the capacity for… • Self-Awareness—recognizing your feelings and behaviors • Self-Management—managing your feelings and behaviors, and staying motivated in spite of setbacks and obstacles • Social Awareness—understanding what others feel • Relationship Management—building rapport and collaborating with others	This definition is broken down into four categories of human behavior that Goleman calls the four domains of emotional intelligence. Delineate these four categories and then show participants the four-domain model on the next slide. (Slide 3 of 5)
	Slide 10 **The Four-Domain Model** 		Personal Competence	Social Competence
Recognition	Self-Awareness	Social Awareness
Regulation	Self-Management	Relationship Management		Show participants this visual graphic of the four-domain model and then briefly recap. There are behaviors that ultimately help us manage our emotional/limbic impulses, and these behaviors fall into four categories that we recognize as the four-domain model of emotional intelligence. Before advancing to the next slide, explain to participants that each of the domains is further broken down into a set of 18 competency behaviors. (Slide 4 of 5)
	Slide 11 **The 18 Competencies** Personal Competence / Social Competence Recognition — Self-Awareness: Emotional Self-Awareness, Accurate Self-Assessment, Self-Confidence / Social Awareness: Empathy, Organizational Awareness, Service Orientation Regulation — Self-Management: Emotional Self-Control, Transparency, Adaptability, Achievement Orientation, Initiative, Optimism / Relationship Skills: Inspirational Leadership, Influence, Developing Others, Change Catalyst, Conflict Management, Teamwork and Collaboration	Share that this is good news, because if you can define something behaviorally, then you can develop it. (Slide 5 of 5)

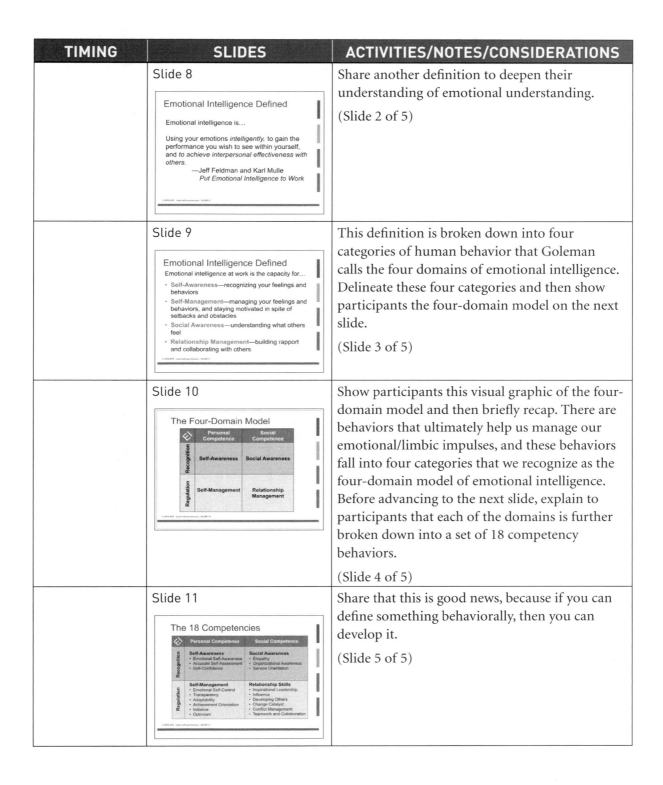

TIMING	SLIDES	ACTIVITIES/NOTES/CONSIDERATIONS
9:35 a.m. (10 min)	Slide 12 Emotional Intelligence Quick Assessment	**Learning Activity 28: Emotional Intelligence Self-Assessment** • **Assessment 3: Emotional Intelligence Quick Assessment** This self-reflection activity helps participants assess which competencies they need to develop to effectively lead others. To debrief, let participants know that they will be revisiting their results later in the workshop when they discuss leadership styles.
9:45 a.m. (1 min) NOTE: Timing for this section (Slides 13–19) can be more organic than suggested here. You have 20 minutes to cover all the content in this section.	Slide 13 Emotional Intelligence and Leadership What does all of this have to do with leadership? The brain is an open loop.	**Learning Content/Discussion** **Emotional Intelligence and Leadership** • **Handout 42: Emotional Intelligence and Leadership** This slide and handout will help introduce the connection between EI and leadership. Briefly overview the content on the handout, emphasizing the idea that we all rely on connections with other people for our emotional stability. The brain's limbic system, its emotional center, is an open-loop system, which relies on connections with people to determine its mood. In short, emotions are contagious. The more positive people's overall mood, the more they will cooperate, and the better the results.
9:46 a.m. (2 min)	Slide 14 Emotional Intelligence and Leadership **Emotional Contagion** The emotions you project will often get reflected back to you in the emotions of others. "Smile and the world smiles with you," as the song goes, but frown and the world frowns with you as well.	**Learning Activity 29: Emotional Contagion** Make sure you look at the faces of the participants while they are watching the video clip.

TIMING	SLIDES	ACTIVITIES/NOTES/CONSIDERATIONS
9:48 a.m. (1 min)	Slide 15 Resonant Leadership The best leaders are "moodivational." The primary task of all effective leadership in organizations is to figure out ways to drive other people's emotions in a positive direction. —Jeff Feldman and Karl Mulle *Put Emotional Intelligence to Work*	**Learning Content/Lecture** **Resonant Leadership** • **Handout 42: Emotional Intelligence and Leadership** Share this quote, which continues to answer the question: What does EI have to do with leadership? Emphasize that the original story of our emotions is also the original story of leadership. The best leaders in any organization are able to drive people's behaviors at the emotional level. They are "moodivational."
9:49 a.m. (8 min)	Slide 16 Resonant Leadership Resonance is a reservoir of positivity that frees the best in people. —Daniel Goleman	**Learning Activity 30: A Person Who Has Made a Difference in My Life** • **Handout 42: Emotional Intelligence and Leadership** Introduce this activity by telling the participants that this connection between leaders and the people they lead is called "resonance"—what Daniel Goleman describes as "a reservoir of positivity that frees up the best in people." The activity will help participants identify the qualities that make a difference in people's lives. Use this slide and the instructions in the learning activity to complete this activity.
9:57 a.m. (1 min)	Slide 17 Dissonant Leadership The Open Loop System Can Also Create Dissonance	**Learning Content/Lecture** **Dissonant Leadership** • **Handout 43: Resonant vs. Dissonant Leadership** Use this slide and handout to introduce the concept of *dissonant* leadership. Dissonant leaders tend to be more authoritative and keep a greater social and emotional distance from employees. While this may help when orders must be executed urgently, it can also leave others anxious or disengaged.

TIMING	SLIDES	ACTIVITIES/NOTES/CONSIDERATIONS
9:58 a.m. (7 min)	Slide 18 Resonant vs. Dissonant Leadership	**Learning Activity 31: Resonant vs. Dissonant Leadership** • **Handout 43: Resonant vs. Dissonant Leadership** In this activity, participants will grasp the difference between resonant and dissonant leadership. This graphic illustrates how *dissonant* leadership works. NOTE: This and the next slide are animated (if you have licensed the custom version of the slides). Click through the animation at the appropriate portion of the script in the learning activity. If you are using the ready-to-use pdf version of the slide deck, simply point out the portion of the slide as you run through the script. (Slide 1 of 2)
	Slide 19 Resonant vs. Dissonant Leadership	Use this slide to illustrate *resonant* leadership. Give participants an opportunity to ask questions, share insights, or relate an experience they have had with managers or supervisors who have modeled either resonant or dissonant leadership. (Slide 2 of 2)

TIMING	SLIDES	ACTIVITIES/NOTES/CONSIDERATIONS
10:05 a.m. (10 min)	Slide 20 Goleman's Six Styles of Leadership	**Learning Activity 32: Goleman's Six Styles of Leadership** • **Handout 44: Goleman's Six Styles of Leadership** Use this activity to introduce Daniel Goleman's six styles of leadership and to explain how they relate to resonant leadership. Here are his six styles: • Visionary • Coaching • Affiliative • Democratic • Pacesetting • Commanding Use the handout to briefly overview each style with the participants. The learning activity includes two different ways that you can present the styles.
10:15 a.m. (15 min)	Slide 21 15-Minute Break	**BREAK**
10:30 a.m. (20 min)	Slide 22 Discussion 1. Describe a situation in which you have used one of the leadership styles effectively. 2. Which leadership style do you use the most? 3. How does this leadership style help you build resonance with others? 4. In what situations do you find this leadership style to be ineffective?	**Learning Activity 33: My Leadership Style** • **Handout 45: Leadership Style Discussion** This small group discussion helps participants identify leadership styles that they do well and those they would like to develop. The goal is for participants to gain clarity around the styles they would like to develop and the emotional competencies that support those styles.

TIMING	SLIDES	ACTIVITIES/NOTES/CONSIDERATIONS
10:50 a.m. (10 min)	Slide 23 Reflection–Action Planning 1. Which leadership style would you like to develop in yourself? 2. What are the underlying EI competencies that support this leadership style? 3. Based on your self-assessment, which of these competencies do you need to focus on for leadership development?	**Learning Activity 34: Leadership Style Action Plan** • **Handout 46: Leadership Style Action Plan** Give participants 10 minutes to reflect and complete the action plan in Handout 46. Use this slide and the instructions in the learning activity to complete this activity.
11:00 a.m. (1 min)	Slide 24 The Big Idea The best leaders find effective ways to understand and improve their own and other people's emotions, which leads to… • Better business results • Retention of Talent • Higher morale • Motivation • Commitment	**Learning Content/Lecture** **Transition to Application: The Big Idea** Use this transition slide to move from assessment to tools and applications. The big idea of the workshop is that effective leaders find ways to understand and improve their own and other people's emotions. So how do we do it? Emphasize that the rest of the course is about developing the emotional competencies that support the resonant leadership styles.
11:01 a.m. (14 min)	Slide 25 EQuip Yourself for Success The Indispensable Competency of Empathy **Think of a time when someone showed you great empathy.** •What specifically did they do? •How did their expression of empathy impact you?	**Learning Activity 35: The Indispensable Competency of Empathy** • **Handout 47: Empathy Discussion** This small group discussion helps participants explore empathy, the emotional competency foundational to all of the resonant leadership styles. Use this slide and the instructions in the learning activity to complete the activity.
11:15 a.m. (1 min)	Slide 26 EQuip Yourself for Success **The Visionary Competencies** 1. Self-Awareness 2. Self-Confidence 3. Change Catalyst 4. Inspirational Leadership	**Learning Content/Lecture** **The Visionary Competencies** This is a transitional slide. Explain to participants that they will now explore the competencies related to the *visionary* leadership style.

TIMING	SLIDES	ACTIVITIES/NOTES/CONSIDERATIONS
11:16 a.m. (4 min)	Slide 27	**Learning Content/Lecture** **The Competency of Self-Awareness** • **Handout 48: The Johari Window** Explain the Johari window and the importance of gaining objective insights by overviewing the notes in the handout. The goal is for participants to realize the importance of seeking feedback to increase their self-awareness. Ask participants this key question: What is the value of increasing the public self? NOTE: This slide is animated (if you have licensed the custom version of the slides). It begins with the Johari window as in the handout and then suggests through each animation that the goal is to increase the public self by seeking feedback from others and disclosing information that could help other people get to know you better. If you are using the ready-to-use pdf version of the slides, cover the same discussion by referring the participants first to the handout version of the window and then to the slide version to help them understand the idea of increasing the public self.
11:20 a.m. (10 min)	Slide 28	**Learning Activity 36: Managing Defensiveness** • **Handout 49: Managing Defensiveness Journaling Exercise** Another key to self-awareness is managing defensiveness. Defensiveness is the opposite of openness and self-awareness; being aware of defensive behaviors is very important. This reflective activity will help participants eliminate defensive habits that can interfere with their leadership. Give participants 8 minutes to complete the handout, which has a brief assessment and question prompts to help them journal their thoughts. (Slide 1 of 2)

TIMING	SLIDES	ACTIVITIES/NOTES/CONSIDERATIONS
	Slide 29 Managing Defensiveness Can you laugh at yourself?	Ask participants the question on the slide. Explain that being able to laugh at yourself can also help you manage defensiveness. In fact, the ability to laugh at yourself is an indication that you have successfully developed the competency of self-awareness. (Slide 2 of 2)
11:30 a.m. (5 min)	Slide 30 Vision and Self-Awareness What does a marshmallow have to do with success?	**Learning Content/Lecture** **Vision and Self-Awareness** • **Handout 50: Visionary Style and the Competency of Self-Awareness** This learning content sets the stage for Learning Activity 37. It helps participants identify basic tools for developing the competencies that support the visionary leadership style. Use this and the next three slides to walk through the information in the handouts with the participants. Briefly tell the story of Walter Mischel's marshmallow experiments with young children in the late 1960s. Part of the story is highlighted in the handout. (Slide 1 of 4)
	Slide 31 Vision and Self-Awareness *The human brain is wired to maximize pleasure and minimize pain.* The *rational* brain says: "No Pain, No Gain." But the *emotional* brain says: "No Pain! No Pain!"	Use this slide to explain how we are challenged to motivate ourselves because the emotional brain tends to crave immediate gratification—emotional junk food. The rational brain says "no pain, no gain," but the emotional brain says "no pain, no pain." This begs two questions: • How do we get ourselves to want the ultimate more than we want the temporary? • How do we generate emotional enthusiasm in the direction of achieving our ultimate goals? (Slide 2 of 4)

TIMING	SLIDES	ACTIVITIES/NOTES/CONSIDERATIONS
	Slide 32 *Never look where you don't want to go.*	This slide helps explain why visionary leadership becomes so critical. Our ability to be clear about what we want is essential to our ability to motivate ourselves to accomplish great things and achieve important goals. This is why golfers say: "Never look where you don't want to go." (Slide 3 of 4)
	Slide 33 Vision and Self-Awareness Introducing… Your Reticular Activating System	Briefly overview the reticular activating system and reemphasize the importance of being clear about what you want. Then lead directly into Learning Activity 37. (Slide 4 of 4)
11:35 a.m. (10 min)	Slide 34 EQuip Yourself for Success **Keep Your Eye on the Grand Marshmallow** 1. What is a two marshmallow goal in your life? Create a clear picture of what it is you desire. 2. What is your motivation for achieving this goal? Why do you want it? What value will its attainment bring to your life? "My best friend is my imagination." —Dan Gable	**Learning Activity 37: Keep Your Eye on the Grand Marshmallow** • **Handout 51: Keep Your Eye on the Grand Marshmallow** This is a reflection and discussion activity. Be sure to reinforce the key learning point here: Motivation is a self-management competency, and anyone can learn how to shift their internal motivation to a positive, energized, purpose-driven, and value-driven outlook. Follow the instructions in the learning activity to complete.
11:45 a.m. (5 min)	Slide 35 A Riddle ???	**Learning Activity 38: The Riddle: The Competency of Self-Confidence** • **Handout 52: Visionary Style and the Competency of Self-Confidence** This very quick activity will introduce the participants to the emotional competency of self-confidence—the second competency that supports the visionary leadership style. Use this slide and the instructions in the learning activity to complete this activity. (Slide 1 of 3)

TIMING	SLIDES	ACTIVITIES/NOTES/CONSIDERATIONS
	Slide 36 Vision and Self-Confidence So…how do you get it? •The level at which you live your life is called *inspiration*, and your inspiration flows primarily from your ability to see your life as meaningful and significant. •The more you can envision the meaning and purpose of your work, the more confidence you will have.	Briefly overview this slide. Emphasize that the more they can envision the meaning and purpose of their work, the more confidence they will have. (Slide 2 of 3)
	Slide 37 Vision and Self-Confidence	Share this story with the participants to help them better understand the links among vision, self-confidence, and engagement: Imagine two people who wake up every morning, go to a job site, and lay bricks for a living. A reporter stops each bricklayer and asks, "What are you doing?" The first bricklayer says, "I am laying bricks. What does it look like I'm doing?" The second bricklayer answers, "I'm building a university. I'm contributing to the future education of our youth. I am changing the world." Both bricklayers are motivated, but only one is motivated by self-confidence that comes from having an inspiring vision. The key is to clearly define what you are doing in terms that let you express your values, fulfill your sense of purpose, or satisfy your innate interests. This means that *anyone* can improve the quality of their motivation by practicing *relational thinking*. The handout has some questions participants can use after the workshop to clarify their values, purpose, and passion. (Slide 3 of 3)

TIMING	SLIDES	ACTIVITIES/NOTES/CONSIDERATIONS
11:50 a.m. (10 min)	Slide 38 **EQuip Yourself for Success** **Practice Relational Thinking** Describe an activity in your life that is fairly important for you to complete, but you have a low motivation to do it, because you are either disinterested, imposed upon, or are only doing it for some external reward. Now, how can relational thinking shift your motivational outlook?	**Learning Activity 39: Practice Relational Thinking** • **Handout 53: Vision, Self-Confidence, and Employee Engagement** This partners activity demonstrates the critical links among vision, self-confidence, and employee engagement. Use this slide and the instructions in the learning activity to complete this activity.
12:00 p.m. (60 min)	Slide 39 Lunch	**LUNCH**
1:00 p.m. (10 min)	Slide 40 The Competency of Change Catalyst	**Learning Content/Lecture** **The Competency of Change Catalyst** • **Handout 54: Visionary Style and the Competency of Change Catalyst** Change catalyst is the third competency of the visionary leadership style. The visionary style is especially effective at helping people manage change. Briefly overview the content in Handout 54, using the graphs in this slide and the next to punctuate your learning points. Point out that change always takes you to a new beginning. (Slide 1 of 2)
	Slide 41 The Competency of Change Catalyst	For something new to begin, something else has to end, and endings are always characterized by loss. This graph shows the emotional roller coaster we all experience as change unfolds, which looks a lot like the grieving process. And that is where visionary leadership comes in. Visionary leaders understand the depths and the heights of performance, morale, and productivity, so they are uniquely positioned to guide others through the pain and uncertainty of change and transition. (Slide 2 of 2)

TIMING	SLIDES	ACTIVITIES/NOTES/CONSIDERATIONS
1:10 p.m. (10 min)	Slide 42 Managing Transition Elements Supporting Transition / Outcome Vision Skills Incentives Resources Actions Skills Incentives Resources Actions Vision Incentives Resources Actions Vision Skills Resources Actions Vision Skills Incentives Actions Vision Skills Incentives Resources	**Learning Activity 40: Visionary Style and Managing Transition** • **Handout 55: Visionary Style and Managing Transition** This small group discussion activity helps participants explore the five elements necessary for managing transition by considering what happens when just one of those elements (vision, skills, incentives, resources, action) is missing. Use this slide and the instructions in the learning activity to complete and debrief this activity.
1:20 p.m. (30 min)	Slide 43 The Competency of Inspirational Leadership **How to Tell a Good Story** **S** ituation **C** omplication **Q** uestion **A** nswer Now, tell your story.....	**Learning Activity 41: Communicating Your Vision** • **Handout 56: The Competency of Inspirational Leadership** Visionary leadership requires the ability to communicate your vision. This activity helps participants practice using a simple storytelling format to communicate vision. There are several variations for facilitating this activity. Use this slide and the instructions in the learning activity to choose the variation you think will be the best fit with your participants.
1:50 p.m. (1 min)	Slide 44 EQuip Yourself for Success **The Coaching Competencies** 1. Empathy 2. Developing Others	**Learning Content/Lecture** **The Coaching Competencies** This is a transitional slide. Explain to participants that now they are going to explore the competencies related to the *coaching* leadership style.
1:51 p.m. (4 min)	Slide 45 The Competency of Empathy **Ask Great Questions...** **???** Change Your Questions, Change Your Life	**Learning Content/Lecture** **Asking Great Questions** • **Handout 57: The Fine Art of Asking Great Questions** To listen and practice empathy, we have to ask great questions of ourselves and others. Reference Marilee Adams' book, *Change Your Questions, Change Your Life*, here as the background for this and the next four slides. (Slide 1 of 5)

TIMING	SLIDES	ACTIVITIES/NOTES/CONSIDERATIONS
1:55 p.m. (10 min)	Slide 46 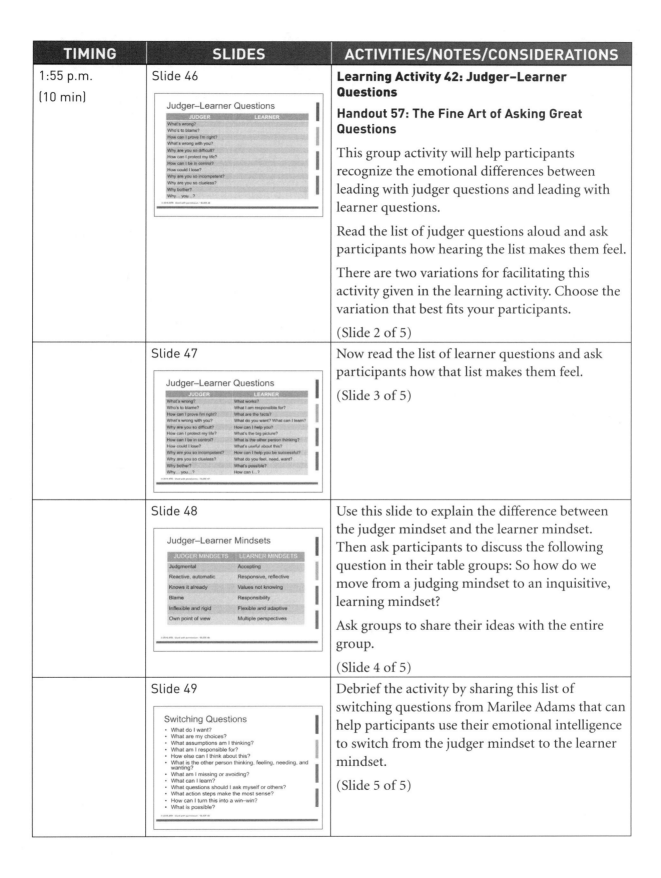	**Learning Activity 42: Judger–Learner Questions** **Handout 57: The Fine Art of Asking Great Questions** This group activity will help participants recognize the emotional differences between leading with judger questions and leading with learner questions. Read the list of judger questions aloud and ask participants how hearing the list makes them feel. There are two variations for facilitating this activity given in the learning activity. Choose the variation that best fits your participants. (Slide 2 of 5)
	Slide 47	Now read the list of learner questions and ask participants how that list makes them feel. (Slide 3 of 5)
	Slide 48	Use this slide to explain the difference between the judger mindset and the learner mindset. Then ask participants to discuss the following question in their table groups: So how do we move from a judging mindset to an inquisitive, learning mindset? Ask groups to share their ideas with the entire group. (Slide 4 of 5)
	Slide 49	Debrief the activity by sharing this list of switching questions from Marilee Adams that can help participants use their emotional intelligence to switch from the judger mindset to the learner mindset. (Slide 5 of 5)

TIMING	SLIDES	ACTIVITIES/NOTES/CONSIDERATIONS
2:05 p.m. (5 min)	Slide 50 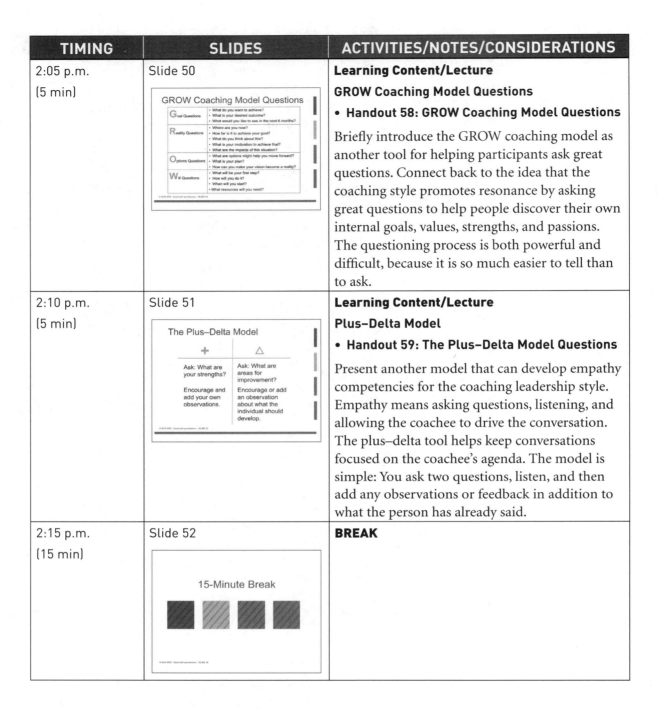	**Learning Content/Lecture** **GROW Coaching Model Questions** • **Handout 58: GROW Coaching Model Questions** Briefly introduce the GROW coaching model as another tool for helping participants ask great questions. Connect back to the idea that the coaching style promotes resonance by asking great questions to help people discover their own internal goals, values, strengths, and passions. The questioning process is both powerful and difficult, because it is so much easier to tell than to ask.
2:10 p.m. (5 min)	Slide 51	**Learning Content/Lecture** **Plus–Delta Model** • **Handout 59: The Plus–Delta Model Questions** Present another model that can develop empathy competencies for the coaching leadership style. Empathy means asking questions, listening, and allowing the coachee to drive the conversation. The plus–delta tool helps keep conversations focused on the coachee's agenda. The model is simple: You ask two questions, listen, and then add any observations or feedback in addition to what the person has already said.
2:15 p.m. (15 min)	Slide 52	**BREAK**

       EMOTIONAL INTELLIGENCE training

TIMING	SLIDES	ACTIVITIES/NOTES/CONSIDERATIONS
2:30 p.m. (40 min)	**Slide 53** Coaching Dialogue: Let's Practice	**Learning Activity 43: Coaching Dialogue** • **Handout 60: Coaching Dialogue Job Aid** This group activity gives participants the opportunity to practice using questions when coaching. It can be conducted in three different ways. Use this slide and the instructions in the learning activity to choose the variation that best fits your participants. (Slide 1 of 3)
	Slide 54 Coaching Dialogue: Interactive Guidelines The Questioning/Problem Identifying Phase 1. One person briefly shares a problem or challenge (23 minutes) 2. Group members start asking questions 3. Try to ask open-ended questions 4. Answer yes/no questions with yes/no answers 5. Keep all other answers as succinct as possible 6. Statements allowed only in response to questions 7. No solutions, and no solutions couched as questions allowed: "Have you tried...?" 8. Listen closely and respect the perceptions of others 9. Build on each other's questions 10. Draw others into the conversation 11. Gain agreement on the problem Remember: The goal of this phase is to problem identify NOT problem solve.	Post the guidelines on this slide while the groups are practicing their coaching dialogues. (Slide 2 of 3)
	Slide 55 Coaching Dialogue: Interactive Guidelines The Creative Ideation/Problem Solving/Action Phase 1. Create choices before you make choices 2. Make sure you have explored the problem and gathered all of the information you need to understand the problem 3. Come up with as many ideas as possible to solve the problem 4. Discuss and evaluate 5. Choose a solution 6. Agree to act on the solution 7. Discuss lessons learned from the coaching dialogue 8. Plan a next time to meet and discuss the action taken and lessons learned Remember: The goal of this phase is to find a collaborative solution, act, and learn.	Use this slide to highlight the difference in questioning during the problem-solving action phase. (Slide 3 of 3)
3:10 p.m. (7 min)	**Slide 56** The Competency of Developing Others **Discussion 1:** Think of the best coaches you have ever partnered with. What was the essence of what they brought to your life? **Discussion 2:** Reflect on yourself as a coach to others, what word or phrase would you use to describe how you see yourself in this role? **Discussion 3:** What coaching skill below represents the one you feel you most need to improve? • Setting clear expectations, goals, and accountabilities • Clearly stating topic and positive intentions • Confronting what needs to be confronted • Sharing constructive, redirecting feedback • Firming up action commitments and follow-through	**Learning Activity 44: The Competency of Developing Others** • **Handout 61: The Competency of Developing Others** This partner activity is designed to get the participants out of their seats and interacting with each other. Have pairs conduct the three rounds of discussions, choosing a new partner for each discussion question.

TIMING	SLIDES	ACTIVITIES/NOTES/CONSIDERATIONS
3:17 p.m. (3 min)	Slide 57 **Coaching Culture** In a coaching culture, all members engage in candid, respectful coaching conversations about how they can improve their working relationships and work performance. Doing annual appraisals is like dieting only one day each year and then wondering why you're not losing any weight.	**Learning Content/Lecture** **Coaching Culture** • **Handout 62: Coaching Culture** Use this slide and handout to define a *coaching culture*. Emphasize the importance of seeking, receiving, and giving feedback as a foundation for creating an organizational culture that engages in candid, respectful coaching conversations to improve working relationships and performance. (Slide 1 of 2)
	Slide 58 **The Importance of Feedback** **The Johari Window: Assessing Self Accurately and Building Trust** 		Known to Self	Not Known to Self
Known to Others	Public Self	Blind Spot
Not Known to Others	Private Self	Unknown		Review what feedback is, using the points from the handout. Then revisit the Johari window briefly and reinforce the importance of seeking, receiving, and giving feedback as a foundation for creating a coaching culture. This slide is intended to help you transition into the next activity. Remind participants of the importance of increasing their own self-awareness through feedback. The same concept holds true for helping others increase their self-awareness. Tell participants that the next activity will help them to understand this concept more clearly. (Slide 2 of 2)
3:20 p.m. (30 min)	Slide 59 **The Hot/Cold Game**	**Learning Activity 45: The Hot/Cold Game** The goal of the hot/cold game is for participants to realize the importance of giving both reinforcing and redirecting feedback to coach others effectively. Use this slide and the instructions in the learning activity to complete this activity. (Slide 1 of 2)
	Slide 60 **Two Types of Feedback** • **Reinforcing Feedback:** tells what you are doing well and what you should continue doing • **Redirecting Feedback:** reveals behaviors that need to change or that need more development	• **Handout 63: Two Types of Feedback** Use this slide *after* debriefing the hot/cold game to emphasize the importance of giving both reinforcing and redirecting feedback. Briefly overview the content on the handout. Try to steer participants away from using the labels *positive* and *negative* when describing feedback. (Slide 2 of 2)

TIMING	SLIDES	ACTIVITIES/NOTES/CONSIDERATIONS
3:50 p.m. (10 min)	Slide 61 Guidelines for Effective Feedback • Specific vs. General • Descriptive vs. Evaluative • Impact vs. Intent • Needs of the Receiver vs. Needs of the Sender • Timely vs. Out of Context • Ensure understanding (*both ways*) • Applicable vs. Useless	**Learning Content/Lecture** **Effective Feedback** • **Handout 64: Guidelines for Effective Feedback** Now that participants have experienced different types of feedback, use this and the next two slides to help them understand how to *deliver* effective feedback. Start by overviewing the guidelines for effective feedback in Handout 64. (Slide 1 of 3)
	Slide 62 Scripting Feedback **S**ituation — 1. Provide the context of the situation **B**ehavior — 2. Describe the specific behavior observed **I**mpact — 3. Describe the impact/consequence of that behavior *Mark, you were really on top of things at the meeting the other day. You seemed to have all of the necessary information right at your fingertips. That kind of preparation really helps us move this project along and makes you stand out within the team.*	Scripting feedback with the situation, behavior, impact (SBI) model can be a helpful coaching tool. Use this slide and the handout to present the SBI model to the participants. Read the sample script on the slide. Ask participants to identify the type of feedback being delivered. (Slide 2 of 3)
	Slide 63 Scripting Feedback **S**ituation — 1. Provide the context of the situation **B**ehavior — 2. Describe the specific behavior observed **I**mpact — 3. Describe the impact/consequence of that behavior *Mark, at the meeting the other day, you were not able to provide some of the details the group needed for making a decision. This made it seem as though you were unprepared and slowed our forward progress in the project.*	Use this slide to demonstrate an example of a redirecting feedback script. Underline that the SBI model helps with scripting, no matter the type of feedback needed. (Slide 3 of 3)
4:00 p.m. (20 min)	Slide 64 Scripting Feedback **S**ituation — 1. Provide the context of the situation **B**ehavior — 2. Describe the specific behavior observed **I**mpact — 3. Describe the impact/consequence of that behavior Now it's your turn…let's practice!	**Learning Activity 46: SBI Practice** • **Handout 65: SBI Practice** This partner activity is designed to give participants practice using the SBI model to script feedback and deliver a feedback conversation. Use this slide and the instructions in the learning activity to complete the activity.

TIMING	SLIDES	ACTIVITIES/NOTES/CONSIDERATIONS
4:20 p.m. (10 min) Ends at 4:30 p.m.	Slide 65 Coaching Action Plan **Complete these action plan prompts:** • One of my primary coaching strengths is… • I will capitalize on this strength by… • A shortcoming in my coaching capability is… • I will develop this competency by… • The positive impact of my efforts to grow as a coach will be…	**Learning Activity 47: Coaching Action Plan and Closing** • **Handout 66: Coaching Action Plan** Give participants 10 minutes to reflect on their coaching strengths and then complete the action prompts on Handout 66. This reflection activity helps participants create alignment between the workshop content and their own personal development plans. Close the activity and Day One of the workshop by asking for volunteers to share their responses to the final prompt on the coaching action plan: What will be the positive impact of their efforts to grow as coaches? Take time to answer any questions about the content you have covered so far in Day One of the workshop and give any reminders for Day Two.

What to Do Between Workshop Days

- Follow-up on any questions or parking lot issues presented during Day One. (A parking lot is a running list that captures issues, ideas, or questions that you couldn't address during the agenda but you want to return to at a later point.)

- Note facilitator lessons learned from the first day of the workshop. Adjust materials for Day Two accordingly, if needed.

- Address any equipment, room setup, or other learning environment issues you weren't able to address during the workshop.

- Debrief with your co-facilitator, if applicable.

Two-Day Workshop Agenda: Day Two

Day Two: (9:00 a.m. to 4:30 p.m.)

TIMING	SLIDES	ACTIVITIES/NOTES/CONSIDERATIONS
Before the Workshop (at least 60 minutes)		**Workshop Setup** Arrive one hour before the start to ensure the room is set up, equipment works, and materials are arranged for the participants. This gives you time to make them feel truly welcomed. Chatting with them builds a trusting relationship and opens them up for learning.
9:00 a.m. (10 min)	Slide 66 **ATD** Workshop Emotional Intelligence The New Science of Leadership Day Two	**Learning Activity 48: Welcome and Lessons Learned** Welcome participants to Day Two and facilitate a group discussion about lessons learned from Day One. Follow the instructions in the learning activity to complete this activity.
9:10 a.m. (5 min)	Slide 67 Learning Objectives: Day Two • Explore a model for deciding how to apply leadership styles to different situations • Learn basic tools for developing competencies that support the *affiliative* leadership style • Manage unconscious bias and create a culture that respects diversity and inclusion • Develop strategies for creating a motivating and engaged culture • Learn basic tools for developing competencies that support the *democratic* leadership style • Identify strategies for win–win collaboration and team decision making	**Learning Objectives: Day Two** • **Handout 67: Learning Objectives: Day Two** Lay out the basic flow of Day Two. Rather than explaining each objective, tell how each objective will be covered. "I will spend some time talking about. . . . And then we will have a small group discussion . . ." Reference participant learning goals as appropriate.

TIMING	SLIDES	ACTIVITIES/NOTES/CONSIDERATIONS
9:15 a.m. (15 min)	**Slide 68** Two Coaching Behaviors **Directive Coaching** Applies telling, instructing, giving advice, offering guidance, providing feedback, and making suggestions to manage the coachee's performance. **Supportive Coaching** A supportive, encouraging, questioning, and listening process for helping someone to solve their own problems where the responsibility for deciding and taking action on the outcome remains with the coachee throughout.	**Learning Content/Lecture** **Two Coaching Behaviors** • **Handout 68: Situational Leadership** In Day One of the workshop you explored two of the four resonant styles of leadership: *visionary* and *coaching*. Today, you will present the *affiliative* and the *democratic* styles. In between you will introduce a situational leadership model that can help participants decide how to blend their coaching behaviors and which style to use with various people. Introduce the situational model by highlighting the two coaching behaviors used in all coaching conversations: directive and supportive. (Slide 1 of 2)
	Slide 69 Tailored Coaching How do I tailor my directive and supportive coaching behaviors to develop high-performing team members? Competence Confidence Motivation High Performance	Next explain the varying degrees of competence, confidence, and motivation that people possess. Read the questions on the slide and then tell participants that the model presented in the next activity will give them a tool to help them work effectively with others. (Slide 2 of 2)
9:30 a.m. (30 min)	**Slide 70** A Meta-Model for Working Effectively With Others High Supportive, Questioning, Encouraging Behaviors Low Direction/ High Support	High Direction/ High Support Low Direction/ Low Support	High Direction/ Low Support Low Low ←——————→ High Directing, Teaching, Training Behaviors	**Learning Activity 49: Discussion of the Meta-Model for Working Effectively With Others** • **Handout 69: A Meta-Model for Working Effectively With Others** This table group discussion activity is designed to help participants learn how to blend supportive and directive coaching based on the competence, confidence, and motivation of the individuals being coached. Briefly explain the model and then ask participants to discuss the scenarios presented in the handout. How would they handle coaching each of the people described in the scenarios? Debrief the activity by asking participants to think of ideas to lead a person who lacks motivation.

TIMING	SLIDES	ACTIVITIES/NOTES/CONSIDERATIONS
10:00 a.m. (5 min)	Slide 71 EQuip Yourself for Success The Affiliative Competencies 1. Empathy 2. Teamwork and Collaboration	**Learning Content/Lecture** **The Affiliative Competencies** This is a transitional slide. Explain to participants that now they will explore the emotional competencies related to the *affiliative* leadership style.
10:05 a.m. (15 min)	Slide 72 Teamwork and Collaboration **Build the tallest, freestanding tower...**	**Learning Activity 50: The Tallest Freestanding Dot Tower** • **Handout 70: The Competency of Teamwork and Collaboration** This fun table group activity supports developing the affiliative competency of teamwork and collaboration. Use this slide and instructions in the learning activity to complete this activity. You will not debrief the activity until *after* you faciliatate the next slide. (Slide 1 of 2)
	Slide 73 Balancing Process and Product Consensus Team Building Brainstorming Ideas Goals Rules Expectations Process Product Results	Define *process* and *product*, the two components of every team undertaking. Explain that even in a 7-minute tower building activity there is time to process what you will do—design your foundation, brainstorm ideas, delineate roles, and so on—and time to produce the end result. Stress the importance of balancing process and product to create effective teamwork and collaboration. Lead a debrief by asking each team to share how well they balanced process and product during the activity. (Slide 2 of 2)

TIMING	SLIDES	ACTIVITIES/NOTES/CONSIDERATIONS
10:20 a.m. (10 min)	Slide 74 Elements of Effective Team Process What are some of the key elements of effective team process?	**Learning Activity 51: The Elements of Effective Team Process** • **Handout 71: EQuip Yourself for Success: The Elements of Team Process** This slide provides either a question to ask of the whole group as part of the learning content or a rhetorical transition, depending on how much time you have at this point in the workshop. Follow the instructions in the learning activity to conduct this exercise. (Slide 1 of 2)
	Slide 75 EQuip Yourself for Success Elements of Team Process 1. Sense of Belonging "Do I belong on this team?" 2. Aligning Strengths "Does my team value my skills?" "Do I get to do what I am good at?" 3. Engagement "Am I engaged?" "Do I bring with passion and commitment to my work and my company?"	Briefly highlight the three elements of team process that you will explore with the participants in the next three learning activities. Emphasize that the affiliative style is particularly effective for facilitating these elements of team process. Mastering these elements produces two sought-after results: • High-performance teams • A highly engaged organizational culture. (Slide 2 of 2)
10:30 a.m. (15 min)	Slide 76 15-Minute Break	**BREAK**

TIMING	SLIDES	ACTIVITIES/NOTES/CONSIDERATIONS
10:45 a.m. (20 min)	Slide 77 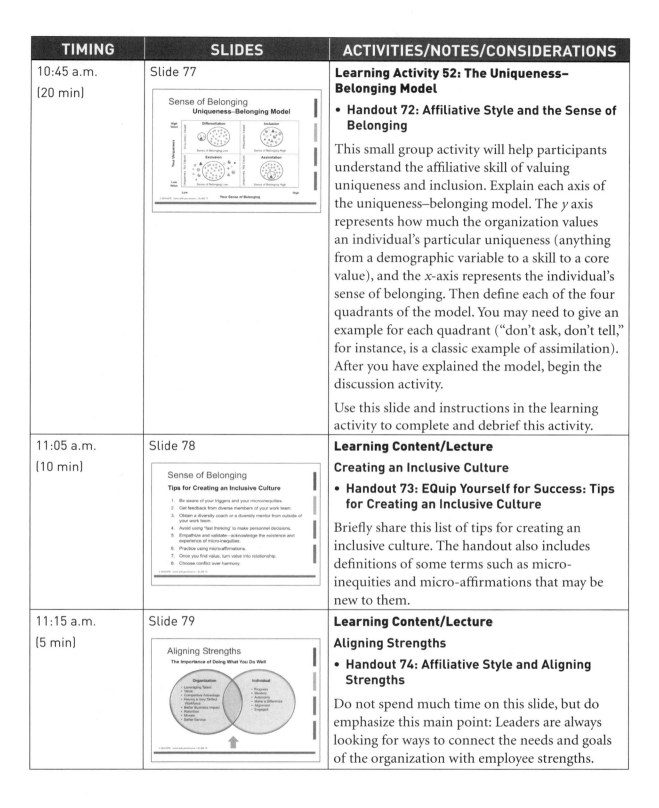	**Learning Activity 52: The Uniqueness–Belonging Model** • **Handout 72: Affiliative Style and the Sense of Belonging** This small group activity will help participants understand the affiliative skill of valuing uniqueness and inclusion. Explain each axis of the uniqueness–belonging model. The y axis represents how much the organization values an individual's particular uniqueness (anything from a demographic variable to a skill to a core value), and the x-axis represents the individual's sense of belonging. Then define each of the four quadrants of the model. You may need to give an example for each quadrant ("don't ask, don't tell," for instance, is a classic example of assimilation). After you have explained the model, begin the discussion activity. Use this slide and instructions in the learning activity to complete and debrief this activity.
11:05 a.m. (10 min)	Slide 78	**Learning Content/Lecture** **Creating an Inclusive Culture** • **Handout 73: EQuip Yourself for Success: Tips for Creating an Inclusive Culture** Briefly share this list of tips for creating an inclusive culture. The handout also includes definitions of some terms such as micro-inequities and micro-affirmations that may be new to them.
11:15 a.m. (5 min)	Slide 79	**Learning Content/Lecture** **Aligning Strengths** • **Handout 74: Affiliative Style and Aligning Strengths** Do not spend much time on this slide, but do emphasize this main point: Leaders are always looking for ways to connect the needs and goals of the organization with employee strengths.

TIMING	SLIDES	ACTIVITIES/NOTES/CONSIDERATIONS
11:20 a.m. (40 min)	Slide 80 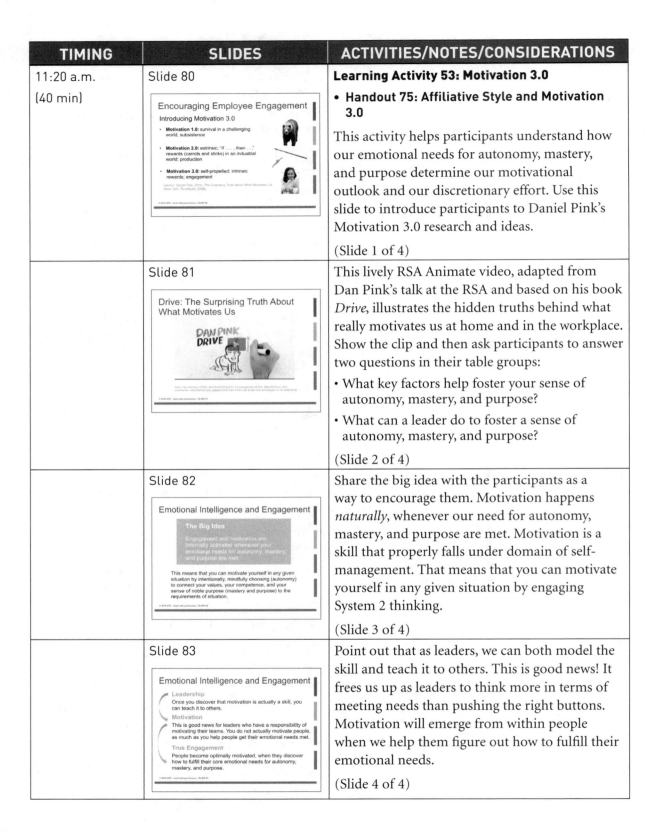 **Encouraging Employee Engagement** Introducing Motivation 3.0 • **Motivation 1.0:** survival in a challenging world; subsistence • **Motivation 2.0:** extrinsic; "If . . . , then . . ." rewards (carrots and sticks) in an industrial world; production • **Motivation 3.0:** self-propelled; intrinsic rewards; engagement	**Learning Activity 53: Motivation 3.0** • **Handout 75: Affiliative Style and Motivation 3.0** This activity helps participants understand how our emotional needs for autonomy, mastery, and purpose determine our motivational outlook and our discretionary effort. Use this slide to introduce participants to Daniel Pink's Motivation 3.0 research and ideas. (Slide 1 of 4)
	Slide 81 Drive: The Surprising Truth About What Motivates Us DAN PINK DRIVE	This lively RSA Animate video, adapted from Dan Pink's talk at the RSA and based on his book *Drive*, illustrates the hidden truths behind what really motivates us at home and in the workplace. Show the clip and then ask participants to answer two questions in their table groups: • What key factors help foster your sense of autonomy, mastery, and purpose? • What can a leader do to foster a sense of autonomy, mastery, and purpose? (Slide 2 of 4)
	Slide 82 Emotional Intelligence and Engagement **The Big Idea** Engagement and motivation are internally activated whenever your emotional needs for autonomy, mastery, and purpose are met. This means that you can motivate yourself in *any* given situation by intentionally, mindfully choosing (autonomy) to connect your values, your competence, and your sense of noble purpose (mastery and purpose) to the requirements of situation.	Share the big idea with the participants as a way to encourage them. Motivation happens *naturally*, whenever our need for autonomy, mastery, and purpose are met. Motivation is a skill that properly falls under domain of self-management. That means that you can motivate yourself in any given situation by engaging System 2 thinking. (Slide 3 of 4)
	Slide 83 Emotional Intelligence and Engagement Leadership Once you discover that motivation is actually a skill, you can teach it to others. Motivation This is good news for leaders who have a responsibility of motivating their teams. You do not actually motivate people, as much as you help people get their emotional needs met. True Engagement People become optimally motivated, when they discover how to fulfill their core emotional needs for autonomy, mastery, and purpose.	Point out that as leaders, we can both model the skill and teach it to others. This is good news! It frees us up as leaders to think more in terms of meeting needs than pushing the right buttons. Motivation will emerge from within people when we help them figure out how to fulfill their emotional needs. (Slide 4 of 4)

TIMING	SLIDES	ACTIVITIES/NOTES/CONSIDERATIONS
12:00 p.m. (60 min)	Slide 84 Lunch	**LUNCH**
1:00 p.m. (20 min)	Slide 85 Using Employee Engagement Surveys	**Learning Content/Lecture** **Using Employee Engagement Surveys** • **Handout 76: Using Employee Engagement Surveys** To help your participants to facilitate discussions with team members and colleagues about motivation and engagement, briefly overview Handout 76, which provides information about using employment engagement surveys.
1:20 p.m. (5 min)	Slide 86 EQuip Yourself for Success The Democratic Competencies 1. Empathy 2. Teamwork and Collaboration 3. Influence 4. Conflict Management	**Learning Content/Lecture** **The Democratic Competencies** This is a transitional slide. Explain to participants that now they will explore the emotional competencies related to the *democratic* leadership style. The democratic competencies include empathy, teamwork and collaboration, influence, and conflict management. This section will focus on influence and conflict management.
1:25 p.m. (15 min)	Slide 87 The Competency of Influence Discussion, Part 1: 1. What is influence? How do you define it? 2. How is influence distinct from persuasion? 3. Is it easier to have influence when you have authority? Is it easier to lead from the top? Discussion, Part 2: • Reflect on the individuals who have the most influence on you in your personal life. What factors gave these individuals their influence?	**Learning Activity 54: The Competency of Influence** • **Handout 77: Democratic Style and the Competency of Influence** This small group discussion activity is conducted in two parts. It introduces the competency of influence to the participants. The debrief of the discussion is a little tricky, so follow the instructions closely in the learning activity.

TIMING	SLIDES	ACTIVITIES/NOTES/CONSIDERATIONS
1:40 p.m. (15 min)	Slide 88 **Six Principles of Influence** 1. Reciprocity 2. Commitment and Consistency 3. Social Proof 4. Liking 5. Authority 6. Scarcity How might you ethically and appropriately leverage these influence principles in the workplace?	**Learning Activity 55: The Six Principles of Influence** • **Handout 78: The Six Principles of Influence** Use this small group discussion activity to introduce Cialdini's six principles of influence, which will help participants develop the competency of influence to support the democratic leadership style. Cialdini, a professor of psychology and researcher, believes that influencing others isn't luck or magic—it's science—and there are proven ways to help anyone be more successful in influencing others. In his seminal book, *Influence*, he highlights six principles of influence: • Reciprocity • Consistency • Social proof • Liking • Authority • Security. Briefly explain the six principles using this slide and the notes in the learning activity. Then ask small groups to brainstorm ways to ethically and appropriately leverage the influence strategies in the workplace. Feel free to mix up the small groups by placing people in different groups for this activity. Use this slide and instructions in the learning activity to complete and debrief this activity.
1:55 p.m. (5 min)	Slide 89 **The Competency of Conflict Management** **Basic Premises** • Your ability to successfully resolve conflicts comes from having access to resources that other people want. • Relationships matter; so build the relationship before you need it. • You must be sincerely willing to yield to agreements, fair arguments, fair principles, and fair procedures.	**Learning Content/Lecture** **The Competency of Conflict Management** • **Handout 79: Democratic Style and the Competency of Conflict Management** Introduce the competency of conflict management and its three basic premises outlined on this slide. (Slide 1 of 2)

TIMING	SLIDES	ACTIVITIES/NOTES/CONSIDERATIONS
2:00 p.m. (25 min)	Slide 90 Sources of Conflict	**Learning Activity 56: Case Studies in Conflict** • **Handout 79: Democratic Style and the Competency of Conflict Management** • **Handout 80: Examples of Conflict Worksheet** This activity helps participants identify examples that they will use to complete the rest of the learning activities in the democratic style section. It is important that they spend time explaining and understanding each other's examples so they will be able to apply the conflict management tools to real-life situations. This activity is facilitated in two parts. In the first part, you will introduce some typical sources of conflict on the slide, illustrating with real-life examples of conflicts from these sources. In the second part, the participants will come up with their own examples of conflicts and then explore them further in their small groups.
2:25 p.m. (5 min)	Slide 91 EQuip Yourself for Success **Four Steps of Conflict Management** 1. Attack the problem not the person 2. Figure out everyone's interests and expectations 3. Brainstorm win–win options 4. Insist on using fair procedures and principles	**Learning Content/Lecture** **Four Steps of Conflict Management** • **Handout 81: EQuip Yourself for Success: Four Steps of Conflict Management** Briefly introduce the steps of conflict management outlined on this slide. Each has several important concepts that are essential to successful completion of the step. Tell the participants that they will explore each step in depth as the workshop unfolds.
2:30 p.m. (15 min)	Slide 92 15-Minute Break	**BREAK**

TIMING	SLIDES	ACTIVITIES/NOTES/CONSIDERATIONS
2:45 p.m. (5 min)	**Slide 93** Step 1: Attack the Problem, Not the Person **Four Important Concepts** 1. Assume there is a win–win solution 2. Use empathy and open questioning to understand 3. Identify and write out the problem 4. Collaborate to solve the problem	**Learning Content/Lecture** **Step 1: Attack the Problem, Not the Person** • **Handout 82: Step 1: Attack the Problem, Not the Person** Share this list of four concepts that are essential to the first step of conflict management. Let participants know that each concept will be addressed either as learning content or a learning activity. (1 of 3)
	Slide 94 Assume There is a Win–Win Solution **The emotional signals of conflict really mean…** • All parties have legitimate concerns. • There is an elegant win–win solution that will resolve the conflict. • The elegant solution has not yet been discovered. • The elegant solution is the best solution because it values the diversity of concerns and perspectives that created the conflict in the first place. *"Conflict is a dangerous opportunity."* —Robert Sutton, People Skills	Remind participants of the first lesson they learned about emotional intelligence: An emotion is a signal to take action. The key idea behind this first concept is that the emotional upset we feel when we are in conflict will control our behaviors and our conversations, *unless* we mindfully treat the signal as if it is asking us to look at our assumptions and curiously seek the win–win opportunity. (2 of 3)
	Slide 95 Use Empathy and Open Questioning	Use this slide to present a metaphor for the power of empathy and open questions, the second concept of Step 1. Explain that if you stand too close to an impressionist painting, you can't figure out what is happening in the picture. The same is true when we stand too close to our problems. We have a difficult time seeing the way out. When we give or receive empathy, we create distance between the person and the problem, and we are better able to see the problem with perspective. Then we can attack the problem and not the person. (3 of 3)

TIMING	SLIDES	ACTIVITIES/NOTES/CONSIDERATIONS
2:50 p.m. (5 min)	Slide 96 Identify and Write Out the Problem Problem	**Learning Activity 57: Step 1 Practice: Identify and Collaborate, Part 1** • **Handout 83: Collaborate to Solve the Problem** This fast-paced, small group activity combines practice on two concepts for Step 1. Use this slide as a cue for Part 1 of the activity: Identify and write out a problem. Have each table group choose one conflict story that is complex and involves several stakeholders, agree on the problem, and then write it in the center of the flipchart. Only give participants 2 minutes to complete this activity. They are only *identifying and writing out the problem, not solving it.* At the end of 2 minutes check in with all groups to make sure they have identified an intractable problem. Then move to the next slide to facilitate Part 2 of the activity.
	Slide 97 Collaborate to Solve the Problem You Stakeholder · Stakeholder Problem Stakeholder · Stakeholder Stakeholder	**Learning Activity 57: Step 1 Practice: Identify and Collaborate, Part 2** • **Handout 83: Collaborate to Solve the Problem** Use this slide and handout to conduct Part 2 of the activity: Collaborate to solve a problem. Instruct table groups to go to the flipchart page that was used to write out the problem and identify all of the stakeholders with whom the problem owner needs to collaborate and write them on their flipcharts. Give participants 2 minutes to complete this activity. Remind them that they are only *identifying stakeholders, not solving the problem.* No debrief is needed for this activity.

TIMING	SLIDES	ACTIVITIES/NOTES/CONSIDERATIONS
2:55 p.m. (10 min)	Slide 98 Step 2: Figure Out Everyone's Interests and Expectations **Five Important Concepts** • Avoid positional arguments and final decisions • Determine what others value and need • Determine what others are willing to contribute • Manage or facilitate the process • Be clear about your own goals and priorities	**Learning Content/Lecture** **Step 2: Figure Out Everyone's Interests and Expectations** • **Handout 84: Step 2: Figure Out Everyone's Interests and Expectations** Briefly introduce the five important concepts for Step 2 of conflict management. Explain the first three concepts, and as you do, refer participants to the takeaway tools in Handout 84. You will present concepts 4 and 5 in the learning activity that follows.
3:05 p.m. (15 min)	Slide 99 Inputs, Outputs, and Managing the Process You Stakeholder Stakeholder Problem Stakeholder Stakeholder Stakeholder	**Learning Activity 58: Step 2 Practice: Inputs, Outputs, and Managing the Process** • **Handout 83: Collaborate to Solve the Problem** • **Handout 84: Step 2: Figure Out Everyone's Interests and Expectations** This small group activity continues the participants' work on the problem they identified in the previous activity. Refer participants back to Handout 83 to complete this activity. Instruct table groups, as best as they can, to work with the problem owner to identify all of the input and output arrows of all of the stakeholders. Emphasize that they are *still not problem solving*, but they are identifying the interests and expectations of the stakeholders. There is no need to debrief this activity, but be sure to explain to participants that the democratic style is all about managing the process and keeping the process collaborative rather than competitive.

TIMING	SLIDES	ACTIVITIES/NOTES/CONSIDERATIONS
3:20 p.m. (5 min)	Slide 100 Be Clear About Your Own Goals and Priorities • Gold Standard • Silver Standard • BATNA	**Learning Content/Lecture** **Be Clear About Your Own Goals and Priorities** • **Handout 85: Know Your BATNA** Now explain concept 5 of Step 2—being clear about your own goals and priorities. Emphasize the balance between inquiring about what others need with expressing what the problem owner needs. Some of the dimensions that affect your choice of how to proceed in a negotiation include identifying your aspirations—your gold standard (pie in the sky outcome), your silver, and your BATNA (best alternative to a negotiated agreement). Walk participants through Handout 85, which introduces the BATNA tool that they can develop ahead of time. Knowing their BATNA can help protect them from making an agreement that should have been rejected.
3:25 p.m. (5 min)	Slide 101 Step 3: Brainstorm Win–Win Options **Three Important Concepts** 1. Create choices before making choices 2. Use 4-8 people of diverse perspectives 3. Use stakeholder needs and interests as a basis for creative ideation	**Learning Content/Lecture** **Step 3: Brainstorm Win–Win Options** • **Handout 86: Step 3: Brainstorm Win–Win Options** Briefly overview the three important concepts for Step 3 of conflict management: brainstorm win–win options. You will explain concepts 1 and 2 on the next slide, and then facilitate a learning activity to explore concept 3 more fully. (Slide 1 of 3)
	Slide 102 Create Choices Before Making Choices DIVERGE CONVERGE CREATE CHOICES MAKE CHOICES	Emphasize these key points: • Concept 1: We need to diverge and create solutions before we converge to pick a solution. • Concept 2: The more diverse our group is, the more diverse our pool of potential solutions. The goal is to generate as many diverse, innovative, creative options to choose from as possible. (Slide 2 of 3)

TIMING	SLIDES	ACTIVITIES/NOTES/CONSIDERATIONS
3:30 p.m. (20 min)	Slide 103 Brainstorming Practice	**Learning Activity 59: Step 3 Practice: Brainstorm** • **Handout 86: Step 3: Brainstorm Win-Win Options** You can choose from two different brainstorming techniques for conducting this activity. Choose whichever tool you like the most, and then lead participants through one brainstorm activity, using the needs and expectations that they identified in Learning Activity 58, as a basis for creative ideation in this activity. (Slide 3 of 3)
3:50 p.m. (5 min)	Slide 104 Step 4: Insist on Using Fair Procedures and Principles **Five Important Concepts** 1. Understand that deciding on the basis of will is costly 2. Frame each issue as a joint search for objective criteria 3. Use valid and reliable decision making tools to keep the process fair and principled 4. Reason and be open to reason as to which standards are most appropriate 5. Never yield to pressure—only to fair principles or fair procedures	**Learning Content/Lecture** **Step 4: Insist on Using Fair Procedures and Principles** • **Handout 87: Step 4: Insist on Using Fair Procedures and Principles** Briefly overview this list of five important concepts for Step 4 of conflict management: insist on using fair procedures or principles. Remember we are still developing the democratic style. Share the big idea here: When the democratic vote ends in a tie, deciding on the basis of will is costly to the relationship. Use of these concepts, therefore, will enable a collaborative agreement. (Slide 1 of 4)
	Slide 105 Fair Principles • Market value • Precedence • Cost efficiency • Scientific judgment • Highest quality • Professional standards • Most compliant • Policy manual • Safest • Equal treatment • Arbitrator decides • HR or SME opinion • Moral standards • Tradition • Fair book value • Reciprocity	Use this slide to expand on concept 2, framing each principle as a joint search for objective criteria. (Slide 2 of 4)

TIMING	SLIDES	ACTIVITIES/NOTES/CONSIDERATIONS
3:55 p.m. (5 min)	Slide 106 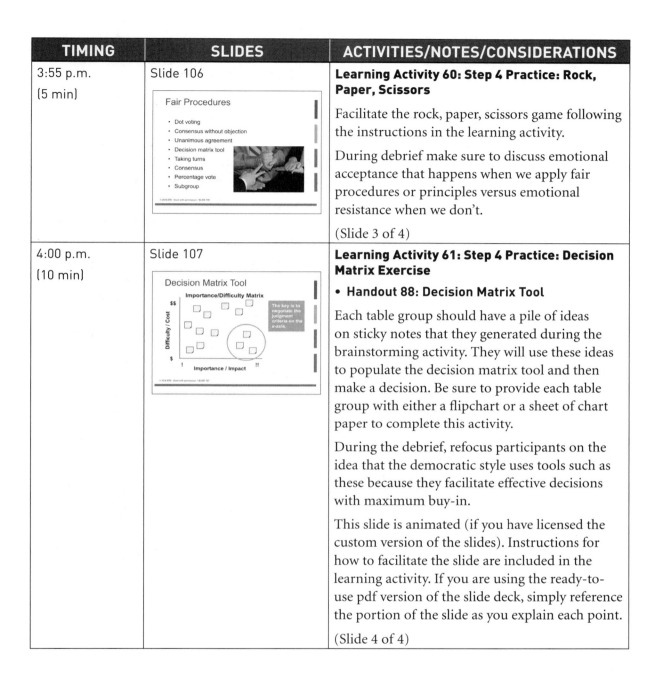	**Learning Activity 60: Step 4 Practice: Rock, Paper, Scissors** Facilitate the rock, paper, scissors game following the instructions in the learning activity. During debrief make sure to discuss emotional acceptance that happens when we apply fair procedures or principles versus emotional resistance when we don't. (Slide 3 of 4)
4:00 p.m. (10 min)	Slide 107	**Learning Activity 61: Step 4 Practice: Decision Matrix Exercise** • **Handout 88: Decision Matrix Tool** Each table group should have a pile of ideas on sticky notes that they generated during the brainstorming activity. They will use these ideas to populate the decision matrix tool and then make a decision. Be sure to provide each table group with either a flipchart or a sheet of chart paper to complete this activity. During the debrief, refocus participants on the idea that the democratic style uses tools such as these because they facilitate effective decisions with maximum buy-in. This slide is animated (if you have licensed the custom version of the slides). Instructions for how to facilitate the slide are included in the learning activity. If you are using the ready-to-use pdf version of the slide deck, simply reference the portion of the slide as you explain each point. (Slide 4 of 4)

TIMING	SLIDES	ACTIVITIES/NOTES/CONSIDERATIONS
4:10 p.m. (5 min)	Slide 108 Q&A	**Learning Content/Lecture** **Q&A** There are three parts to facilitating the Q&A: First, let participants know the workshop is *not* over yet. Say: "Before I give you time to work on your action plan, what questions do you have about today's workshop?" Second, wait a full 7 seconds to give people time to reflect and process. Third, if there is time after you have addressed their questions, revisit any learning goals that participants discussed at the beginning of the workshop (and that you recorded on the flipchart) that were not covered by the program. Refer participants to the half-day or one-day program, if appropriate.
4:15 p.m. (10 min)	Slide 109 Action Plan IDEA PLAN ACTION SUCCESS	**Learning Activity 62: EQuip Yourself for Success: Action Plan** • **Handout 89: EQuip Yourself for Success: Action Plan** This activity is designed to create alignment between the workshop content and the individual participant's development plan. Give participants 10 minutes to reflect on lessons learned and to fill out the action plan as outlined in Handout 89.

TIMING	SLIDES	ACTIVITIES/NOTES/CONSIDERATIONS
4:25 p.m. (5 min) Ends at 4:30 p.m.	Slide 110 Wrap-Up Key Learning Points	**Wrap-Up** • **Assessment 1: Workshop Evaluation** Close the workshop on a positive note. Distribute the workshop evaluations. As they are completing the evaluations, ask them to think about the most valuable idea or strategy they learned today. When you have all the evaluations, ask everyone to form a circle. Start by sharing something that *you* learned today. Then toss a soft throwing object such as a Koosh ball to one participant and ask him or her to share a key learning point. Continue tossing the ball around the circle until everyone who is willing to share has shared. Be available to answer any questions participants may still have about the workshop content. Share plans for follow-up coaching, if applicable (see Chapter 10 for ideas to follow up the training with support and activities). Thank participants for their contributions and wish them well.

What to Do Next

- Determine the schedule for training workshops; reserve location and catering you may wish to provide.

- Identify and invite participants.

- Inform participants about any pre-work, if applicable, that you want completed before the workshop begins.

- Review the workshop objectives, activities, and handouts to plan the content you will use.

- Prepare copies of the participant materials and any activity-related materials you may need. Refer to Chapter 14 for information about how to access and use the supplemental materials provided for this workshop.

- Gather tactile items, such as Koosh balls, crayons, magnets, Play-Doh, or others, that you wish to place on the tables for tactile learners. See Chapter 8 for other ideas to enhance the learning environment of your workshop.

- Prepare yourself both emotionally and physically. Confirm that you have addressed scheduling and personal concerns so that you can be fully present to facilitate the workshop.

References

Adams, M. (2016). *Change Your Questions, Change Your Life: 12 Powerful Tools for Leadership, Coaching, and Life*, 3rd ed. San Francisco: Berrett-Koehler.

Bridges, W. (2004). *Transitions: Making Sense of Life's Changes*, 2nd ed. Boston: Da Capo.

Cialdini, R. (1995). *Influence: The Psychology of Persuasion*, rev. ed. New York: William Morrow.

Feldman, J., and K. Mulle. (2007). *Put Emotional Intelligence to Work: EQuip Yourself for Success*. Alexandria, VA: ASTD Press.

Goleman, D. (1998). *Working With Emotional Intelligence*. New York: Bloomsbury.

Goleman, D. (2000). "Leadership That Gets Results." *Harvard Business Review*, 82-83.

Goleman, D., R. Boyatzis, and A. McKee. (2002). *Primal Leadership: Realizing the Power of Emotional Intelligence*. Boston: Harvard Business Press.

Mischel, W. (2014). *The Marshmallow Test: Mastering Self-Control*. New York: Little, Brown.

Pink, D. (2009). *Drive: The Surprising Truth About What Motivates Us*. New York: Riverhead.

Chapter 4

Customizing the Emotional Intelligence Workshops

What's in This Chapter

- Ideas for creating customized emotional intelligence workshops
- Ideas for lunch-and-learn formats or two-hour workshops
- Suggestions for designing theme-based workshops

Many organizations are challenged by having employees away from the workplace for an entire day or two, even if it is for professional development. As a result, you may need to adjust and adapt your workshop to the scheduling needs of the organization. Additionally, the content and topics of your workshop truly must match the needs of the participants attending the training. Therefore, your training needs analysis will help you select the workshop best suited to your participants' needs and guide your decisions in customizing the content and activities. For more on needs analysis, see Chapter 5.

The materials in this ATD Workshop Series volume are designed to meet a variety of training needs. They cover multiple topics within three key aspects of emotional intelligence training and can be offered in many timeframes and formats. By using the learning content and activities provided here as a foundation, you can modify and adapt the learning experience by customizing the content and activities, customizing the workshop format, and customizing the delivery with technology.

Customizing the Content and Activities

The requirement to provide a customized workshop experience is usually driven by the needs of the requesting organization. A training need, for example, might include a request to build a program around the emotional competencies of self-awareness, teamwork and collaboration, transparency, and change catalyst. This begs the question: Does any random combination of three or four competencies seamlessly integrate into one cohesive program? Although any of these four competencies could easily be offered as a stand-alone delivery, it is difficult to imagine how to integrate them together into a customized half-day or even full-day workshop.

The easiest way to think about designing a customized emotional intelligence workshop is to begin with the foundation of simply defining and explaining what emotional intelligence is. The human tendency to make fast, automatic decisions serves us well when we are under severe threat or in danger but not so well when dealing with an angry customer. So the tendency to be emotionally reactive needs to be managed, and we do it with the four building blocks of emotional intelligence: self-awareness, self-management, social awareness, and relationship management. Each workshop in this series begins with the same foundational material and then diverges into one of three very distinct areas of focus: personal success, interpersonal success, and leadership. This pattern of beginning with the four-domain model and then diverging into a unique focus can be repeated in customized formats, with each workshop focusing on a different relationship topic.

Let's return to the hypothetical request for a customized program that includes the four emotional competencies of self-awareness, teamwork and collaboration, transparency, and change catalyst. Rather than one workshop, this material might be better designed and delivered as two workshops:

- Emotional Intelligence: Focus on Teamwork and Collaboration
- Emotional Intelligence: Focus on Managing Change

As you tailor the content in this book for your own workshops, be sure to carefully think through the content to create a meaningful learning experience. Start with a good foundation of emotional intelligence, and then focus on developing competencies that complement or reinforce each other. Resist the temptation to include a laundry list of emotional intelligence competencies in your design. There is no one way to flow emotional intelligence content, but you must ensure that the topics build on one another and that you solidly connect the concepts and ideas together to leverage the most of the learning opportunity.

Finally, research on adult learning and retention overwhelmingly points to the need for activity-based learning. Even in a one-hour format, there should be at least one activity to reinforce the content. The key to customizing the activities is for you to *own* the material as you facilitate it. As you become more comfortable with both the topic and the timing of each component, you will be able to introduce more of your own personal style into the workshop. You may find that you would introduce a particular topic with an activity instead of a lecture format, or that you have a variation on an activity that works better with your training style. The most important variable for keeping the material relevant and ensuring that learning happens is for you to customize in a way that preserves your authentic style.

Customizing the Workshop Format

Although extended immersion in the learning environment can increase the depth of learning experiences, workplace realities sometimes require the training be conducted in short, small doses. All of the topics described in this series can be delivered in one- or two-hour formats. However, just like there isn't really a "10-minute workout" to get in shape, the one-hour workshop that will completely exercise one's emotional intelligence muscle does not really exist. Realistically, the only goal that you will accomplish in one hour is to define the four quadrants. If the one- or two-hour format is the only option that an organization has for employee training, then the best way to deliver the topic of emotional intelligence is to suggest a *series* of one- or two-hour sessions.

One-Hour, Themed Sessions

Table 4-1 breaks down some of the content in this book into 12 one-hour sessions based on selected themes to be offered as stand-alone events. You can also consider stringing a few of them together to offer as a series. If you have the opportunity to offer these one-hour sessions as a series, then you will not need to begin each session discussing the anatomy of an emotion, which will leave you more time to devote to activities.

Table 4-1. Sample One-Hour Formats

ONE-HOUR TOPIC	RESOURCES
Emotional Intelligence: The New Science of Success	
• The Anatomy of an Emotion	Handout 18
• The Definition of Emotional Intelligence	Handout 20
• The Four-Domain Model	Handout 20
• The 18 Competencies	Handouts 21–24; Learning Activities 11–14
Emotional Intelligence: Self-Awareness	
• The Anatomy of an Emotion	Handout 18
• The Definition of Emotional Intelligence	Handout 20
• The Four-Domain Model	Handout 20
• The E-Motion Chart	Handout 19; Learning Activity 10
Emotional Intelligence: Self-Management	
• The Anatomy of an Emotion	Handout 18
• The Definition of Emotional Intelligence	Handout 20
• The Four-Domain Model	Handout 20
• Emotions, Thoughts, and Behaviors	Handout 7
• Behavioral Strategies	Handout 8; Learning Activity 3
• Cognitive Strategies	Handouts 9, 10; Learning Activity 5
Emotional Intelligence: Self-Motivation	
• The Anatomy of an Emotion	Handout 18
• The Definition of Emotional Intelligence	Handout 20
• The Four-Domain Model	Handout 20
• The Marshmallow Story	Handouts 50–52; Learning Activity 38
• Relational Thinking	Handouts 52, 53; Learning Activity 39
Emotional Intelligence: Social-Awareness	
• The Anatomy of an Emotion	Handout 18
• The Definition of Emotional Intelligence	Handout 20
• The Four-Domain Model	Handout 20
• Defining the Emotional Competency of Empathy	Handout 25; Learning Activity 15
• Three Listening Skills	Handout 26; Learning Activity 16
Emotional Intelligence: Resonant Leadership	
• The Anatomy of an Emotion	Handout 18
• The Definition of Emotional Intelligence	Handout 20
• The Four-Domain Model	Handout 20
• Resonant vs. Dissonant Leadership	Handout 43; Learning Activity 31
• The Six Styles of Leadership	Handouts 44, 45; Learning Activites 32, 33

ONE-HOUR TOPIC	RESOURCES
Emotional Intelligence: Influence	
• The Anatomy of an Emotion	Handout 18
• The Definition of Emotional Intelligence	Handout 20
• The Four-Domain Model	Handout 20
• The Competency of Influence	Handout 77; Learning Activity 54
• The Two Messages	Handout 35; Learning Activity 24
• Six Principles of Influence	Handout 78
Emotional Intelligence: Developing Others	
• The Anatomy of an Emotion	Handout 18
• The Definition of Emotional Intelligence	Handout 20
• The Four-Domain Model	Handout 20
• The Competency of Developing Others	Handouts 61, 62; Learning Activity 44
• The Johari Window and the Importance of Feedback	Handout 48
• The SBI Model	Handouts 63, 64
Emotional Intelligence: Change Catalyst	
• The Anatomy of an Emotion	Handout 18
• The Definition of Emotional Intelligence	Handout 20
• The Four-Domain Model	Handout 20
• The Competency of Change Catalyst	Handout 54
• The Change Model	Handout 54
• Managing Transition	Handout 55; Learning Activity 40
Emotional Intelligence: Conflict Management	
• The Anatomy of an Emotion	Handout 18
• The Definition of Emotional Intelligence	Handout 20
• The Four-Domain Model	Handout 20
• The Competency of Conflict Management	Handout 36
• Who Needs to Initiate Conflict Resolution?	Handout 36
• XYZ Talk	Handout 37; Learning Activity 26
Emotional Intelligence: Teamwork and Collaboration	
• The Anatomy of an Emotion	Handout 18
• The Definition of Emotional Intelligence	Handout 20
• The Four-Domain Model	Handout 20
• The Competency of Teamwork and Collaboration	Handout 70
• Balancing Process and Product	Handout 71; Learning Activities 50, 51
Emotional Intelligence: Employee Engagement	
• The Anatomy of an Emotion	Handout 18
• The Definition of Emotional Intelligence	Handout 20
• The Four-Domain Model	Handout 20
• Discretionary Emotional Energy	Handout 29; Learning Activity 19
• Motivation and Employee Engagement	Handouts 75, 76; Learning Activity 53

Two-Hour, Themed Sessions

Table 4-2 breaks down some of the content in this book into 12 two-hour sessions based on selected themes to be offered as stand-alone events. The two-hour sessions are the same as the one-hour sessions, with the addition of one or two more content points and more activity. The additional content is noted by a + bullet point. You may also string these two-hour sessions together to offer as a series.

Table 4-2. Sample Two-Hour Formats

TWO-HOUR TOPIC	RESOURCES
Emotional Intelligence: The New Science of Success	
• The Anatomy of an Emotion	Handout 18
+ The E-Motion Chart	Handout 19; Learning Activity 10
• The Definition of Emotional Intelligence	Handout 20
• The Four-Domain Model	Handout 20
• The 18 Competencies	Handouts 21–24; Learning Activities 11–14
+ Emotional Intelligence Self-Assessment	Assessment 3
Emotional Intelligence: Self-Awareness	
• The Anatomy of an Emotion	Handout 18
• The Definition of Emotional Intelligence	Handout 20
• The Four-Domain Model	Handout 20
• The E-Motion Chart	Handout 19; Learning Activity 10
+ System 1 vs. System 2 Thinking	Handouts 2, 4–6; Learning Activity 2
Emotional Intelligence: Self-Management	
• The Anatomy of an Emotion	Handout 18
• The Definition of Emotional Intelligence	Handout 20
• The Four-Domain Model	Handout 20
• Emotions, Thoughts, and Behaviors	Handout 7
• Behavioral Strategies	Handout 8; Learning Activity 3
• Cognitive Strategies	Handout 9; Learning Activity 5
+ More Cognitive Strategies	Handouts 11–13, 15; Learning Activities 6, 8

TWO-HOUR TOPIC	RESOURCES
Emotional Intelligence: Self-Motivation	
• The Anatomy of an Emotion	Handout 18
• The Definition of Emotional Intelligence	Handout 20
• The Four-Domain Model	Handout 20
• The Marshmallow Story	Handouts 50, 51; Learning Activity 38
• Relational Thinking	Handouts 52, 53; Learning Activity 39
+ Encouraging Employee Engagement	Handouts 75, 76; Learning Activity 53
Emotional Intelligence: Social-Awareness	
• The Anatomy of an Emotion	Handout 18
• The Definition of Emotional Intelligence	Handout 20
• The Four-Domain Model	Handout 20
• Defining the Emotional Competency of Empathy	Handout 25; Learning Activity 15
• Three Listening Skills	Handout 26; Learning Activity 16
+ Collaborative Intention	Handout 27; Assessment 2; Learning Activity 17
+ Managing Defensiveness	Handout 49; Learning Activity 36
+ How to Ask Great Questions	Handouts 57, 58; Learning Activity 42
Emotional Intelligence: Resonant Leadership	
• The Anatomy of an Emotion	Handout 18
• The Definition of Emotional Intelligence	Handout 20
• The Four-Domain Model	Handout 20
• Resonant vs. Dissonant Leadership	Handout 43; Learning Activity 31
• The Six Styles of Leadership	Handouts 44, 45; Learning Activities 32, 33
+ Emotional Intelligence Self-Assessment	Assessment 3; Learning Activity 34
+ Situational Leadership Model	Handouts 68, 69; Learning Activity 49
Emotional Intelligence: Influence	
• The Anatomy of an Emotion	Handout 18
• The Definition of Emotional Intelligence	Handout 20
• The Four-Domain Model	Handout 20
• The Competency of Influence	Handout 77; Learning Activity 54
• The Two Messages	Handout 35; Learning Activity 24
• Six Principles of Influence	Handout 78
+ Map Your Personal Influence Network	Handout 30; Learning Activity 20

Continued on next page

Table 4-2. Sample Two-Hour Formats, *continued*

TWO-HOUR TOPIC	RESOURCES
Emotional Intelligence: Developing Others	
• The Anatomy of an Emotion	Handout 18
• The Definition of Emotional Intelligence	Handout 20
• The Four-Domain Model	Handout 20
• The Competency of Developing Others	Handouts 61, 62; Learning Activity 44
• The Johari Window and the Importance of Feedback	Handout 48; Learning Activity 45
• The SBI Model	Handouts 63, 64
+ Practice Giving Performance Feedback	Handout 65; Learning Activity 46
Emotional Intelligence: Change Catalyst	
• The Anatomy of an Emotion	Handout 18
• The Definition of Emotional Intelligence	Handout 20
• The Four-Domain Model	Handout 20
• The Competency of Change Catalyst	Handout 54
• The Change Model	Handout 54
• Managing Transition	Handout 55, Learning Activity 40
+ Communicating Your Vision	Handout 56; Learning Activity 41
Emotional Intelligence: Conflict Management	
• The Anatomy of an Emotion	Handout 18
• The Definition of Emotional Intelligence	Handout 20
• The Four-Domain Model	Handout 20
• The Competency of Conflict Management	Handout 36
• Who Needs to Initiate Conflict Resolution?	Handout 36
• XYZ Talk	Handout 37; Learning Activity 26
+ Personal Case Study	Handouts 79–87; Learning Activities 56–58
Emotional Intelligence: Teamwork and Collaboration	
• The Anatomy of an Emotion	Handout 18
• The Definition of Emotional Intelligence	Handout 20
• The Four-Domain Model	Handout 20
• The Competency of Teamwork and Collaboration	Handout 70
• Balancing Process and Product	Handout 71; Learning Activities 50, 51
+ The Uniqueness–Belonging Model	Handouts 72, 73; Learning Activity 52

TWO-HOUR TOPIC	RESOURCES
Emotional Intelligence: Employee Engagement	
• The Anatomy of an Emotion	Handout 18
• The Definition of Emotional Intelligence	Handout 20
• The Four-Domain Model	Handout 20
• Discretionary Emotional Energy	Handout 29; Learning Activity 19
• Motivation and Employee Engagement	Handouts 75, 76; Learning Activity 53
+ Relational Thinking	Handouts 52, 53; Learning Activities 38, 39

One-Day, Themed Sessions

Table 4-3 breaks down some of the content in this book into 12 one-day sessions based on selected themes to be offered as stand-alone events. Each of these one-day training events focuses on a specific relationship skill. The first part of each of these programs is formatted very similarly to the half-day workshop in this series, with the addition of a section on social awareness and empathy. Then the second half of each themed session focuses on the theme.

Table 4-3. Sample One-Day Themed Sessions

ONE-DAY TOPIC	RESOURCES
Emotional Intelligence: The New Science of Success	
Teach self-awareness, self-management, and social awareness during the first 5 hours of training	
• The Anatomy of an Emotion	Handout 18
• The Definition of Emotional Intelligence	Handout 20
• The Four-Domain Model	Handout 20
• The 18 Competencies	Handouts 21–24
• The E-Motion Chart	Handout 19; Learning Activity 10
• System 1 vs. System 2 Thinking	Handout 4–6; Learning Activity 2
• Emotions, Thoughts, and Behaviors	Handout 7
• Behavioral Strategies	Handout 8; Learning Activity 3
• Cognitive Strategies	Handout 9; Learning Activity 5
• More Cognitive Strategies	Handouts 11–13, 15; Learning Activities 6, 8
• Defining the Emotional Competency of Empathy	Handout 25; Learning Activity 15
• Three Listening Skills	Handout 26; Learning Activity 16
• Collaborative Intention	Handout 27; Assessment 2; Learning Activity 17
• Managing Defensiveness	Handout 49; Learning Activity 36
• How to Ask Great Questions	Handouts 57, 58; Learning Activity 42

Continued on next page

Table 4-3. Sample One-Day Themed Sessions, *continued*

ONE-DAY TOPIC	RESOURCES
Emotional Intelligence: Focus on Resonant Leadership	
Focus on the relationship theme during the last 2 hours of training	
• Resonant vs. Dissonant Leadership	Handout 43; Learning Activity 31
• The Six Styles of Leadership	Handout 44, 45; Learning Activity 32, 33
• Emotional Intelligence Self-Assessment	Handout 46; Assessment 3; Learning Activity 34
• Situational Leadership Model	Handouts 68, 69; Learning Activity 49
Emotional Intelligence: Focus on Influence	
• The Competency of Influence	Handout 77; Learning Activity 54
• The Two Messages	Handout 35; Learning Activity 24
• Six Principles of Influence	Handout 78
• Map Your Personal Influence Network	Handout 30; Learning Activity 20
Emotional Intelligence: Focus on Developing Others	
• The Competency of Developing Others	Handouts 61, 62; Learning Activity 44
• The Johari Window and the Importance of Feedback	Handout 48; Learning Activity 45
• The SBI Model	Handouts 63, 64
• Practice Giving Performance Feedback	Handout 65; Learning Activity 46
Emotional Intelligence: Focus on Change Catalyst	
• The Competency of Change Catalyst	Handout 54
• The Change Model	Handout 54
• Managing Transition	Handout 55; Learning Activity 40
• Communicating Your Vision	Handout 56; Learning Activity 41
Emotional Intelligence: Focus on Conflict Management	
• The Competency of Conflict Management	Handout 36
• Who Needs to Initiate Conflict Resolution?	Handout 36
• XYZ Talk	Handout 37; Learning Activity 26
• Personal Case study	Handouts 79–87; Learning Activities 56–58
Emotional Intelligence: Focus on Teamwork and Collaboration	
• The Competency of Teamwork and Collaboration	Handout 70
• Balancing Process and Product	Handout 71; Learning Activities 50, 51
• The Uniqueness–Belonging Model	Handouts 72, 73; Learning Activity 52

EMOTIONAL INTELLIGENCE training

ONE-DAY TOPIC	RESOURCES
Emotional Intelligence: Focus on Personality	
• Temperament Styles and Personality	Handout 32
• Priority Styles and Personality	Handout 32
• The Four Quadrant Model (Practice Personality Talk)	Handout 32
• Develop the Competency of Teamwork	Handouts 32–34; Learning Activities 22, 23
Emotional Intelligence: Focus on Employee Engagement	
• Discretionary Emotional Energy	Handout 29; Learning Activity 19
• Motivation and Employee Engagement	Handouts 75, 76; Learning Activity 53
• The Marshmallow Story	Handouts 50, 51; Learning Activity 38
• Relational Thinking	Handouts 52, 53; Learning Activities 38, 39

Customizing Delivery With Technology

Learning technologies can play an important role in adapting workshops to fit your organization. They have the potential to enhance learners' abilities to understand and apply workshop concepts. Examples include webinars, wikis, email groups, online surveys, and teleconferencing, to name just a few. Learn more about how to use technology to maximize learning in Chapter 7 of this book.

The Bare Minimum

With any of these customization options, always keep in mind the essentials of training design (Chapter 6) and delivery (Chapter 8). At a bare minimum, remember these basics:

- **Prepare, prepare, prepare.** Ready the room, the handouts, the equipment, and you. Familiarize yourself with the content, materials, and equipment. Practice can only make you a better facilitator. The more comfortable you feel, the more open and relaxed you will be for your participants. Many things can go wrong: Equipment can fail, the hotel can double-book your room, your Internet connection may not work, or 10 more participants may show up. You simply can't control it all. You can, however, control 100 percent of how much you prepare.

- **Start with a bang.** The beginning of your session is crucial to the dynamics of the workshop. How participants respond to you can set the mood for the remainder of the workshop. Get to the classroom *at least* an hour before the session begins. Be ready to welcome and greet the participants. Have everything ready so that you are available to learn something about them and their needs. Ask them simple questions to build rapport. After introducing yourself, introduce participants to each other or provide an activity in which participants can meet each other. The more time they spend getting to know you and each other, the more all of you will benefit when the session begins. Once the session starts conduct an opening icebreaker that introduces the topic, ensures participants learn more about each other, and sets the stage for the rest of the seminar by letting participants know that this will be an active learning session. Try a provocative opening to get their attention.

- **Don't lecture without interaction.** Your learners like to have fun and participate in interactive learning opportunities. Be sure to vary the learning and teaching methods to maintain engagement. There will be times when you need to deliver information, but be sure to include participants by asking questions, posing critical incidents, incorporating a survey question, or a dozen other ways.

- **End strong.** Providing time for participants to reflect and create an action plan at the end of a module or the session will help establish learning. Don't skip this opportunity to encourage participants to take action on something they have learned. Several of the activities in the workshop help participants develop a plan for next steps. Stress the importance of implementing what they learned upon returning to the workplace.

What to Do Next

- When customizing a workshop it is important to have a clear understanding of the learning objectives. Conduct a needs analysis to identify the gap between what the organization needs and what the employees are able to do and then determine how best to bridge the gap. At the minimum, identify who wants the training, how the results will be defined, why the training is being requested now, and what the budget is. Chapter 5 provides more guidance on identifying training needs.

- Modify or add your own content to an existing agenda from Chapters 1–3 or create your own agenda using the learning support documents included in this book. There is no one way to flow emotional intelligence content, but you must ensure that the topics build on one another and that you solidly connect the concepts and ideas together to leverage the most of the learning opportunity.

- Make sure to incorporate interactive practice activities into the design of the workshop.

- Compile and review all learning activities, handouts, and slides you will use for the session.

- Add your own slides or your own touches to the slides provided.

- Build a detailed plan for preparing for this session, including scheduling and room reservations, invitations, supply list, teaching notes, and time estimates.

SECTION II

ESSENTIALS OF EFFECTIVE EMOTIONAL INTELLIGENCE TRAINING

Chapter 5

Identifying Needs for Emotional Intelligence Training

What's in This Chapter

- Discovering the purpose of needs analysis
- Introducing some data-gathering methods
- Determining the bare minimum needed to deliver training

Ideally, you should always carry out a needs analysis before designing and creating a workshop to address a performance gap. The cost of *not* identifying and carefully considering the performance requirement can be high: wasted training dollars, unhappy staff going to boring or useless sessions, increased disengagement of employees, and so forth. But the world of training is rarely ideal, and the existence of this book, which essentially provides a workshop in a box, is testament to that. This chapter describes the essential theory and techniques for a complete needs analysis to provide the fundamentals of the process and explain how it fits into designing learning. However, because the decision to train may already be out of your hands, the last part of this chapter provides a bare-bones list of things you need to know to train effectively even if someone just handed you this book and told you to put on a workshop.

Why Needs Analysis?

In short, as a trainer, learning professional, performance consultant, or whatever job title you hold, your role is to ensure that the employees of your organization know how to do the work that will make the organization succeed. That means you must first identify the skills, knowledge, and abilities that the employees need for optimal performance and then determine where these are lacking in the employee population to bridge that gap. However, the most important reason for needs assessment is that it is not your learning experience. You may deliver it, but the learning belongs to the learner. Making decisions for learners about what performance they need without working with them is inappropriate. If you are an experienced facilitator, you have a large repository of PowerPoint decks at your disposal. Resist the urge while talking with your customers to listen for words that allow you just to grab what you already have. Be open to the possibilities. A training needs analysis helps you do this (see Figure 5-1). Methods to identify this information include strategic needs analysis, structured interviews, focus groups, and surveys.

Strategic Needs Analysis

An analysis of future directions usually identifies emerging issues and trends with a major potential effect on a business and its customers over a two- to three-year period. The analysis

Figure 5-1. Introducing the ADDIE Model

A needs analysis is the first step in the classic instructional design model called ADDIE, which is named after its steps: analysis, design, development, implementation, and evaluation. Roughly speaking, the tasks involved in ADDIE are

1. **Analysis:** Gather data about organizational and individual needs as well as the gap between the goals the organization means to accomplish and the skills and knowledge needed to accomplish those goals.

2. **Design:** Identify and plan the topics and sequence of learning to accomplish the desired learning.

3. **Development:** Create the components of the learning event, such as learning activities and materials.

4. **Implementation:** Put on the learning event or launch the learning materials.

5. **Evaluation:** Gather data to determine the outcome of the learning to improve future iterations of the learning, enhance materials and facilitation, and justify budget decisions.

Instructional design models such as ADDIE are a systematic approach to developing learning and could also be viewed as a project management framework for the project phases involved in creating learning events.

helps a business develop goals and programs that proactively anticipate and position the organization to influence the future.

To conduct such an analysis, organizations look at issues such as expected changes within the business (for example, technology and professional requirements) and expected changes outside the company (for example, the economy, demographics, politics, and the environment).

Results of an analysis provide a rationale for developing company and departmental goals and for making policy and budgetary decisions. From the analysis comes a summary of key change dynamics that will affect the business.

These questions often are asked in strategic needs analysis:

- What information did previous organizational analyses impart?
- Are those issues and trends still relevant?
- Do the results point to what may need to be done differently in the future?
- How has the organization performed in achieving results?
- What is the present workforce like?
- How will it change or need to change?
- What does the organization know about future changes in customer needs?
- Are customer surveys conducted and, if so, what do they reveal?
- How might the organization have to change to serve customers better?
- Is the company's organizational structure working to achieve results?
- What are the strengths and limitations of the company?
- What are the opportunities for positive change?
- What do competitors do or say that might have implications for the organization?
- What are the most important opportunities for the future?
- What are the biggest problems?
- Is the organization in a competitive marketplace?
- How does the organization compare with competitors?

The results can be summarized in a SWOT analysis model (strengths, weaknesses, opportunities, threats—see Figure 5-2). Action plans are then developed to increase the strengths, overcome the weaknesses, plan for the opportunities, and decrease the threats.

Figure 5-2. SWOT Analysis Model

	STRENGTHS	WEAKNESSES
INTERNAL		
	OPPORTUNITIES	THREATS
EXTERNAL		

Structured Interviews

Start structured interviews as high up in the organization as you can go, with the CEO if possible. Make sure that you include input from human resource personnel and line or operations managers and supervisors. Managers and supervisors will want to tell you what they have seen and what they consider the most pressing issues in the organization.

Focus Groups

Focus groups can be set up to give people opportunities to brainstorm ideas about issues in the organization and to realize the potential of team involvement. One comment may spark another and so on. Focus groups should begin with questions that you prepare. It is important to record the responses and comments on a flipchart so everyone can see them. If that is not possible, you may simply take notes. Results of the sessions should be compiled.

Surveys

Surveys, whether paper or web based, gather information from a large or geographically dispersed group of employees. The advantages of surveys are speed of data collection, objectivity, repeatability, and ease of analysis.

Individual Learning Needs Analysis

While identifying organizational learning needs is critical to making the best use of an organization's training budget, analyzing individual learning needs is also important. Understanding the training group's current skills and knowledge can help to focus the training on those areas that require most work—this also helps to avoid going over what the individuals already know, thus wasting their time, or losing them by jumping in at too advanced a level. In addition, individual learning needs analysis can uncover unfavorable attitudes about training that trainers will be better able to address if they are prepared for them. For example, some learners may see the training as a waste of time, as an interruption to their normal work, or as a sign of potentially frightening organizational change.

Many of the same methods used to gather data for organizational learning needs are used for individual learning needs analysis. Analyzing employee learning needs should be carried out in a thoughtful, sensitive, and inclusive manner. Here are potential pitfalls to avoid:

- **Don't analyze needs you can't meet.** Training needs analysis raises expectations. It sends a message to employees that the organization expects them to be competent in particular areas.

- **Involve employees directly.** Sometimes employees don't see a value in participating in training. In assessing needs, trainers need to prepare employees to buy into the training. Asking useful questions and listening carefully to stated needs are excellent methods for accomplishing both of those goals. Ask these questions: "To what degree would you like to learn how to do [X] more effectively?" and "To what degree would you seriously consider participating in training to improve your competency in [X]?"

- **Make the identified needs an obvious part of your training design.** Participants should be able to see that they have influenced the content and emphasis of the training session. A good practice is briefly to summarize the local trends discovered in the training needs analysis when you introduce the goals of the session.

- **Don't think of training as a "magic bullet."** Sometimes a given employee needs coaching, counseling, or consulting, which is best carried out one on one and customized to the individual and the situation. Still other times, the problem is caused by equipment or processes that need upgrading, not people who need training.

The Bare Minimum

As noted, in an ideal world, you would have gathered all this data about the needs of the organization and the employees and determined that training was the right way to connect those dots.

However, even if the decision to put on this workshop has already been made, you still need a bare minimum of information to be successful:

- **Who is your project sponsor (who wants to do this, provides the budget, and so on)?** In fact, if you don't have a project sponsor, *stop* the project. Lack of a project sponsor indicates that the project isn't important to the business. Optimally, the project sponsor should come from the business side of the organization. If the project sponsor is the head of training, then the mentality behind the training—"build it and they will come"—is likely wrong. Even compliance training should have a functional sponsor.

- **What does the sponsor want the learners to be able to do when they are done with training?** How does the sponsor define measures of success? Answering these critical questions brings clarity to the sponsor's expectations and thus to the workshop design.

- **What are the objectives of the training?** What, specifically, do you want participants to be able to *do* after the workshop? Build clear, specific, and measurable learning objectives and then develop learning activities that directly support them. A good resource for writing objectives is Bloom's Taxonomy; if you use it, aim to create Application-level or higher objectives. Knowledge- and Comprehension-level objectives have their place, but learning events need to go beyond these levels of learning to effectively change behaviors in the workplace.

- **Why does the sponsor want this right now?** Is something going on in the organization of which you should be aware?

- **What is the budget?** How much time and money will be invested in the training?

Key Points

- Needs analysis identifies the gap between what the organization needs and what the employees are able to do and then determines how best to bridge that gap.

- Methods of data gathering for needs analysis include strategic needs analysis, structured interviews, surveys, focus groups, and others.

- Sometimes, needs analysis is not an option, but some minimum information is necessary, including who wants the training, how the results will be defined, why the training is being requested now, and what the budget is.

What to Do Next

- If you have the option, carry out a needs analysis to determine if this training is really what your organization requires to succeed. If it isn't, prepare to argue against wasting time, money, and effort on training that will not support the organization's goals.

- If you don't have the option of a needs analysis, make sure that you seek out at least the bare minimum information to conduct effective training.

- Prepare learning objectives that are measurable, clear, and specific.

- If you have little training background, read the next chapter (Chapter 6) to learn about the theories and concepts that are at the root of training design. If you are an experienced trainer, skim Chapter 6 on design theory or go straight to Chapters 7 and 8 for tips on leveraging technology and delivering training, respectively.

Additional Resources

Biech, E., ed. (2008). *ASTD Handbook for Workplace Learning Professionals.* Alexandria, VA: ASTD Press.

Biech, E., ed. (2014). *ASTD Handbook: The Definitive Reference for Training & Development.* Alexandria, VA: ASTD Press.

Russo, C. "Be a Better Needs Analyst." ASTD *Infoline* no. 258502. Alexandria, VA: ASTD Press.

Tobey, D. (2005). *Needs Assessment Basics.* Alexandria, VA: ASTD Press.

Chapter 6

Understanding the Foundations of Training Design

What's in This Chapter

- Introducing adult learning theory
- Exploring multiple intelligences
- Incorporating whole brain learning
- Learning how theory enters into practice

Because this book provides fully designed workshops, you don't need to know all the details of designing a course—the design has already been done for you. However, understanding some of the principal design and learning theories that underpin these workshops is useful and helpful—especially if you are somewhat new to the field of workplace training and development. To effectively deliver training to learners requires a core understanding of how and why people learn. This gives you the flexibility to adapt a course to the unique learners in the room as needed.

When designing a workshop, paying attention to content flow is especially important. While there is no one right way to flow emotional intelligence content, you must ensure that the topics build on one another and that you solidly connect the concepts and ideas together so you leverage the most of the learning opportunity. New skills require practice, so always include interactive practice sessions in the design of the workshop. Short but well-designed activities can have significant impact.

Basic Adult Learning Theory

The individual participant addressed in these workshops is typically an adult with learning needs that differ in many (but not all) ways from children. Much has been documented about how adults learn best. A key figure in adult education is Malcolm Knowles, who is often regarded as the father of adult learning. Knowles made several contributions to the field but is best known for popularizing the term *andragogy*, which refers to the art and science of teaching adults. Here are six assumptions about adult learners noted in *The Adult Learner: A Neglected Species* (Knowles 1984):

- Adults need to know why learning something is important before they learn it.
- Adults have a concept of self and do not like others imposing their will on them.
- Adults have a wealth of knowledge and experience and want that knowledge to be recognized.
- Adults open up to learning when they think that the learning will help them with real problems.
- Adults want to know how the learning will help them in their personal lives.
- Adults respond to internal motivations.

Given these principles of adult learning, designing sessions that are highly interactive and engaging is critical (see sidebar for more tips). Forcing anyone to learn anything is impossible, so the goal of effective training design is to provide every opportunity and encouragement to the potential learner. Involvement of the learner is the key. As an old Chinese proverb says, "Tell me and I will forget. Show me and I may remember. Involve me and I will understand." The designs in this book use several methods to convey information and engage participants. By incorporating varied training media—such as presentation media, discussion sessions, small-group work, structured exercises, and self-assessments—these designs maximize active participant involvement and offer something for every learning style.

Tips for Adult Learning

To reach adult learners, incorporate these ideas into your next training session:

- Incorporate self-directed learning activities in the session design.
- Avoid overuse of lectures and "talking to"; emphasize discussion.
- Use interactive methods such as case studies, role playing, and so forth.
- Make the content and materials closely fit assessed needs.
- Allow plenty of time to "process" the learning activities.
- Promote inquiry into problems and affirm the experience of participants.
- Give participants a rationale for becoming involved and provide opportunities for success.
- Promote getting acquainted and interpersonal linkages.
- Diagnose and prioritize learning needs and preferences before and during the session.
- Use learning groups as "home bases" for participants.
- Include interpersonal feedback exercises and opportunities to experiment.
- Use subgroups to provide safety and readiness to engage in open interchange.
- Make all learner assessment self-directed.
- Provide activities that focus on cognitive, affective, and behavioral change.

In addition to engaging the interest of the learner, interactive training allows you to tap into another source of learning content: the participants themselves. In a group-learning situation, a good learning environment encourages participants to share with others in the group so the entire group's cumulative knowledge can be used.

More Theoretical Ideas Important to Learning

Research on how people learn and how the brain works occurs continuously. A few ideas that come up frequently in training design and delivery are multiple intelligences and whole brain learning.

Multiple Intelligences

Multiple intelligences reflect how people prefer to process information. Howard Gardner, from Harvard University, has been challenging the basic beliefs about intelligence since the early

1980s. Gardner initially described a list of seven intelligences. Later, he added three additional intelligences to his list, and he expects the list to continue to grow (Gardner 2011). The intelligences are

- **interpersonal:** aptitude for working with others
- **logical/mathematical:** aptitude for math, logic, and deduction
- **spatial/visual:** aptitude for picturing, seeing
- **musical:** aptitude for musical expression
- **linguistic/verbal:** aptitude for the written and spoken word
- **intrapersonal:** aptitude for working alone
- **bodily kinesthetic:** aptitude for being physical
- **emotional:** aptitude for identifying emotion
- **naturalist:** aptitude for being with nature
- **existential:** aptitude for understanding one's purpose.

How do multiple intelligences affect your learning? Gardner suggests that most people are comfortable in three or four of these intelligences and avoid the others. For example, if you are not comfortable working with other people, doing group case studies may interfere with your ability to process new material. Video-based instruction will not be good for people with lower spatial/visual aptitudes. People with strong bodily/kinesthetic aptitudes prefer to move around while they are learning.

Allowing your learners to use their own strengths and weaknesses helps them process and learn. Here's an example: Suppose you are debriefing one of the exercises in the material. The exercise has been highly interpersonal (team activity), linguistic (lots of talking), spatial/visual (the participants built an object), musical (music was playing), logical/mathematical (there were rules and structure), and kinesthetic (people moved around). You've honored all the processing styles except intrapersonal, so the people who process information in this manner probably need a return to their strength of working alone. Start the debriefing by asking people to quietly work on their own, writing down five observations of the activity. Then ask them to share as a group.

Whole Brain Learning

Ned Herrmann pioneered the concept of whole brain learning in the 1970s, developing the Herrmann Whole Brain Model, which divides the brain into four distinct types of thinking: analytical, sequential, interpersonal, and imaginative. Each individual tends to favor one type of thinking over another, and this thinking preference evolves continually throughout a person's life. In fact, the brain changes all the time with new input and new ways of thinking—a feature that is known as *plasticity*.

Although each person has a preferred thinking style, he or she may prefer it to varying degrees. To identify a person's thinking preference, Herrmann developed the Herrmann Brain Dominance Instrument in 1979. Learning about your own thinking and learning preferences can motivate you to learn new ways to learn and think. For trainers and facilitators, learning about your own preferences can help you identify where you may be neglecting other styles or preferences in your training design and delivery. As Ann Herrmann-Nehdi, daughter of Ned Herrmann and researcher in her own right, notes in the *ASTD Handbook for Workplace Learning Professionals*, "Effective learning is whole brained—designing, delivering, and evaluating the learning to best meet the varying needs of diverse learners" (2008, p. 215).

Herrmann-Nehdi continues, "Our knowledge of the brain and its inherent uniqueness shows that each individual is a unique learner with learning experiences, preferences, and avoidances that will be different from those of other learners. This means that learning designs must somehow factor in the uniqueness of the individual learner" (2008, p. 221). That is to say that effective facilitation must provide a blend of learning activities that addresses various thinking processes from analytical to sequential to interpersonal to imaginative. Because each individual has a unique combination of varying preferences for different types of learning, such a blend can engage most learners even when they are not directly learning in their preferred style. Engaging varied thinking styles ensures *whole brain learning*, rather than a narrow focus on one or two thinking styles.

Here are some tips for incorporating whole brain learning into your facilitation:

- Identify your own thinking preferences to avoid getting too one-sided in your presentation. Deliberately include styles you don't typically prefer.
- Recognize that your learners have unique brains that have continually changed as a result of a lifetime of experiences, learning, and ways of thinking.
- Address those variations in learning and thinking preferences by identifying different ways to deliver learning, including facts, case studies, metaphors, brainstorming, simulations, quizzes, outlines, procedures, group learning, role plays, and so on to engage their whole brains.
- Avoid diminishing learners' motivation to learn.
- Avoid overwhelming the brain or causing stress. Stick to need-to-know rather than nice-to-know.

Theory Into Practice

These theories (and more that are not addressed here) affect the way the content of the workshops are put together. Some examples of training features that derive from these theories include handouts, research references, and presentation media to read; quiet time to write notes and reflect; opportunities for listening and talking; and exercises for practicing skills. The workshop activities and materials for the programs in this book have taken these theories to heart in their design, providing content, activities, and tools that will appeal to and engage many learning and thinking styles. Additional ways to translate learning and design theory into practice include the following:

Establishing a Framework

For learners to understand the goals of training and how material relates to real work situations, a framework can be helpful. When presenting the training in the context of a framework, trainers should provide an overview of why the organization has decided to undertake the training and why it is important. This explanation should also highlight what the trainer hopes to accomplish and how the skills learned in this training will be useful back on the job.

Objectives and goals of the programs and learning activities are described in this workbook; share those objectives with the learners when discussing the purposes of specific exercises. Handouts will also help provide a framework for participants.

Identifying Behaviors

Within any training goal are many behaviors. For example, listening and giving clear directions are necessary behaviors for good customer service. Customer service does not improve simply because employees are told to do so—participants need to understand the reasons and see the relevant parts of the equation. For these reasons, facilitators should identify and discuss relevant behaviors throughout the program.

Training helps people identify the behaviors that are important, so that those behaviors can be targeted for improvement. Learning activities enable participants to analyze different skills and behaviors and to separate the parts from the whole. The learning activities in this book, with their clearly stated objectives, have been carefully crafted to take these considerations into account.

Practicing

Practice is crucial for learning because learning takes place by doing and by seeing. In the training designs included in this workbook, practice occurs in written exercises, verbal exercises, and role playing. Role playing helps participants actually practice the behaviors that are being addressed. Role-play exercises bring skills and behaviors to life for those acting out particular roles and for those observing the scenarios.

Learning a new skill takes a lot of practice. Some participants learn skills more quickly than others. Some people's attitudes might prevent them from being open to trying new behaviors. Your job is to facilitate the session to the best of your ability, taking different learning styles into account. The rest is up to the participants.

Providing Feedback

A key aspect of training is the feedback trainers give to participants. If delivered in a supportive and constructive manner, feedback helps learners develop a deeper understanding of the content you are presenting and the behaviors they are practicing. Feedback in role plays is especially powerful because this is where "the rubber hits the road." In role plays, observers can see if people are able to practice the behaviors that have been discussed, or whether habitual responses will prevail.

Making It Relevant

Throughout the program you will discuss how to use skills and new behaviors on the job. These discussions will help answer the question "So what?" Exercises and action plans help participants bring new skills back to actual work situations. This is also important in addressing the adult need for relevancy in learning.

The Bare Minimum

- **Keep the focus on self-reflection.** Be purposeful in designing content that encourages participants to analyze their own behaviors instead of what others do wrong.
- **Build practice into the design.** Provide your participants with hands-on, engaging opportunities to practice the correct skills.

Key Points

- Adults have specific learning needs that must be addressed in training to make it successful.

- People also have different intelligences; that is, different areas in which they are more comfortable and competent. Addressing different intelligences in the workshop keeps more people engaged in more ways.

- People take in new information in different ways; addressing a variety of different thinking styles can help everyone learn more effectively.

- Bring theory into practice by creating a framework, identifying behaviors, practicing, providing feedback, and making the learning relevant.

What to Do Next

- Look through the training materials to identify how they address the learning theories presented in this book. If you make modifications to the material, consider whether those modifications leave out an intelligence or a thinking style. Can you address more intelligences without making the material cumbersome?

- Read the next chapter to identify how to incorporate technology into the workshop to make it more effective.

Additional Resources

Biech, E., ed. (2008). *ASTD Handbook for Workplace Learning Professionals*. Alexandria, VA: ASTD Press.

Biech, E., ed. (2014). *ASTD Handbook: The Definitive Reference for Training & Development,* 2nd edition. Alexandria, VA: ASTD Press.

Gardner, H. (2006). *Multiple Intelligences: New Horizons in Theory and Practice*. New York: Basic Books.

Gardner, H. (2011). *Frames of Mind: The Theory of Multiple Intelligences*. New York: Basic Books.

Herrmann, N. (1988). *Creative Brain*. Lake Lure, NC: Brain Books.

Herrmann, N. , and A. Herrmann-Nehdi. (2015). *Whole Brain Business Book,* 2nd edition. San Francisco: McGraw-Hill.

Herrmann-Nehdi, A. (2008). "The Learner: What We Need to Know." In E. Biech, ed., *ASTD Handbook for Workplace Learning Professionals*. Alexandria, VA: ASTD Press.

Jones, J.E., W.L. Bearley, and D.C. Watsabaugh. (1996). *The New Fieldbook for Trainers: Tips, Tools, and Techniques*. Amherst, MA: HRD Press.

Knowles, M.S. (1984). *The Adult Learner: A Neglected Species*. Houston, TX: Gulf Publishing.

Russell, L. (1999). *The Accelerated Learning Fieldbook: Making the Instructional Process Fast, Flexible, and Fun*. San Francisco: Jossey-Bass/Pfeiffer.

Chapter 7

Leveraging Technology to Maximize and Support Design and Delivery

What's in This Chapter

- Recognizing the importance of technology tools
- Determining when to use learning technologies
- Identifying types of learning technologies
- Enhancing learner engagement
- Deepening learner understanding
- Increasing learning application

The workshops offered in this book are designed to be facilitated in person. Even so, learning technologies can and should play a role in adapting workshops to fit your organization, reinforce learning, and measure effectiveness. Technology is an important learning component, but it can also become an expensive distraction. The key is whether and how well technology enhances learners' abilities to understand and apply workshop concepts.

Your use of technology should also align with your organization's culture and readiness. For example, using webinars and wikis in a high-tech environment where employees are familiar with these tools may be logical and welcome, but you might need to introduce these tools more slowly at another company where email is the primary technology used for communication (see Figure 7-1 for some dos and don'ts of recording webinars).

The most important factor to consider when deciding whether to use learning technologies is how they can best support your workshop's learning objectives. This is particularly critical (and not at all straightforward) when delivering these workshops' soft skills training because personal and interpersonal habits and skills tend to require participants to challenge their beliefs and shift their mindsets. This deeper level of self-reflection, though tougher to do in a virtual setting, can be done if you select the right tool and use it at the right time in the learning process.

In the previous chapter, you learned about the adult learning theories and learning styles that underpin the workshops in this volume. Keep these in mind as you assess and weigh opportunities to use learning technologies. In this chapter, you will explore where technology can augment learning transfer and application in your workshop. Please note that the information has been kept general for two reasons. First, each organization has access to specific and limited technologies, and you should learn about them and creatively use what you have. Second, recommendations for specific technologies are likely to become obsolete quickly; so instead, focus on the types of learning technologies that might best augment in-person workshops.

Figure 7-1. Dos and Don'ts of Recording Webinars

To increase your chances of a successful webinar, consider and incorporate these tips.

Do

- Introduce yourself and the topic.
- Keep recorded webinars short—ideally 20 minutes or less.
- Use a conversational voice to increase interest.
- Use adequate numbers of slides so that you do not stay on one slide for more than 30 or 45 seconds.
- Address simple, focused topics with five or fewer key points.
- Use pictures and minimal text on slides.

Don't

- Use your computer's microphone to record; instead, invest in a good headset.
- Use a recorded webinar that has poor audio quality; instead, re-record if needed.
- Use too much text or small fonts.
- Assume that participants are just watching the webinar; you have to keep their interest or they will get distracted.
- Try to cover a complex topic using a recorded webinar; the webinar should focus on one topic with a few main points.

Why Consider Learning Technologies?

You have decided to provide in-person workshops and will use the agendas offered in this book to plan and conduct the training. Learning technologies can be essential tools in your tool kit. Most behavior change does not occur in the classroom. The workshop is important, but it must be supported by strong pre- and post-course reinforcement. To learn something, learners need many points of contact with the new skills and concepts, such as presentation, reflection, discussion, practice, feedback, and exploration. Moreover, most of your participants are very busy and unable to attend multiple in-person pre- or post-course sessions. So to ensure learning transfer, you can augment in-person activities with technology-based engagement. The good news is that you can use technology in many ways to enhance learning, even of soft skills.

Opportunities to Use Learning Technologies

Whether you have many or few technology resources upon which to draw for learning, start by asking yourself this question: For this topic or series, how can I best use technology to increase learner engagement, understanding, and application? You will use these criteria to discover and evaluate potential ways technology might provide value in the learning process, including

- when designing the training
- before the training
- during the training
- after the training
- while building a learner community.

Note that this chapter offers ways to use technology to enhance traditional learning workshops (blended learning). It is important that you consult with a technology partner if you are considering a technology-driven training program—such as a workplace simulation or self-directed online learning. That said, the content found in this training series could be adapted for use in an online learning platform. For more information on how to use the online tools and downloads, see Chapter 14.

When Designing Training

The ATD Workshop Series offers fully designed training you can use with minimal preparation and solid facilitation skills. Even so, you will be creating a learning implementation plan that is an important part of the design process.

To increase engagement: You have to know your audience members to engage them, because engagement is a choice driven by interest, challenge, and relevance of the topic. Use learning technologies to ensure that you understand where your audience is coming from and the learning approaches they will most value. Email groups, online surveys, teleconferencing, and web meetings with polling can help you ascertain their wants and needs before you solidify your training plan.

To deepen understanding: When in the planning stage, make sure that you have not tried to cram too much presentation into the learning process and that you have planned sufficient time and attention to engaging participants. Flowcharting or mind-mapping software can help you visualize and communicate your learning plan and ensure that you allow for maximum engagement and practice.

To increase application: Increasing retention and application requires buy-in from sponsors and managers to ensure that what is learned is welcomed and applied on the job. Use email groups, online surveys, teleconferencing, and web meetings with polling to communicate with sponsors and managers about what they want out of the training and to identify ways to apply the learning back on the job. Having this information is also valuable in developing the training plan.

Before Training

You want to prime your participants' minds for the topic you will be presenting during the workshop. Pre-work does not have to be something arduous and unwelcome. In fact, a great pre-work assignment can help maximize precious time in the classroom and allow you to focus on the topics that require thorough discussion.

To increase engagement: Tap into the most fascinating aspects of the workshop topic and introduce these through video clips, blog posts, and online resources (see Figure 7-2 about the legal use of video clips, images, and so forth). Avoid boring participants with long "how-to" articles or book chapters before the workshop. In fact, do the opposite and ensure that the pre-work is interesting, provocative (even controversial), and brief. You might select a blog post or video clip that offers a counterpoint to the training or something that inspires your participants to think about the topic before attending training.

To deepen understanding: If you know that the workshop topic will be challenging to some of your participants, prepare and share a brief recorded webinar, video clip, or article that introduces the topic. For example, if your managers tend to tell versus coach, try sharing one or two external resources that discuss the value of service-oriented coaching conversations.

To increase application: You can improve the chances that your participants will apply what they learn by ensuring they identify real-world work challenges in which they can apply their new skills. Start with a one- or two-question pre-workshop survey (using Survey Monkey or similar) that requires they identify these opportunities and then use the responses to enhance your in-workshop discussions. If your organization has an internal social network or ways to create collaboration groups, use the pre-work questions to begin an online discussion of the topic. The conversations will help your participants think about the topic and will help you prepare for a great workshop (and will give you a beneficial "heads-up" on potential areas of conflict or disagreement).

During Training

Learning technologies can help make your workshops more interesting and can help enhance understanding of the material. Beware, however, that you always want to have a "Plan B" in case of technology glitches or breakdowns. Another critical point to make here is that technology does not change how people learn. Learning and performance drive the technology choice, not the other way around.

To increase engagement: The perennial favorite technology for spicing up a workshop is the use of a great video. Boring videos don't help! If you can find short video clips that reinforce your

Figure 7-2. Copyright Beware

Copyright law is a sticky, complex area that is beyond the scope of this book to address in detail. For legal advice, consult your legal department.

However, it's very important to note a few things about copyright, fair use, and intellectual property:

- Just because you found an image, article, music, or video online doesn't mean that you can use it in training without permission. Make sure you obtain permission from the copyright owner before you use it (sometimes the copyright owner is not obvious and you will need to do some research).

- Fair use is pretty limited. Although most fair use allows an educational exception, that does *not* include corporate or organizational training. Other exceptions relate to how much material relative to the original was used, the nature of the original work (creative work generally has more protection), and the effect on the market for the original (Swindling and Partridge 2008). Once again, your best bet is to get written permission.

- Just because something doesn't have a copyright notice on it doesn't mean that it isn't copyright protected. All original material is protected under copyright law as soon as it is published or created.

Don't despair. Plenty of online sources of images, videos, text, and so forth exist that you can use for free or for a minimal fee. Just search on the terms "copyright free" or "open source." Another place to look is Wikimedia Commons, which has millions of freely usable media files. For more information about how copyright law affects your use of materials in this volume, please see Chapter 14 on how to use the online materials and downloads.

most important points, please do so. In addition to adding contrast to the workshop flow, having other "experts" say what you want participants to hear is helpful. Another way to increase engagement is to use some kind of audience-response system or electronic polling. Although this might not be practical for small groups (the technology can be a bit pricey), some less expensive alternatives use texting schemas you might want to check out. Your participants will love seeing their collective responses instantly populate your PowerPoint charts. (For more on PowerPoint, see Figure 7-3 and Chapter 8.)

To deepen understanding: Videos can also help improve understanding. If your participants have access to computers during the workshop, consider short technology-based games and short simulations that reinforce the points. You can also ask participants to fill out worksheets and surveys online during the class. Share animated models, flowcharts, or mind maps to help explain key concepts or how they connect together.

To increase application: Learning simulations and practice sessions help prepare participants to apply new skills. You can do these in person, and you can use technology to facilitate practices. This depends a lot on the topic.

After Training

Your participants are busy, and the new skills and concepts they learned in the workshop will become a distant memory without follow-up. Just as you did before the training, you can and should use learning technologies to augment the learning that occurs during the workshop.

Figure 7-3. PowerPoint or Prezi or Other?

Although PowerPoint is the most common presentation software, other platforms you might want to consider include Prezi, GoAnimate, Google Docs, mind-mapping programs, or others. Here are a few key considerations that will help you choose:

- Aside from the in-class workshop, where will you want to share the presentation?
- If you will be sharing the presentation with others, consider whether new software will be required.
- Which presentation platform is best for the content you are presenting, or does it matter?
- What are the costs and resources required for each platform?
- Which platform will partner well with technology tools you will use to reinforce the learning?
- What might be the advantage of using two or more platforms throughout the learning process?

To increase engagement: Learners engage when they perceive something as interesting, relevant right now, or challenging. Use tools such as video, blogs, social networks, chat, websites, and email to increase interest in the topic and to provide challenge.

To deepen understanding: Use post-workshop surveys and polling tools to assess understanding so you can address any gap. Add to the participants' understanding of the topic by posting materials on a SharePoint site or through blog posts that you push to their email inboxes using an RSS feed.

To increase application: Provide a just-in-time online resource where participants find quick reference sheets and get application tips using a group site, social network, or SharePoint site. Request or require that participants report how they have used new skills through an online project management collaboration site, wiki, or email group.

While Building a Learning Community

Creating an ongoing network of learners is extremely valuable, especially for soft skills. The in-person workshop is just the beginning of the learning journey and so keeping learners engaged is helpful. In addition, you want to create a safe place where learners can discuss challenges, provide encouragement, and share their best practices. Learning technologies are particularly useful for building community among learners and teams.

To increase engagement: Busy people value community but often can't make the time to attend follow-up sessions or network with peers. They might, however, be able to take 10 minutes to check in on an internal social network, group site, or blog to learn from and share with others. If your organization does not have social networking or collaboration software, you might need to get creative. Talk to your technology department about the tools you do have—whether they are SharePoint, blog software, internal messaging, a wiki-type project management collaboration tool, or other. You can even use email groups to connect learners. Look for ways you can create pull (they choose when to engage) and push (they get updates), such as using RSS feeds.

To deepen understanding: After the workshop, use web meetings, teleconferencing, and messaging to connect learning partners or mentors and facilitate their sharing real-time application stories. Periodically facilitate online discussion groups to reinforce the learning and bring participants back together.

To increase application: Use a collaborative online project site or social network to set expectations about post-workshop peer discussions and reinforce engagement. Poll participants and assign sub-teams to lead a portion of each web meeting.

The Bare Minimum

- **Know what resources you have available.** Many organizations have widely varying resources; don't assume that you know everything that is available.

- **Stretch yourself.** Be willing to try something new; develop your skills to use technology in innovative ways to facilitate learning.

- **Know your participants.** They may be far ahead of you in their skills with technology or they may be far behind. If you plan to use learning technologies, do your best to assess their skill level before designing the workshop.

- **Be prepared for challenges.** No matter the skill level of the group, technology glitches are unavoidable. Be sure to cultivate good working relationships with technology support staff.

Key Points

- Most behavior change does not happen in a classroom but through multiple points of reinforcement. Learning technologies are an efficient way to augment learning.

- You can use learning technologies your organization already has if you are creative and partner with your technology team.

- Use learning technologies throughout the learning process to increase engagement, understanding, and application.

What to Do Next

- **Highlight the portions of this chapter that seem most relevant to your learning plan.** Meet with your technology team and get its input on the most applicable tools you might use.

- **Create a plan for how you will use learning technologies to reinforce your workshop.** Ensure that you select only those tools and activities that will enhance the overall learning objectives and be mindful of your organization's culture and comfort level with technology.

- **Test, test, test!** Practice using technology tools to ensure they will deliver what you hope.

- **Read the next chapter to learn ways you can improve your facilitation skills.** Many of these skills will also be useful when using learning technologies, especially collaboration tools.

Additional Resources

Bozarth, J. (2014). "Effective Social Media for Learning." In E. Biech, ed., *ASTD Handbook: The Definitive Reference for Training & Development,* 2nd edition. Alexandria, VA: ASTD Press.

Chen, J. (2012). *50 Digital Team-Building Games: Fast, Fun Meeting Openers, Group Activities and Adventures Using Social Media, Smart Phones, GPS, Tablets, and More.* Hoboken, NJ: Wiley.

Halls, J. (2012). *Rapid Video Development for Trainers: How to Create Learning Videos Fast and Affordably.* Alexandria, VA: ASTD Press.

Kapp, K. (2013). *The Gamification of Learning and Instruction Fieldbook: Ideas Into Practice.* San Francisco: Wiley.

Palloff, R.M., and K. Pratt. (2009). *Building Online Learning Communities: Effective Strategies for the Virtual Classroom.* San Francisco: Jossey-Bass.

Quinn, C. (2014). "M-Thinking: There's an App for That." In E. Biech, ed., *ASTD Handbook: The Definitive Reference for Training & Development,* 2nd edition. Alexandria, VA: ASTD Press.

Swindling, L.B., and M.V.B. Partridge. (2008). "Intellectual Property: Protect What Is Yours and Avoid Taking What Belongs to Someone Else." In E. Biech, *ASTD Handbook for Workplace Learning Professionals.* Alexandria, VA: ASTD Press.

Toth, T. (2006). *Technology for Trainers.* Alexandria, VA: ASTD Press.

Udell, C. (2012). *Learning Everywhere: How Mobile Content Strategies Are Transforming Training.* Nashville, TN: Rockbench Publishing.

Chapter 8

Delivering Your Emotional Intelligence Workshop: Be a Great Facilitator

What's in This Chapter

- Defining the facilitator's role

- Creating an effective learning environment

- Preparing participant materials

- Using program preparation checklists

- Starting and ending on a strong note

- Managing participant behaviors

Let's get one thing clear from the get-go: Facilitating a workshop—facilitating learning—is *not* lecturing. The title of ATD's bestselling book says it all: *Telling Ain't Training* (Stolovitch and Keeps 2011). A facilitator is the person who helps learners open themselves to new learning and makes the process easier. The role requires that you avoid projecting yourself as a subject matter expert (SME) and that you prepare activities that foster learning through "hands-on" experience and interaction.

Before you can help someone else learn, you must understand the roles you will embody when you deliver training: trainer, facilitator, and learner. When a workshop begins, you are the trainer, bringing to the learning event a plan, structure, experience, and objectives. This is only possible because you have a strong, repeatable logistics process. As you ask the learners to prioritize the learning objectives, you slowly release control, inviting them to become partners in their own learning. As you move from the trainer role into the facilitator role, the objectives are the contract between the learners and the facilitator. All great facilitators also have a third role in the classroom—the role of learner. If you are open, you can learn many new things when you are in class. If you believe you must be the expert as a learning facilitator, you will not be very effective.

To be most successful as a learning facilitator, consider this checklist:

- ☐ Identify the beliefs that limit your ability to learn and, therefore, to teach.
- ☐ Learning is a gift for you and from you to others.
- ☐ Choose carefully what you call yourself and what you call your outcomes.
- ☐ Clarify your purpose to better honor your roles at a learning event.
- ☐ If you can't teach with passion, don't do it.

This last point is especially important. Not everyone is destined to be a great facilitator and teacher, but you can still have enormous impact if you are passionate about the topic, about the process, and about helping people improve their working lives. If you are serious about becoming a great facilitator, Chapter 12 provides a comprehensive assessment instrument to help you manage your personal development and increase the effectiveness of your training (see Assessment 4). You can use this instrument for self-assessment, end-of-course feedback, observer feedback, or as a professional growth tracker.

With these points firmly in mind—facilitating is not lecturing and passion can get you past many facilitator deficiencies—let's look at some other important aspects of facilitating, starting with how to create an engaging and effective learning environment.

The Learning Environment

Colors, seating, tools, environmental considerations (such as temperature, ventilation, lighting), and your attitude, dress, preparation, and passion all enhance—or detract from—an effective and positive learning environment. This section describes some ways to maximize learning through environmental factors.

Color. Research has shown that bland, neutral environments are so unlike the real world that learning achieved in these "sensory deprivation chambers" cannot be transferred to the job. Color can be a powerful way to engage the limbic part of the brain and create long-term retention. It can align the right and left brains. Ways to incorporate color include artwork, plants, and pictures that help people feel comfortable and visually stimulated. Consider printing your handouts and assessments in color. The training support materials provided in this book are designed in color but can be printed in either color or grayscale (to reduce reproduction costs).

Room Setup. Because much learning requires both individual reflection and role playing, consider seating that promotes personal thought and group sharing. One way to accomplish this is to set up groups of three to five at round or square tables, with each chair positioned so the projection screen can easily be seen. Leave plenty of room for each person so that when he or she does need to reflect, there is a feeling of privacy. Keep in mind that comfortable chairs and places to write help people relax to learn. Figure 8-1 details more room configurations that you can use to accomplish specific tasks or purposes in training.

Tools of the Trade. Lots of flipcharts (one per table is optimal) with brightly colored markers create an interactive environment. Flipcharts are about as basic and low tech as tools get, but they are also low cost and do the trick. Consider putting colorful hard candy on the tables (include sugar-free options), with bright cups of markers, pencils, and pens. Gather pads of colorful sticky notes and "fidgets" (quiet toys such as chenille stems, Koosh balls, and others) to place on the table as well. For the right level of trust to exist, your learners must feel welcome.

Your Secret Weapon. Finally, the key to establishing the optimal learning environment is *you*. You set the tone by your attitude, the way you greet people, the clothes you wear, your passion, and your interest and care for the participants. You set the stage for learning with four conditions that only you as the facilitator can create to maximize learning:

1. **Confidentiality.** Establish the expectation that anything shared during the training program will remain confidential among participants and that as the facilitator you are committed to creating a safe environment. An important step in learning is first admitting ignorance, which has some inherent risk. Adult learners may resist admitting their learning needs because they fear the repercussions of showing their weaknesses. You can alleviate these concerns by assuring participants that the sole purpose of the training is to build their skills, and that no evaluations will take place. Your workshop must be a safe place to learn and take risks.

Figure 8-1. Seating Configurations

Select a room setup that will best support the needs of your learners:

- **Rounds.** Circular tables are particularly useful for small-group work when you have 16 to 24 participants.

- **U-Shaped.** This setup features three long rectangular tables set up to form a U, with you at the open end. It is good for overall group interaction and small-group work (two to three people). This setup also helps you establish rapport with your learners.

- **Classroom.** This setup is a traditional grade-school format characterized by rows of tables with all the participants facing forward toward the trainer. Avoid this setup as much as possible because you become the focal point rather than the learners, and your ability to interact with learners is extremely limited. Problems of visibility also occur when rows in the back are blocked by rows in the front.

- **Chevron.** Chevron setup features rows of tables as in the classroom setup but the tables are angled to form a V-shape. This opens up the room to allow you to interact more with the learners and accommodates a larger group of learners without sacrificing visibility. However, it shares many of the drawbacks of the classroom setup.

- **Hybrid or Fishbone.** This setup combines a U-shaped configuration with that of a chevron. It is useful when there are too many learners to form a good U and there is room enough to broaden the U to allow tables to be set up as chevrons in the center of the U. This hybrid approach allows for interaction and enables the trainer to move around.

Source: Drawn from McCain (2015).

2. **Freedom from distractions.** Work and personal demands cannot be ignored during training, but to maximize each participant's learning, and as a courtesy to others, outside demands should be minimized:

   a. Select a training site away from the workplace to help reduce distractions.

   b. Acknowledge that participants probably feel they shouldn't be away from work; remind them that the purpose of the training is to improve their work lives.

   c. Ask that mobile devices be turned off or set to silent alerts.

   d. Emphasize that because they are spending this time in training, trainees should immerse themselves in the learning experience and thereby maximize the value of their time, because far from being time "away from work responsibilities," it *is* a work responsibility.

3. **Personal responsibility for learning.** A facilitator can only create the *opportunity* for learning. Experiential learning requires that participants actively engage with and commit to learning—they cannot sit back and soak up information like sponges.

4. **Group participation.** Each participant brings relevant knowledge to the training program. Through discussion and sharing of information, a successful training session will

tap into the knowledge of each participant. Encourage all participants to accept responsibility for helping others learn.

Program Preparation Checklist

Preparation is power when it comes to facilitating a successful workshop, and a checklist is a powerful tool for effective preparation. This checklist of activities will help you prepare your workshop:

☐ Write down all location and workshop details when scheduling the workshop.

☐ Make travel reservations early (to save money, too), if applicable.

☐ Send a contract to the client to confirm details, or if you are an internal facilitator, develop guidelines and a workshop structure in conjunction with appropriate supervisors and managers.

☐ Specify room and equipment details in writing and then confirm by telephone.

☐ Define goals and expectations for the workshop.

☐ Get a list of participants, titles, roles, and responsibilities.

☐ Send participants a questionnaire that requires them to confirm their goals for the workshop.

☐ Send the client (or the participants, if you are an internal facilitator) an agenda for the workshop, with times for breaks and meals.

☐ Recommend that lunch or dinner be offered in-house, with nutritious food provided.

☐ Make a list of materials that you will need in the room (pads of paper, pens, pencils, markers, flipcharts, and so forth). Make sure to plan for some extras.

☐ Design the room layout (for example, rounds, U-shaped, classroom, chevron, or hybrid).

☐ Confirm whether you or your internal/external client will prepare copies of the workshop handouts. The workshop handouts should include all tools, training instruments, assessments, and worksheets. You may choose also to include copies of the presentation slides as part of the participant guide. All the supplemental materials you need to conduct the workshops in this book are available for download (see Chapter 14 for instructions).

☐ Find out if participants would like to receive pre-reading materials electronically before the session.

☐ Prepare assessments, tools, training instruments, and workshop materials at least one week before the workshop so that you have time to peruse and check them and assemble any equipment you may need (see the next two sections).

Participant Materials

Participant materials support participant learning throughout the workshop and provide continuing references after the workshop has ended. There are several kinds of participant materials. Here are some options:

Handouts

The development and "look" of your handouts are vital to help participants understand the information they convey. To compile the handouts properly, first gather all assessments, tools, training instruments, activities, and presentation slides and arrange them in the order they appear in the workshop. Then bind them together in some fashion. There are several options for compiling your material, ranging from inexpensive to deluxe. The kind of binding is your choice—materials can be stapled, spiral bound, or gathered in a ring binder—but remember that a professional look supports success. Your choice of binding will depend on your budget for the project. Because first appearances count, provide a cover with eye-catching colors and appropriate graphics.

Using the agendas in Chapters 1–3, select the presentation slides, learning activities, handouts, tools, and assessments appropriate to your workshop (see Chapter 14). If you choose to print out the presentation slides for your participants, consider printing no more than three slides per handout page to keep your content simple with sufficient white space for the participants to write their own notes. Use the learning objectives for each workshop to provide clarity for the participants at the outset. Remember to number the pages, to add graphics for interest (and humor), and to include tabs for easy reference if the packet of materials has multiple sections.

Some participants like to receive the handouts before the workshop begins. You may want to email participants to determine if they would like to receive the handouts electronically.

Presentation Slides

This ATD Workshop Series book includes presentation slides to support the two-day, one-day, and half-day agendas. They have been crafted to adhere to presentation best practices. If you choose to reorder or otherwise modify the slides, keep in mind these important concepts.

When you use PowerPoint software as a teaching tool, be judicious in the number of slides that you prepare. In a scientific lecture, slides are usually a necessity for explaining formulas or results, but a workshop relies on interaction so keep the slide information simple. Also, do not include more than five or six bullet points per slide. See more tips for effective PowerPoint slides in Figure 8-2.

A message can be conveyed quickly through the use of simple graphics. For example, an illustration of two people in conversation may highlight interpersonal communication, whereas a photo of a boardroom-style meeting may illustrate a group engaged in negotiation. Please note that any use of the images in the presentation slides provided with this book other than as part of your presentation is strictly prohibited by law.

When you use presentation slides ask yourself: What will a slide add to my presentation? Ensure that the answer that comes back is "it will enhance the message." If slides are simply used to make the workshop look more sophisticated or technical, the process may not achieve the desired results.

It can be frustrating when a facilitator shows a slide for every page that the participants have in front of them. The dynamics of the class are likely to disconnect. If the information you are teaching is in the handouts or workbook, work from those media alone and keep the workshop personally interactive.

Workbooks and Journals

A participant journal can be included in the binder with your handouts, or it may be a separate entity. Throughout the workshop participants can assess their progress and advance their development by entering details of their personal learning in the journal. The benefit of this journal to participants is that they can separate their personal discoveries and development from the main workshop handouts and use this journal as an action plan if desired.

Videos

If you show a video in your workshop, ensure that the skills it contains are up to date and that the video is less than 20 minutes long. Provide questions that will lead to a discussion of the information viewed. Short video clips can be effective learning tools.

Toys, Noisemakers, and Other Props

Experienced facilitators understand the value of gadgets and games that advance the learning, provide a break from learning, or both.

Figure 8-2. Tips for Effective PowerPoint Slides

Presentation slides can enhance your presentation. They can also detract from it by being too cluttered, monotonous, or hard to read. Here are some tips for clear, effective slides:

Fonts

- Use sans-serif fonts such as Arial, Calibri, or Helvetica; other fonts are blurry when viewed from 20 feet or more and are more easily read on LCD screens and in video/web presentations.
- Use the same sans-serif font for most (if not all) of the presentation.
- Use a font size no smaller than 24 points. (This will also help keep the number of bullets per slide down.)
- Consider using a 32-point font—this is the easiest for web/video transmission.
- Limit yourself to one font size per slide.

Colors

- Font colors should be black or dark blue for light backgrounds and white or yellow on dark backgrounds. Think high contrast for clarity and visual impact.
- Avoid using red or green. It doesn't project well, doesn't transfer well when used in a webinar, and causes issues for people who suffer color blindness.

Text and Paragraphs

- Align text left or right, not centered.
- Avoid cluttering a slide—use a single headline and a few bullet points.
- Use no more than six words to a line; avoid long sentences.
- Use sentence case—ALL CAPS ARE DIFFICULT TO READ AND CAN FEEL LIKE YELLING.
- Avoid abbreviations and acronyms.
- Limit use of punctuation marks.

Source: Developed by Cat Russo.

Adults love to play. When their minds are open they learn quickly and effectively. Something as simple as tossing a rubber ball from person to person as questions are asked about topics studied can liven up the workshop and help people remember what they've learned.

Case studies and lively exercises accelerate learning. Bells and whistles are forms of communication; use them when you pit two teams against each other or to indicate the end of an activity.

Facilitator Equipment and Materials

When all details for the workshop have been confirmed, it is time to prepare for the actual facilitation of the workshop at the site. You may know the site well because you are providing in-house facilitation. If, however, you are traveling off site to facilitate, important elements enter the planning. Here's a checklist of things to consider:

- ☐ Pack a data-storage device that contains your handouts and all relevant workshop materials. In the event that your printed materials do not reach the workshop location, you will have the electronic files to reprint on site.

- ☐ Pack the proper power cords, a spare battery for the laptop, and a bulb for the LCD or overhead projector in the event that these items are not available at the workshop location. This requires obtaining the make and model of all audiovisual and electronic equipment from the client or the training facility during your planning process.

- ☐ Bring an extension cord.

- ☐ Bring reference materials, books, article reprints, and ancillary content. Take advantage of all technology options, such as tablets or other readers to store reference materials. As a facilitator, you will occasionally need to refer to materials other than your own for additional information. Having the materials with you not only provides correct information about authors and articles, but it also positively reinforces participants' impressions of your knowledge, training, openness to learning, and preparedness.

- ☐ Bring flipcharts, painter's tape, and sticky notes.

- ☐ Pack toys and games for the workshop, a timer or bell, and extra marking pens.

- ☐ Bring duct tape. You may need it to tape extension cords to the floor as a safety precaution. The strength of duct tape also ensures that any flipchart pages hung on walls (with permission) will hold fast.

You can ship these items to the workshop in advance, but recognize that the shipment may not arrive in time, and that even if it does arrive on time, you may have to track it down at the venue. Also, take some time identifying backups or alternatives in case the materials, technology, and so on do not conform to plan. What are the worst-case scenarios? How could you manage such situations? Prepare to be flexible and creative.

A Strong Start: Introduction, Icebreakers, and Openers

The start of a session is a crucial time in the workshop dynamic. How the participants respond to you, the facilitator, can set the mood for the remainder of the workshop. To get things off on the right foot, get to the training room early, at least 30 to 60 minutes before the workshop. This gives you time not only to set up the room if that has not already been done, but also to test the environment, the seating plan, the equipment, and your place in the room. Find out where the restrooms are. When participants begin to arrive (and some of them come very early), be ready to welcome them. Don't be distracted with problems or issues; be free and available to your participants.

While they are settling in, engage them with simple questions:

- How was your commute?
- Have you traveled far for this workshop?
- Was it easy to find this room?
- May I help you with anything?

When the participants have arrived and settled, introduce yourself. Write a humorous introduction, if that's your style, because this will help you be more approachable. Talk more about what you want to accomplish in the workshop than about your accomplishments. If you have a short biographical piece included in the handouts or in the workbook, it may serve as your personal introduction.

At the conclusion of your introduction, provide an activity in which participants can meet each other (often called an icebreaker). Because participants sometimes come into a training session feeling inexperienced, skeptical, reluctant, or scared, using icebreaker activities to open training enables participants to interact in a fun and nonthreatening way and to warm up the group before approaching more serious content. Don't limit the time on this too much unless you have an extremely tight schedule. The more time participants spend getting to know each other at the beginning of the workshop, the more all of you will benefit as the session proceeds.

Feedback

Feedback is the quickest, surest way for you, the facilitator, to learn if the messages and instruction are reaching the participants and if the participants are absorbing the content. It is also important for you to evaluate the participants' rate of progress and learning. Answers to the questions you ask throughout the workshop will help you identify much of the progress, but these answers come from only a few of the participants at a time. They're not a global snapshot of the entire group's comprehension and skills mastery.

When you lead a workshop, the participants walk a fine line between retention and deflection of knowledge. Continuing evaluations ensure that learning is taking root. Three levels of questions—learning comprehension, skills mastery, and skills application—help you determine where the training may not be achieving the intended results.

- Learning comprehension checks that the participants understand and grasp the skills being taught (see Figure 8-3).

- Skills mastery means that the participants are able to demonstrate their newly acquired knowledge by some activity, such as teaching a portion of a module to their fellow participants or delivering their interpretation of topic specifics to the class (see Figure 8-4).

- Skills application is the real test. You may choose to substantiate this through role plays or group case studies. When the participants have the opportunity to verbally communicate the skills learned and to reach desired results through such application, then skills application is established (see Figure 8-5).

The questions in Figures 8-3 to 8-5 are designed for written answers so you can incorporate them into the takeaway workbook you create. The questions concerning skills mastery and skills application could be used as a job-based assignment if the workshop is longer than one day. Keep in mind that you will also reevaluate after each day of a multiday session.

Let's now look at other forms of in-class learning assessments: role plays, participant presentations, ball toss, and journaling.

Role Plays

Role plays are an effective tool for assessing learning comprehension. If two or more participants conduct a role play that reveals their understanding of the information, with an outcome that reflects that understanding, then it becomes a "live feed," instantaneous learning for all.

You must set up the role play carefully. It is often wise for you to be a part of the first role-play experience to show participants how it's done and to make them more comfortable with the activity. Ensure that you explain all the steps of the role play and the desired outcome. It is insightful to role-play a negative version first, followed by participant discussion; then role-play a positive aspect the second time. For example, if confrontational communication is the topic

Figure 8-3. Learning Comprehension Questions

Here are some questions that can be asked to determine each participant's level of *learning comprehension*:
• Give a brief overview of your learning in this workshop. Begin your phrases with "I have learned. . . ." This will assist you in focusing your responses.
• How/where will you apply this knowledge in your workplace?
• Did you acquire this knowledge through lectures/practice/discussion or a combination of all methods?
• Do you feel sufficiently confident to pass on this knowledge to your colleagues?
• Are there any areas that will require additional learning for you to feel sufficiently confident?

Figure 8-4. Skills Mastery Questions

Now let's look at some questions you can use to evaluate your participants' *skills mastery*:

- If you were asked to teach one skill in this workshop, which skill would it be?
- What would your three key message points be for that skill?
- Describe the steps you would take to instruct each message point (for example, lecture, group discussion, PowerPoint presentation, and so forth).
- What methods would you use to ensure that your participants comprehend your instruction?
- Would feedback from your participants, both positive and negative, affect the development of your skills mastery? If yes, illustrate your response and the changes you would make.

Figure 8-5. Skills Application Questions

And finally, let's consider some questions that identify participants' *ability to apply the skills* they've learned in the workshop:

- Please describe a situation at your workplace where you could employ one specific skill from this workshop.
- How would you introduce this skill to your colleagues?
- How would you set goals to measure the improvement in this skill?
- Describe the input and participation you would expect from your colleagues.
- How would you exemplify mastery of the skill?

and the situation under discussion involves a line manager and his or her supervisor, first enact the role play using the verbal and body language that is causing the negative result. Discuss this as a class to identify the specific language that needs improvement. Then enact the role play again, this time using positive language.

Frequently it is helpful for a participant who has been on the receiving end of negative communication in his or her workplace to adopt the role of deliverer. Walking in the other person's shoes leads to a quicker understanding of the transaction. This positive role play should also be followed by whole-group discussion of the elements that worked. Participants can be invited to write about the process and its results to give them a real-life example to take back to the workplace.

Participant Presentations

You might ask a participant to present a module of learning to the group. This allows you to observe the participants from a different perspective—both as a contributor to the conversation and as a presenter leading the discussion. Be ready to assist or to answer questions. For example, a participant may choose assertive communication as his or her module, and the specific issue on return to the workplace may be a request for promotion. The participant defines and delivers the steps required to ask for the promotion while the facilitator and other participants observe and evaluate the success of the approach and demonstration of confidence and assertiveness.

Ball Toss

A quick method for evaluating a class's knowledge of the material presented is to ask the participants to form a standing circle. The facilitator throws out a soft rubber ball to an individual and asks a question about the previous learning activity. When the catcher gives the right answer, he or she throws the ball to another participant who answers another question. The facilitator can step out of this circle and let the participants ask as well as answer questions to review the skills as a group. Candy for all as a reward for contributions is always enjoyed by the participants (consider keeping some sugar-free treats on hand as well).

Journaling

Keeping a journal is a quiet, introspective way for participants to get a grip on their learning. When you complete an activity, have everyone take five minutes to write a summary of the skill just learned and then ask them to share what they've written with a partner. Invite the partner to correct and improve the material if necessary or appropriate.

Responding to Questions

When participants are asking questions, they are engaged and interested. Your responses to questions will augment the learning atmosphere. The way in which you respond is extremely important. Answers that are evasive can disturb a class because they cast doubts on your credibility. Glib or curt answers are insulting. Lengthy responses break the rhythm of the class and often go off track. When dealing with questions, the value of effective communication is in hearing the question, answering the question asked, and moving on. Repeat questions so that all participants hear them. In addition, this can ensure that you have heard the question correctly.

However, don't rush to answer. Take time to let everyone absorb the information. When time is of the essence, don't be tempted to give long, complicated answers that embrace additional topics. Be courteous and clear. Check that your answer has been understood. When a question comes up that could possibly derail the session or that is beyond the scope of the topic, you can choose to record it on a "parking lot" list and then revisit it later at an assigned time. A parking lot can be as simple as a list on a flipchart. However, whenever possible, answer a question at the time it is asked. Consider answering with analogies when they are appropriate because these often help elucidate challenging concepts.

You are likely aware that effective questions that prompt answers are open ended. Here are some that you might ask:

- What have you learned so far?
- How do you feel about this concept?
- How would you handle this situation?

Any question that begins with "what" or "how" promotes a more extensive answer. Do you also know, though, that questions that begin with "why"—as in "why do you think that way?"—can promote defensiveness? So what is a facilitator to do when asked a "why" question?

When a participant asks a confrontational or negative question, handle it with dignity and do not become aggressive. It's helpful to ask open-ended questions of the participant to try to clarify the original question. For example, ask, "What do you mean by . . . ?" or "Which part of the activity do you find challenging?" This form of open-ended questioning requires additional accountability from the participant. The reason for the confrontation may have arisen from confusion about the information or the need to hear his or her own thoughts aloud. When you are calm and patient, the altercation is more likely to be resolved. If the participant persists, you may wish to ask him or her to discuss the specifics in a private setting. More ideas for dealing with difficult participants are provided later in this chapter.

Some participants enjoy being questioned because it gives them an opportunity to show their knowledge. Others are reticent for fear of looking foolish if they don't know the answer. Because your participants have unique styles and personalities, always have a purpose for asking questions: Will these questions test the participants' knowledge? Are these questions appropriate? Are you asking them in the style that suits the participant?

Training Room and Participant Management

When everything is in place and ready for the session, it's time to review the "soft skills" portion of your responsibilities—that is, how you conduct the workshop and interact with participants. Here are some things to consider:

- **"Respect and respond" should be a facilitator's mantra.** At all times respect the participants and respond in a timely manner.

- **Learn participants' names at the beginning of the workshop.** Focus on each participant, give a firm handshake, and repeat the name in your greeting. Paying attention to the details they share during your greeting, and thereby getting to know them on a personal level, makes learning names much easier. When you have time, survey the room and write down every name without looking at nametags or name tents on the tables.

- **Manage workshop program time.** This is vital because it ensures that the goals will be met in the time allotted.

- **Read the participants' body language.** This will help you know when to pause and ask questions or to give them a stretch break.

- **Answer questions fully and effectively.** If you don't know an answer, open the question up to the participants or offer to get back to the questioner. Make a note to remind yourself to do so.

- **Add a "parking lot" to the room**—a large sheet of paper taped to one of the walls (use your own artistic prowess to draw a vehicle of some sort). When questions arise that are out of step with the current activity, ask the participant to write the question on a sticky note and put it in the parking lot. When the current activity is completed, you can address the questions parked there.

- **Control unruly participants through assertiveness of vocal tone and message.** When appropriate, invite them to help you with tasks because frequently they just need to be more physically involved. If the unruliness gets out of hand, accompany the person out of the room to discuss the situation.

- **Be sure to monitor a participant who is slower to assimilate the information.** If time permits, give that person some one-on-one time with you.

- **Keep your energy high.** Inject humor wherever possible. Ensure the learning is taking root.

A Word About Dealing With Difficult Participants

Much of the preparation you do before a training session will help you minimize disruptive behavior in your training session. But, sadly, you are still likely at some point to have difficult participants in your training room. Beyond preparation, you may need some specific strategies to help you manage disruptions and keep the learning on track. Figure 8-6, drawn from McCain's second edition of *Facilitation Basics* (2015), identifies many of these behaviors and gives strategies for nipping them in the bud.

Figure 8-6. Managing Difficult Participants

THE PROBLEM	THE SOLUTION
Carrying on a Side Conversation	• Don't assume the talkers are being disrespectful; depersonalize the behavior by thinking: "Maybe they are unclear about a point in the material, or the material is not relevant to their needs." • Ask the talkers if they don't understand something. • Walk toward the talkers as you continue to make your point; this stops many conversations dead in their tracks.
Monopolizing the Discussion	• Some participants tend to take over the conversation; while the enthusiasm is great, you don't want to leave other learners out. • Tell the monopolizer that her comments are valuable and interesting and that you would like to open up the discussion to others in the group. Then call on another person by name. • Enlist the monopolizer to help you by being a gatekeeper and ensuring that no one monopolizes the conversation.
Complaining	• Don't assume someone who complains doesn't have a valid reason to do so. • Ask the rest of the group if they feel the same way. If they do, try to address the issue as appropriate. If they don't, talk to the individual in the hallway during the break.
Challenging Your Knowledge	• Determine if this person really knows more than you do, or is just trying to act as though he does. • If he does know more, try to enlist his help in the training. If he doesn't, ask him to provide expertise, and he will usually realize he can't and back down.
Daydreaming	• Use the person's name in an example to get her attention. • Switch to something more active. • If behavior affects more than just one person, try to find out if something work related is causing it and have a brief discussion about it.
Heckling	• Don't get upset or start volleying remarks. • Try giving the person learning-oriented attention: "John, you clearly have some background in this area; would you care to share your thoughts with the rest of the group?" • Get the attention off you by switching to a group-oriented activity.
Clowning Around	• Give the person attention in a learning-oriented way by calling on her to answer a question or be a team leader. • If a joke is intended to relieve tension in the room and others seem to be experiencing it, deal with the tension head on by bringing it up. • If it is just a joke, and it's funny and appropriate, laugh!

EMOTIONAL INTELLIGENCE training

THE PROBLEM	THE SOLUTION
Making an Insensitive Remark	• Remember that if the person truly didn't intend offense, you don't want to humiliate him. But you do need to ensure that the person and everyone else in the room know that you will not tolerate bigoted or otherwise inappropriate remarks.
	• Give the person a chance to retract what he said by asking if that is what he meant to say. If it wasn't, then move on. If it was, you need to let the person know that the comment is not in line with the values of your organization and it can't be allowed to continue.
	• If the person persists, speak to him in the hallway, or as a last resort, ask him to leave.
Doing Other Work	• Talk to the person at a break to find out if the workshop is meeting her needs.
	• If the person is truly under too much pressure, offer to have her come to another session.
Not Talking	• If you can tell the person is engaged because he is taking notes, maintaining eye contact, or leaning forward, let him alone.
	• Give the person opportunities to interact at a greater comfort level by participating in small groups or in pairs.
Withdrawing	• Talk to the person at break to find out if something is going on. Deal with the issue as appropriate.
	• If the person feels excluded, have her act as a team leader for a turn, or ensure that all members of teams are given opportunities to participate.
Missing the Point	• If someone misses the point, be sensitive in dealing with him. Try to find something to agree with in his point.
	• Try to identify what the person is having trouble grasping and clear up the point with an analogy or an example.
	• Never laugh at the person or otherwise humiliate him.
Playing With Technology	• Minimize distractions by setting specific ground rules for technology use in the training room. (See Chapter 7 for creative ways to use technology to enhance training.)
	• Direct a training-related question to the person.
	• If the behavior persists, talk to the person at break to determine if there is an issue with which you can help.

Source: McCain (2015).

When all else fails, you have a few last resorts, although you would clearly rather not get to that point. One option is to simply pull aside the individual who is disrupting the class and talk to her privately. Dick Grote (1998) suggests in "Dealing With Miscreants, Snivelers, and Adversaries" that you can often catch someone off guard by asking: "Is it personal?" The direct question will usually cause the individual to deny that it is personal. Next, you tell the person that the behavior is unacceptable and that you will speak to a supervisor or training sponsor if it continues. This often works.

However, if it does not work, you can ask to have the person removed or cancel the program and speak to the person's supervisor. Clearly, these options are not to be taken lightly, but realize that they are available when you are faced with truly recalcitrant behavior.

Follow up when you have faced a difficult situation. Take some time to reflect on the event and write down the details of what happened. If possible, get perspectives and feedback from participants who witnessed it. If outside perspectives are not an option, think about the event from the points of view of the disruptive individual and other participants and ask yourself: What went wrong? What went well? How could I manage the situation better next time?

An Unforgettable End

In Biech (2008), contributor Mel Silberman explains that

> [m]any training programs run out of steam in the end. In some cases, participants are marking time until the close is near. In other cases, facilitators are valiantly trying to cover what they haven't got to before time runs out. How unfortunate! What happens at the end needs to be "unforgettable." You want participants to remember what they've learned. You also want participants to think what they've learned has been special. (p. 315)

Silberman suggests considering four areas when preparing to end your workshop:

- How will participants review what you've taught them?
- How will participants assess what they have learned?
- What will participants do about what they have learned?
- How will participants celebrate their accomplishments?

For example, consider what you've learned in this chapter. You've developed a well-rounded picture of what it takes to create an optimal, effective learning environment, from creating an inviting and engaging space to preparing and gathering materials that will make you feel like an organizational champ. You're ready to get the training off to a productive start, to manage difficult participants and situations, and to pull it all together in a powerful way. Now review the bullet points that follow to determine what the next steps are and take pride in the preparation that will enable you to adapt and thrive in the training room.

The Bare Minimum

- **Keep things moving.** Create an engaging, interactive environment.
- **Pay attention to the energy in the room.** Be prepared to adjust the activities as needed. Build in content that can be delivered standing or through networking activities to get participants out of their seats when needed.
- **Have fun!** If you create an upbeat tone and enjoy yourself, the participants are likely to have fun as well.

Key Points

- Facilitation is not lecturing. It's providing learning activities and support to make learning easier for the participant.
- Facilitation is not about the facilitator—it's about the learner.
- An inviting space and a safe, collaborative environment are necessary for learning to occur.
- Good facilitation starts with passion and significant attention to preparation.
- A good start sets the tone for the whole training session.
- A strong ending helps learners to remember the training and carry lessons forward into their work.

What to Do Next

- Prepare, modify, and review the training agenda. Use one of the agendas in Section I as a starting point.
- Review the program preparation checklist and work through it step by step.
- Make a list of required participant materials and facilitator equipment and begin assembling them.
- Review all learning activities included in the agenda and start preparing for your delivery.

Additional Resources

Biech, E. (2006). *90 World-Class Activities by 90 World-Class Trainers.* San Francisco: John Wiley/Pfeiffer.

Biech, E. (2008). *10 Steps to Successful Training.* Alexandria, VA: ASTD Press.

Biech, E., ed. (2008). *ASTD Handbook for Workplace Learning Professionals.* Alexandria, VA: ASTD Press.

Biech, E., ed. (2014). *ASTD Handbook: The Definitive Reference for Training & Development.* Alexandria, VA: ASTD Press.

Biech, E. (2015). *Training and Development for Dummies.* Hoboken, NJ: Wiley.

Duarte, N. (2010). *Resonate: Present Visual Stories That Transform Audiences.* Hoboken, NJ: Wiley.

Grote, D. (1998). "Dealing With Miscreants, Snivelers, and Adversaries," *Training & Development,* 52(10), October.

McCain, D.V. (2015). *Facilitation Basics,* 2nd edition. Alexandria, VA: ASTD Press.

Stolovitch, H.D., and E.J. Keeps. (2011). *Telling Ain't Training,* 2nd edition. Alexandria, VA: ASTD Press.

Thiagarajan, S. (2005). *Thiagi's Interactive Lectures: Power Up Your Training With Interactive Games and Exercises.* Alexandria, VA: ASTD Press.

Thiagarajan, S. (2006). *Thiagi's 100 Favorite Games.* San Francisco: John Wiley/Pfeiffer.

Chapter 9
Evaluating Workshop Results

What's in This Chapter

- Exploring the reasons to evaluate your program
- Introducing the levels of measurement and what they measure

---

Evaluation represents the last letter of the ADDIE cycle of instructional design (analysis, design, development, implementation, and evaluation). Although evaluation is placed at the end of the model, an argument could be made for including it far earlier, as early as the design and development phase and perhaps even in the analysis phase. Why? Because the goals of the training, or the learning objectives (see Chapter 5), provide insight into what the purpose of the evaluation should be. In fact, business goals, learning goals, and evaluation of those goals are useful subjects to address with organizational leaders or the training sponsor. Trainers often begin a program without thinking about how the program fits into a strategic plan or how it supports and promotes specific business goals, but these are critical to consider before implementing the program.

However, this chapter is not about that upfront evaluation of the program design and materials; it is about evaluating the program after it has been delivered and reporting the results back to the training sponsor. This form of evaluation allows you to determine whether the program objectives were achieved and whether the learning was applied on the job and had an impact on the business. Evaluation can also serve as the basis for future program and budget discussions with training sponsors.

Levels of Measurement

No discussion of measurement would be complete without an introduction to the concepts that underpin the field of evaluation. The following is a brief primer on a very large and detailed subject that can be somewhat overwhelming. If your organization is committed to measuring beyond Level 2, take some time to read the classics of evaluation.

In 1956–57, Donald Kirkpatrick, one of the leading experts in measuring training results, identified four levels of measurement and evaluation. These four levels build successively from the simplest (Level 1) to the most complex (Level 4) and are based on information gathered at previous levels. For that reason, determining upfront at what level to evaluate a program is important. A general rule of thumb is that the more important or fundamental the training is and the greater the investment in it, the higher the level of evaluation to use. The four basic levels of evaluation are

- **Level 1—Reaction:** Measures how participants react to the workshop.
- **Level 2—Learning:** Measures whether participants have learned and understood the content of the workshop.
- **Level 3—Behavior (also referred to as application):** Measures on-the-job changes that have occurred because of the learning.
- **Level 4—Results:** Measures the impact of training on the bottom line.

These four levels correspond with the evaluation methods described below.

Level 1: Measuring Participant Reactions

One of the most common ways trainers measure participants' reactions is by administering end-of-session evaluation forms, often called "smile sheets" (for a sample, see Assessment 1). The main benefit of using smile sheets is that they are easy to create and administer. If you choose this method, consider the following suggestions, but first decide the purpose of evaluating. Do you want to know if the participants enjoyed the presentation? How they felt about the facilities? Or how they reacted to the content?

Here are a few suggestions for creating evaluation forms:

- Limit the form to one page.
- Make your questions brief.
- Leave adequate space for comments.

- Group types of questions into categories (for example, cluster questions about content, questions about the instructor, and questions about materials).

- Provide variety in types of questions (include multiple-choice, true-false, short-answer, and open-ended items).

- Include relevant decision makers in your questionnaire design.

- Plan how you will use and analyze the data and create a design that will facilitate your analysis.

- Use positively worded items (such as "I listen to others," instead of "I don't listen to others").

You can find additional tips for creating evaluation sheets and evaluating their results in the *Infoline* "Making Smile Sheets Count" by Nancy S. Kristiansen (2004).

Although evaluation sheets are used frequently, they have some inherent limitations. For example, participants cannot judge the *effectiveness* of training techniques. In addition, results can be overly influenced by the personality of the facilitator or participants' feelings about having to attend training. Be cautious of relying solely on Level 1 evaluations.

Level 2: Measuring the Extent to Which Participants Have Learned

If you want to determine the extent to which participants have understood the content of your workshop, testing is an option. Comparing pre-training and post-training test results indicates the amount of knowledge gained. Or you can give a quiz that tests conceptual information 30 to 60 days after the training to see if people remember the concepts. Because most adult learners do not generally like the idea of tests, you might want to refer to these evaluations as "assessments."

Another model of testing is criterion-referenced testing (CRT), which tests the learner's performance against a given standard, such as "greets the customer and offers assistance within one minute of entering the store" or "initiates the landing gear at the proper time and altitude." Such testing can be important in determining whether a learner can carry out the task, determining the efficacy of the training materials, and providing a foundation for further levels of evaluation. Coscarelli and Shrock (2008) describe a five-step method for developing CRTs that includes

1. Determining what to test (analysis)

2. Determining if the test measures what it purports to measure (validity)

3. Writing test items

4. Establishing a cut-off or mastery score

5. Showing that the test provides consistent results (reliability).

Level 3: Measuring the Results of Training Back on the Job

The next level of evaluation identifies whether the learning was actually used back on the job. It is important to recognize that application on the job is where learning begins to have real-world effects and that application is not solely up to the learner. Many elements affect transfer and application, including follow-up, manager support, and so forth. For example, consider a sales training attendee who attends training and learns a new, more efficient way to identify sales leads. However, upon returning to work, the attendee's manager does not allow the time for the attendee to practice applying those new skills in the workplace. Over time, the training is forgotten, and any value it may have had does not accrue.

Methods for collecting data regarding performance back on the job include reports by people who manage participants, reports from staff and peers, observations, quality monitors, and other quality and efficiency measures. In "The Four Levels of Evaluation," Kirkpatrick (2007) provides some guidelines for carrying out Level 3 evaluations:

- Use a control group, if practical.
- Allow time for behavior change to take place.
- Evaluate before and after the program, if possible.
- Interview learners, their immediate managers, and possibly their subordinates and anyone else who observes their work or behavior.
- Repeat the evaluation at appropriate times.

Level 4: Measuring the Organizational Impact of Training

Level 4 identifies how learning affects business measures. Consider an example related to management training. Let's say a manager attends management training and learns several new and valuable techniques to engage employees and help keep them on track. Upon return, the manager gets support in applying the new skills and behaviors. As time passes, the learning starts to have measurable results: Retention has increased, employees are demonstrably more engaged and are producing better-quality goods, and sales increase because the quality has increased. Retention, engagement, quality, and sales are all measurable business results improved as a result of the training.

Measuring such organizational impact requires working with leaders to create and implement a plan to collect the data you need. Possible methods include customer surveys, measurements of sales, studies of customer retention or turnover, employee satisfaction surveys, and other measurements of issues pertinent to the organization.

Robert Brinkerhoff, well-known author and researcher of evaluation methods, has suggested the following method to obtain information relevant to results:

- Send out questionnaires to people who have gone through training, asking: To what extent have you used your training in a way that has made a significant business impact? (This question can elicit information that will point to business benefits and ways to use other data to measure accomplishments.)
- When you get responses back, conduct interviews to get more information.

Return on Investment

Measuring return on investment (ROI)—sometimes referred to as Level 5 evaluation—is useful and can help "sell" training to leaders. ROI measures the monetary value of business benefits such as those noted in the discussion about Level 4 and compares them with the fully loaded costs of training to provide a percentage return on training investment. Hard numbers such as these can be helpful in discussions with organizational executives about conducting further training and raise the profile of training.

ROI was popularized by Jack Phillips. More in-depth information can be found in the *ASTD Handbook of Measuring and Evaluating Training* (Phillips 2010).

Reporting Results

An important and often under-considered component of both ROI and Level 4 evaluations is reporting results. Results from these types of evaluation studies have several different audiences, and it is important to take time to plan the layout of the evaluation report and the method of delivery with the audience in question. Consider the following factors in preparing communications:

- **Purpose:** The purposes for communicating program results depend on the specific program, the setting, and unique organizational needs.
- **Audience:** For each target audience, understand the audience and find out what information is needed and why. Take into account audience bias, and then tailor the communication to each group.

- **Timing:** Lay the groundwork for communication before program implementation. Avoid delivering a message, particularly a negative message, to an audience unprepared to hear the story and unaware of the methods that generated the results.
- **Reporting format:** The type of formal evaluation report depends on how much detailed information is presented to target audiences. Brief summaries may be sufficient for some communication efforts. In other cases, particularly those programs that require significant funding, more detail may be important.

The Bare Minimum

- If formal measurement techniques are not possible, consider using simple, interactive, informal measurement activities such as a quick pulse-check during the workshop.
- Empower the participants to create an action plan to capture the new skills and ideas they plan to use. Ultimately, the success of any training event will rest on lasting positive change in participants' behavior.

Key Points

- The four basic levels of evaluation cover reaction, learning, application, and organizational impact.
- A fifth level covers return on investment.
- Reporting results is as important as measuring them. Be strategic in crafting your results document, taking into consideration purpose, audience, timing, and format.

What to Do Next

- Identify the purpose and level of evaluation based on the learning objectives and learning goals.
- Prepare a training evaluation form, or use the one provided in Chapter 12.
- If required, develop plans for follow-up evaluations to determine skills mastery, on-the-job application, and business impact.

Additional Resources

Biech, E., ed. (2014). *ASTD Handbook: The Definitive Reference for Training & Development,* 2nd edition. Alexandria, VA: ASTD Press.

Brinkerhoff, R.O. (2006). *Telling Training's Story: Evaluation Made Simple, Credible, and Effective.* San Francisco: Berrett-Koehler.

EMOTIONAL INTELLIGENCE training

Coscarelli, W., and S. Shrock. (2008). "Level 2: Learning—Five Essential Steps for Creating Your Tests and Two Cautionary Tales." In E. Biech, ed., *ASTD Handbook for Workplace Learning Professionals.* Alexandria, VA: ASTD Press.

Kirkpatrick, D.L. (2007). "The Four Levels of Evaluation." *Infoline* No. 0701, Alexandria, VA: ASTD Press.

Kirkpatrick, D., and J.D. Kirkpatrick. (2006). *Evaluating Training Programs: The Four Levels,* 3rd edition. San Francisco: Berrett-Koehler.

Kirkpatrick, D., and J.D. Kirkpatrick. (2007). *Implementing the Four Levels: A Practical Guide for Effective Evaluation of Training Programs.* San Francisco: Berrett-Koehler.

Kristiansen, N.S. (2004). "Making Smile Sheets Count." *Infoline* No. 0402, Alexandria, VA: ASTD Press.

Phillips, P.P., ed. (2010). *ASTD Handbook of Measuring and Evaluating Training.* Alexandria, VA: ASTD Press.

SECTION III
POST-WORKSHOP LEARNING

Chapter 10
The Follow-Up Coach

What's in This Chapter

- Reinforcing emotional intelligence training to ensure success
- The importance of feedback and encouragement in the follow-up process
- Forming habits out of action plan goals

According to research studies, self-awareness is foundational for growth and change, but it does not guarantee it. At the end of a one- or two-day workshop, participants usually have a lot of self-awareness, but actual skill development and change requires additional support and on-the-job application. That means that training does not end when participants leave the session. Unfortunately, too many trainers and managers forget an essential step—following up to ensure transfer of training.

Reinforce Employee Learning to Ensure Success

Here are some effective techniques to reinforce the training message after the workshop:

- **Ask participants to write certain teaching points in their handouts.** Encourage them to take away *hand-written* notes that summarize key information from the training session. During the training session, ask participants to underline, fill in blanks, and write down key ideas that you are presenting. Make sure you give them time for reflection, journaling, and action planning. The simple act of writing down information increases learning and retention over just hearing it. Participants are also more likely to revisit their handouts if they have taken notes and journaled in them.

- **Provide enough time during the workshop for participants to complete their action plans.** Resistance to change on the part of some participants is formidable, and they might need encouragement to put the skills they learn into practice. Action plans operate like accountability partners for participants. The very act of writing down a learning goal tends to shift the process of learning from contemplation (this is something I would like to learn) to intentionality (this is something I intend to learn). A good action plan can serve as a guide for application of skills by requiring each participant to specify what he or she will do, with whom, by such and such a date, and so on. Additionally, action plans usually include a place to journal the action taken and lessons learned. Action plans not only clarify what participants intend to do but also increase the level of self-efficacy, which improves the likelihood of behavioral change. Finally, participants can choose to share their action plans with managers, mentors, and team members creating a baseline set of learning agreements as well as the opportunity to invite feedback and measure progress around learning goals.

- **Make the trainee a trainer.** Teaching is a great way to reinforce learning. Retention increases when you go from writing something down in your notes to actually teaching it to other people. Organizations can maximize their investment in employees' training by giving them opportunities to facilitate a portion of the learning content for co-workers. This is particularly effective if they supplement whatever they teach with actual post-workshop experiences such as these:

  ◦ Talk about how newly acquired skills and knowledge are improving as they are being used on the job

  ◦ Discuss any problems in transferring skills and knowledge from the training session to the job

  ◦ Invite questions or feedback from other co-workers.

- **Reinforce training messages through workplace communication channels.** Employee newsletters, blogs, intranet sites, or posters are great communication tools that reinforce key learning concepts. Any e-collaboration technology that helps participants share additional tips, success stories, research articles, assessments, job aids, links to TED Talks, and other learning resources can serve as a means for workshop participants to apply and refine what they've learned.

Provide Feedback and Encouragement in the Follow-Up Process

Learners can become greatly discouraged when they are trying to learn a new skill and their progress never seems to register in the perceptions of the people who know them best. The people they most hope will notice may not seem to give them credit for their behavioral changes and growth. To eliminate this source of discouragement, partner with participants' supervisors and managers to support learning success in their employees. Encourage supervisors to attend the workshops to increase their own emotional intelligence skills and so they understand what their employees have been learning.

Conduct Follow-Up Coaching Sessions

Encourage supervisors to proactively schedule at least two follow-up coaching sessions to let participants know that they will look for opportunities to provide feedback that reinforces progress and growth.

Coaching Session 1: During the first follow-up coaching session, supervisors can review the participant's action plan goals, including strengths to build on and areas for development. This information gives managers what they need to both reinforce strengths and provide feedback and encouragement around growth goals. They should conduct this first coaching session within three weeks of the training. Urge supervisors to discuss any applications and lessons learned since the completion of the workshop.

Coaching Session 2: After the initial follow-up coaching session, employee and supervisor should agree to a time interval in which the participant will practice and learn, and then schedule another coaching session after that time interval (usually 3 to 6 weeks), to provide progress encouragement around the participant's growth goals. Encourage coaches to give situation-specific feedback that lets the learner know that they have noticed change and growth. If the coach observed the individual applying a learning goal during a conversation with a customer, for example, then the feedback conversation should both highlight the observed behavior and recognize the impact that the new skill is having on customer satisfaction.

Avoid Evaluative Praise

You may need to coach the coaches. Make sure that supervisors grasp the difference between encouragement and evaluative praise. People are internally motivated to learn when they experience progress and growth toward a learning goal. Internal motivation tends to spur on additional growth and continued learning. Once the results of lessons learned are experienced, the supervisors' role in encouraging the progress is to be thankful and to simply observe the impact that the growth is having on real workplace concerns, such as team success, achieving goals, providing customer service, fulfilling the mission, managing one's career, or achieving a noble purpose.

Motivation will shift from internally rewarding to externally imposed if supervisors provide too much evaluative praise. Evaluative praise is something like approval. It happens when we judge what we see ("You are doing great now," or "You are okay, now that your behaviors are in alignment with these standards") instead of just describing it: "Your contributions at the team meeting today really helped us to address this issue with the customer that we have been trying to resolve." It is unfortunately what parents often do with children, and it creates a kind of addiction to authority approval, instead of an internal confidence that is activated by the more natural process of learning and getting better at something. There is a fine line between internal motivation: "I am learning because I love to learn" and externally imposed motivation: "I am learning because these things are expected of me, and if I don't do it I might lose my job."

Emphasize with supervisors that the key to encouragement is to be descriptive and to simply let their thoughtful words sit with the receiver. Urge them to describe the impact that new behaviors are having on project results, team success, service to others, company mission, the learner's sense of purpose, the learner's value system, or the learner's desire for supervisors to observe progress.

Share these suggestions with supervisors to help them make their praise and encouragement more descriptive:

- **Be specific.** Throw out the list of character traits for labeling behavior and simply describe what you observe: "Yesterday, when we were discussing the budget numbers, you shared an idea about how we can save money in our marketing department."

- **Show appreciation.** Name exactly what the person did and how it supports the team, customer, mission, and so on: "That was just what we needed to hear to be able to make the budget work. Thank you!"

- **Avoid emphasizing the word *you*.** Emphasizing "you" creates defensiveness, as in "when *you* did this. . . ." Use "I" statements or focus on the action and the impact but not the person: "When you took the time to show Sarah how to run the new program, it was just what she needed. She is really looking forward to her new role on this project."

- **Ask more questions.** Instead of telling, consider asking a question that shows a respect for the growth and development that the individual is working on: "What are your thoughts about how we can improve our onboarding process?" Make sure to ask in a spirit of curiosity.

- **What would I say to my boss?** Supervisors and managers tend to speak differently to bosses. For example, one does not approach a boss and say: "Wow! Great job. You are really developing your emotional intelligence." Observations to bosses are usually more appreciative: "I am really glad you took the time to explain the situation to me. It really helped to focus the proposal."

- **Be observant.** Use specific and descriptive behavioral language, which means starting with observing. When details are not observed, then feedback gets *lazy*, and encouragement often reverts to flattery: "You are doing great!" Flattery is usually appreciated and won't typically damage a relationship, but it doesn't give the learner the kind of specific observations and insights that can be used for continual growth and development. As mentioned, learners can become discouraged when they do not sense that their progress is being noticed.

Form Habits Out of Action Plan Goals

In the world of learning, David Kolb (1984) has demonstrated that learning involves taking an abstract concept and applying it in a range of situations. Each application then provides a real-life experience that one can reflect on and translate into a lesson that refines the process of learning the concept. Learning a new skill is thus a continual cycle of understanding a concept, intentionally applying it in a real-life situation, reflecting on the experience, and fine-tuning the results for the next application.

Participants can form lifelong habits out of their action plan learning goals by following four simple principles and consciously managing their learning process during the first three weeks following a training event: set intentions, create an experience, reflect, and follow the 7/21 rule.

Set Intentions

What participants actually take away from a one- or two-day learning event is a set of abstract concepts and a list of intentions that are defined through the action plan. Even if the agenda is activity based and includes generous amounts of discussion and group learning, most of these abstract concepts are understood but not yet applied. The real learning takes place *after* the workshop when participants make good on their intentions by *practicing* the concept in the workplace. To this end, the likelihood that participants will overcome well-formed habits and learn a new skill increases when the new behavior is preceded by effortful, intentional planning. Action plans don't need to be elaborate, but they must include a response to this statement: "This is how I intend to apply these concepts back at work."

Create an Experience

Once an intention has been set, the key to learning is action, post-action experience, and reflection. Imagine a participant comes out of the two-day workshop on emotional intelligence and leadership with an intention to work on the competency of developing others by asking more questions. The participant decides that her weekly mentoring conversation with one of the new hires is a good place to start. And so a cup of coffee and an hour-long discussion becomes the next phase of learning this very important skill. She is more or less successful at applying the concept; the decision to act creates an *experience* that serves to further the learning process.

Reflect on the Experience

The experience provides food for thought. Continuing with our example above, as the participant reflects on the mentoring discussion, she is able to answer several questions:

- What did I learn about the power of asking questions?
- What questions were the most effective?
- What was the difference between open-ended and closed questions?
- What was the best question I asked?
- What was difficult?
- What do I need to do next time?

To make reflection a valuable stage in the learning process, remind learners to avoid the tendency to become self-critical and second guess what they *should have* or *could have* done better. There is no need for learners to be perfect: There are no mistakes, only feedback. Reflection is simply looking back on the experience to learn lessons that can be carried forward to the next action.

Follow the 7/21 Rule

The conventional wisdom is that doing something for 21 consecutive days will make it a habit. My colleague Tom Dearth (n.d.) has shared a piece of research that I find helps people avoid becoming discouraged because they were only successful 17 out of 21 days. The real secret to making new information your own is to use what you have learned seven times within a 21-day timeframe. This means that if intention, experience, and reflection are exercised seven times over the three weeks following a training event, then the desired growth becomes a new habit and a true transfer of learning will occur.

The Bare Minimum

Remember that most learning occurs after the workshop once participants have a chance to try out the content in the real world. You can reinforce learning in several ways:

- Give learners the support they need to implement ideas and concepts learned in the emotional intelligence workshops.

- Explain to supervisors and managers how critical it is for them to be a part of the participants' continued growth.

- Encourage learners to continue learning by using other resources, mentoring, coaching, and other growth opportunities such as those listed here.

What to Do Next

Many ideas are presented here. Decide which ones you will do based on these guidelines:

- **Determine what is and what is not in your control.** You can't force managers to do anything they don't want to do. And if it isn't in the budget, then it probably isn't going to happen.

- **Maintain momentum.** Decide the best ways to get managers involved to maintain the momentum for their participants.

- **Be choosy.** You can't do everything. Decide which actions will have the best results.

- **Select something that would be a stretch for you—yes you.** Remember, you are a lifelong learner too.

- **Stay connected.** Select follow-up activities that allow you to stay in touch with your learners.

References

Dearth, T. (n.d.). Business Presentation Skills Course. Lakewood, CO: Spotwood Communications. More info at www.tomdearth.com.

Kolb, D. (1984). *Experiential Learning: Experience as a Source of Learning and Development.* Englewood Cliffs, NJ: Prentice Hall.

SECTION IV

WORKSHOP SUPPORTING DOCUMENTS AND ONLINE SUPPORT

Chapter 11
Learning Activities

What's in This Chapter

- Sixty-two learning activities to use in your workshops
- Complete step-by-step instructions to use for each activity

---

The learning activities in this chapter are provided to help you engage participants through a variety of activity-based learning events. The experiences provided by the learning activities serve to deepen the participant's knowledge and retention of the material. Most of the activities are discussions that balance what you as the facilitator bring to the workshop with the individual experiences and expertise of the participants.

Each learning activity provides detailed information about learning objectives, materials required, timeframe, step-by-step instructions, and debriefing questions. The step-by-step instructions are often designed to get participants into their role, *before* providing additional instruction. This is very intentional because participants tend to pay closer attention to instructions *after* they are placed in their roles. Refer to Chapter 14 for instructions on how to download these workshop support materials.

Learning Activities Included in *Emotional Intelligence Training*

Half-Day Workshop: The New Science of Success

Learning Activity 1: When Emotions Get the Best of Us

Learning Activity 2: System 1 vs. System 2 Thinking

Learning Activity 3: Three Behavioral Principles

Learning Activity 4: Behavior Strategies

Learning Activity 5: Emotional Triggers Exercise

Learning Activity 6: EQuip Yourself for Success: Managing Expectations Discussion

Learning Activity 7: EQuip Yourself for Success: Practice Asking System 2 Questions

Learning Activity 8: EQuip Yourself for Success: Reframe

Learning Activity 9: EQuip Yourself for Success: Action Plan

One-Day Workshop: The New Science of Relationships

Learning Activity 10: The E-Motion Chart

Learning Activity 11: Self-Awareness Competencies

Learning Activity 12: Self-Management Competencies

Learning Activity 13: Social Awareness Competencies

Learning Activity 14: Relationship Management Competencies

Learning Activity 15: The Emotional Competency of Empathy

Learning Activity 16: Effective Listening Exercise

Learning Activity 17: Collaborative Intention Self-Assessment

Learning Activity 18: Empathy and Feeling Blockers

Learning Activity 19: Discretionary Emotional Energy

Learning Activity 20: Map Your Personal Influence Network

Two-Day Workshop: The New Science of Leadership

Learning Activity 1: When Emotions Get the Best of Us

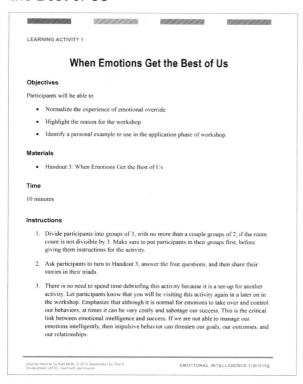

LEARNING ACTIVITY 1

When Emotions Get the Best of Us

Objectives

Participants will be able to

- Normalize the experience of emotional override
- Highlight the reason for the workshop
- Identify a personal example to use in the application phase of workshop.

Materials

- Handout 3: When Emotions Get the Best of Us

Time

10 minutes

Instructions

1. Divide participants into groups of 3, with no more than a couple groups of 2, if the room count is not divisible by 3. Make sure to put participants in their groups first, before giving them instructions for the activity.

2. Ask participants to turn to Handout 3, answer the four questions, and then share their stories in their triads.

3. There is no need to spend time debriefing this activity because it is a set-up for another activity. Let participants know that you will be visiting this activity again in a later on in the workshop. Emphasize that although it is normal for emotions to take over and control our behaviors, at times it can be very costly and sabotage our success. This is the critical link between emotional intelligence and success. If we are not able to manage our emotions intelligently, then impulsive behavior can threaten our goals, our outcomes, and our relationships.

Original material by Karl Mulle, © 2016 Association for Talent Development (ATD). Used with permission.   EMOTIONAL INTELLIGENCE training

Learning Activity 2: System 1 vs. System 2 Thinking

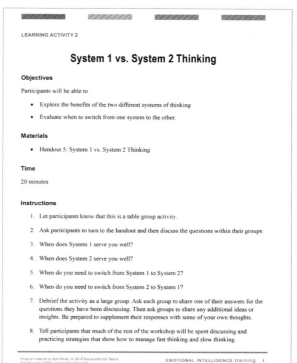

LEARNING ACTIVITY 2

System 1 vs. System 2 Thinking

Objectives

Participants will be able to

- Explore the benefits of the two different systems of thinking
- Evaluate when to switch from one system to the other.

Materials

- Handout 5: System 1 vs. System 2 Thinking

Time

20 minutes

Instructions

1. Let participants know that this is a table group activity.

2. Ask participants to turn to the handout and then discuss the questions within their groups:

3. When does System 1 serve you well?

4. When does System 2 serve you well?

5. When do you need to switch from System 1 to System 2?

6. When do you need to switch from System 2 to System 1?

7. Debrief the activity as a large group. Ask each group to share one of their answers for the questions they have been discussing. Then ask groups to share any additional ideas or insights. Be prepared to supplement their responses with some of your own thoughts.

8. Tell participants that much of the rest of the workshop will be spent discussing and practicing strategies that show how to manage fast thinking and slow thinking.

Original material by Karl Mulle, © 2016 Association for Talent Development (ATD). Used with permission.   EMOTIONAL INTELLIGENCE training   1

Learning Activity 2: System 1 vs. System 2 Thinking, *continued*

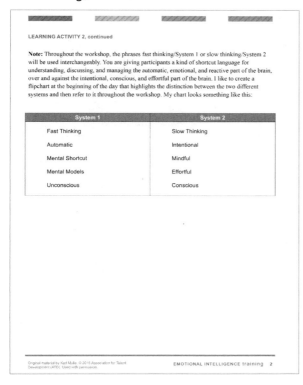

LEARNING ACTIVITY 2, continued

Note: Throughout the workshop, the phrases fast thinking/System 1 or slow thinking/System 2 will be used interchangeably. You are giving participants a kind of shortcut language for understanding, discussing, and managing the automatic, emotional, and reactive part of the brain, over and against the intentional, conscious, and effortful part of the brain. I like to create a flipchart at the beginning of the day that highlights the distinction between the two different systems and then refer to it throughout the workshop. My chart looks something like this:

System 1	System 2
Fast Thinking	Slow Thinking
Automatic	Intentional
Mental Shortcut	Mindful
Mental Models	Effortful
Unconscious	Conscious

Original material by Karl Mulle, © 2016 Association for Talent Development (ATD). Used with permission.   EMOTIONAL INTELLIGENCE training   2

Learning Activity 3: Three Behavioral Principles

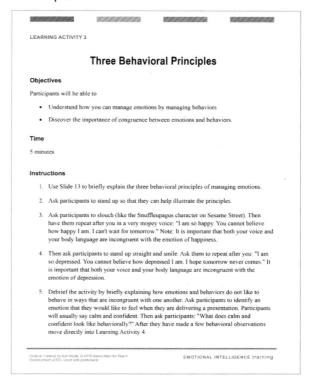

LEARNING ACTIVITY 3

Three Behavioral Principles

Objectives

Participants will be able to

- Understand how you can manage emotions by managing behaviors
- Discover the importance of congruence between emotions and behaviors.

Time

5 minutes

Instructions

1. Use Slide 13 to briefly explain the three behavioral principles of managing emotions.

2. Ask participants to stand up so that they can help illustrate the principles.

3. Ask participants to slouch (like the Snuffleupagus character on Sesame Street). Then have them repeat after you in a very mopey voice: "I am so happy. You cannot believe how happy I am. I can't wait for tomorrow." Note: It is important that both your voice and your body language are incongruent with the emotion of happiness.

4. Then ask participants to stand up straight and smile. Ask them to repeat after you: "I am so depressed. You cannot believe how depressed I am. I hope tomorrow never comes." It is important that both your voice and your body language are incongruent with the emotion of depression.

5. Debrief the activity by briefly explaining how emotions and behaviors do not like to behave in ways that are incongruent with one another. Ask participants to identify an emotion that they would like to feel when they are delivering a presentation. Participants will usually say calm and confident. Then ask participants: "What does calm and confident look like behaviorally?" After they have made a few behavioral observations move directly into Learning Activity 4.

Original material by Karl Mulle, © 2016 Association for Talent Development (ATD). Used with permission.   EMOTIONAL INTELLIGENCE training

Learning Activity 4: Behavior Strategies

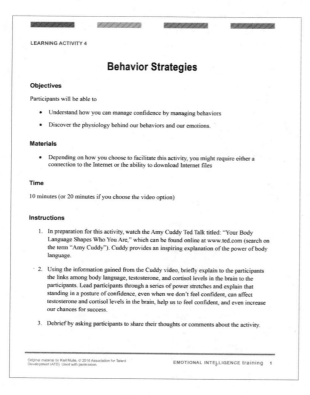

Behavior Strategies

Objectives

Participants will be able to

- Understand how you can manage confidence by managing behaviors
- Discover the physiology behind our behaviors and our emotions.

Materials

- Depending on how you choose to facilitate this activity, you might require either a connection to the Internet or the ability to download Internet files

Time

10 minutes (or 20 minutes if you choose the video option)

Instructions

1. In preparation for this activity, watch the Amy Cuddy Ted Talk titled: "Your Body Language Shapes Who You Are," which can be found online at www.ted.com (search on the term "Amy Cuddy"). Cuddy provides an inspiring explanation of the power of body language.

2. Using the information gained from the Cuddy video, briefly explain to the participants the links among body language, testosterone, and cortisol levels in the brain to the participants. Lead participants through a series of power stretches and explain that standing in a posture of confidence, even when we don't feel confident, can affect testosterone and cortisol levels in the brain, help us to feel confident, and even increase our chances for success.

3. Debrief by asking participants to share their thoughts or comments about the activity.

Original material by Karl Mulle, © 2016 Association for Talent Development (ATD). Used with permission.

EMOTIONAL INTELLIGENCE training 1

Learning Activity 4: Behavior Strategies, *continued*

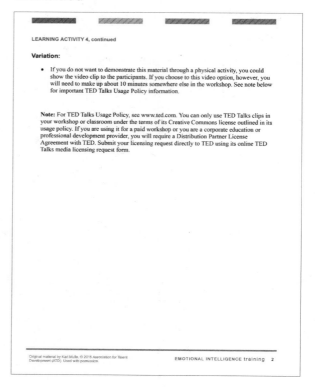

Variation:

- If you do not want to demonstrate this material through a physical activity, you could show the video clip to the participants. If you choose to this video option, however, you will need to make up about 10 minutes somewhere else in the workshop. See note below for important TED Talks Usage Policy information.

Note: For TED Talks Usage Policy, see www.ted.com. You can only use TED Talks clips in your workshop or classroom under the terms of its Creative Commons license outlined in its usage policy. If you are using it for a paid workshop or you are a corporate education or professional development provider, you will require a Distribution Partner License Agreement with TED. Submit your licensing request directly to TED using its online TED Talks media licensing request form.

Original material by Karl Mulle, © 2016 Association for Talent Development (ATD). Used with permission.

EMOTIONAL INTELLIGENCE training 2

Learning Activity 5: Emotional Triggers Exercise

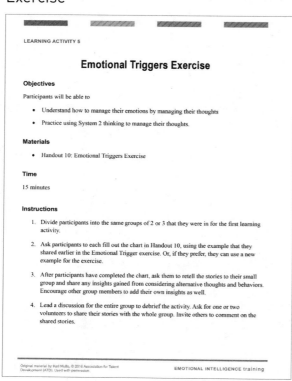

Emotional Triggers Exercise

Objectives

Participants will be able to

- Understand how to manage their emotions by managing their thoughts
- Practice using System 2 thinking to manage their thoughts.

Materials

- Handout 10: Emotional Triggers Exercise

Time

15 minutes

Instructions

1. Divide participants into the same groups of 2 or 3 that they were in for the first learning activity.

2. Ask participants to each fill out the chart in Handout 10, using the example that they shared earlier in the Emotional Trigger exercise. Or, if they prefer, they can use a new example for the exercise.

3. After participants have completed the chart, ask them to retell the stories to their small group and share any insights gained from considering alternative thoughts and behaviors. Encourage other group members to add their own insights as well.

4. Lead a discussion for the entire group to debrief the activity. Ask for one or two volunteers to share their stories with the whole group. Invite others to comment on the shared stories.

Original material by Karl Mulle, © 2016 Association for Talent Development (ATD). Used with permission.

EMOTIONAL INTELLIGENCE training

Learning Activity 6: EQuip Yourself for Success: Managing Expectations Discussion

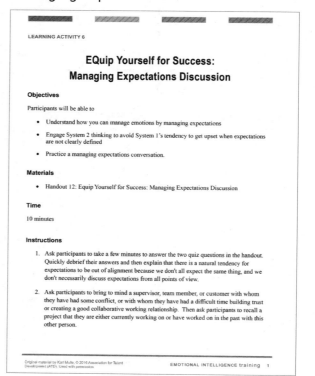

EQuip Yourself for Success:
Managing Expectations Discussion

Objectives

Participants will be able to

- Understand how you can manage emotions by managing expectations
- Engage System 2 thinking to avoid System 1's tendency to get upset when expectations are not clearly defined
- Practice a managing expectations conversation.

Materials

- Handout 12: Equip Yourself for Success: Managing Expectations Discussion

Time

10 minutes

Instructions

1. Ask participants to take a few minutes to answer the two quiz questions in the handout. Quickly debrief their answers and then explain that there is a natural tendency for expectations to be out of alignment because we don't all expect the same thing, and we don't necessarily discuss expectations from all points of view.

2. Ask participants to bring to mind a supervisor, team member, or customer with whom they have had some conflict, or with whom they have had a difficult time building trust or creating a good collaborative working relationship. Then ask participants to recall a project that they are either currently working on or have worked on in the past with this other person.

Original material by Karl Mulle, © 2016 Association for Talent Development (ATD). Used with permission.

EMOTIONAL INTELLIGENCE training 1

Learning Activity 6: EQuip Yourself for Success: Managing Expectations Discussion, *continued*

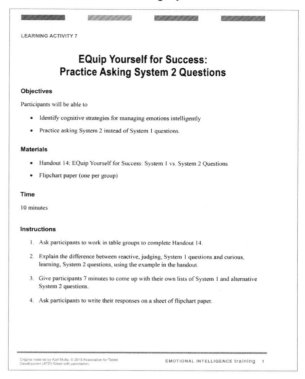

LEARNING ACTIVITY 6, continued

3. Have participants to try to answer these first two questions as best as they can from the other person's perspective and in the context of the project:

   - What does this person expect of himself or herself?

   - What does this person expect of you?

4. Now, ask participants to answer these two questions from their perspective and in the context of the project:

   - What does this person expect of himself or herself?

   - What does this person expect of you?

5. Debrief the activity as a large group discussion. It is important to discuss the idea that our expectation conversations are often "top down," so we don't always tap into the emotional energy and enthusiasms of our colleagues and team members. Also, what people expect of themselves is usually closely connected with their true motivations. Use the discussion questions below to help guide your debrief..

Discussion Questions for Debriefing

   - Were you able to answer all four questions?

   - Have you actually had the four conversations with your supervisor, team member, or customer? What was that conversation like?

   - Did you reach an agreement about what to expect of each other?

EMOTIONAL INTELLIGENCE training   2

Learning Activity 7: EQuip Yourself for Success: Practice Asking System 2 Questions

LEARNING ACTIVITY 7

EQuip Yourself for Success: Practice Asking System 2 Questions

Objectives

Participants will be able to

   - Identify cognitive strategies for managing emotions intelligently

   - Practice asking System 2 instead of System 1 questions.

Materials

   - Handout 14: EQuip Yourself for Success: System 1 vs. System 2 Questions

   - Flipchart paper (one per group)

Time

10 minutes

Instructions

1. Ask participants to work in table groups to complete Handout 14.

2. Explain the difference between reactive, judging, System 1 questions and curious, learning, System 2 questions, using the example in the handout.

3. Give participants 7 minutes to come up with their own lists of System 1 and alternative System 2 questions.

4. Ask participants to write their responses on a sheet of flipchart paper.

EMOTIONAL INTELLIGENCE training   1

Learning Activity 7: EQuip Yourself for Success: Practice Asking System 2 Questions, *continued*

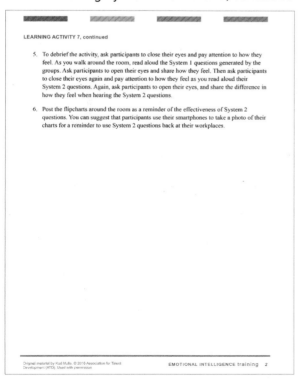

LEARNING ACTIVITY 7, continued

5. To debrief the activity, ask participants to close their eyes and pay attention to how they feel. As you walk around the room, read aloud the System 1 questions generated by the groups. Ask participants to open their eyes and share how they feel. Then ask participants to close their eyes again and pay attention to how they feel as you read aloud their System 2 questions. Again, ask participants to open their eyes, and share the difference in how they feel when hearing the System 2 questions.

6. Post the flipcharts around the room as a reminder of the effectiveness of System 2 questions. You can suggest that participants use their smartphones to take a photo of their charts for a reminder to use System 2 questions back at their workplaces.

EMOTIONAL INTELLIGENCE training   2

Learning Activity 8: EQuip Yourself for Success: Reframe

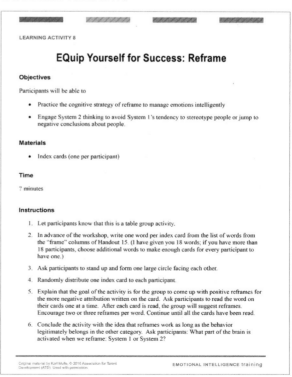

LEARNING ACTIVITY 8

EQuip Yourself for Success: Reframe

Objectives

Participants will be able to

   - Practice the cognitive strategy of reframe to manage emotions intelligently

   - Engage System 2 thinking to avoid System 1's tendency to stereotype people or jump to negative conclusions about people.

Materials

   - Index cards (one per participant)

Time

? minutes

Instructions

1. Let participants know that this is a table group activity.

2. In advance of the workshop, write one word per index card from the list of words from the "frame" columns of Handout 15. (I have given you 18 words; if you have more than 18 participants, choose additional words to make enough cards for every participant to have one.)

3. Ask participants to stand up and form one large circle facing each other.

4. Randomly distribute one index card to each participant.

5. Explain that the goal of the activity is for the group to come up with positive reframes for the more negative attribution written on the card. Ask participants to read the word on their cards one at a time. After each card is read, the group will suggest reframes. Encourage two or three reframes per word. Continue until all the cards have been read.

6. Conclude the activity with the idea that reframes work as long as the behavior legitimately belongs in the other category. Ask participants: What part of the brain is activated when we reframe: System 1 or System 2?

EMOTIONAL INTELLIGENCE training

Learning Activity 9: EQuip Yourself for Success: Action Plan

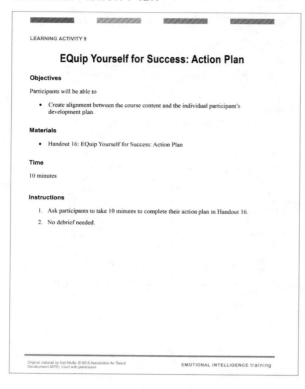

LEARNING ACTIVITY 9

EQuip Yourself for Success: Action Plan

Objectives

Participants will be able to

- Create alignment between the course content and the individual participant's development plan.

Materials

- Handout 16: EQuip Yourself for Success: Action Plan

Time

10 minutes

Instructions

1. Ask participants to take 10 minutes to complete their action plan in Handout 16.
2. No debrief needed.

Original material by Karl Mulle, © 2016 Association for Talent Development (ATD). Used with permission.

EMOTIONAL INTELLIGENCE training

Learning Activity 10: The E-Motion Chart

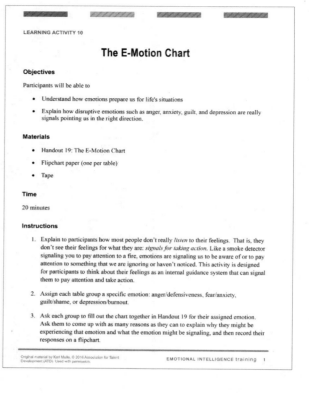

LEARNING ACTIVITY 10

The E-Motion Chart

Objectives

Participants will be able to

- Understand how emotions prepare us for life's situations
- Explain how disruptive emotions such as anger, anxiety, guilt, and depression are really signals pointing us in the right direction.

Materials

- Handout 19: The E-Motion Chart
- Flipchart paper (one per table)
- Tape

Time

20 minutes

Instructions

1. Explain to participants how most people don't really *listen* to their feelings. That is, they don't see their feelings for what they are: *signals for taking action*. Like a smoke detector signaling you to pay attention to a fire, emotions are signaling us to be aware of or to pay attention to something that we are ignoring or haven't noticed. This activity is designed for participants to think about their feelings as an internal guidance system that can signal them to pay attention and take action.

2. Assign each table group a specific emotion: anger/defensiveness, fear/anxiety, guilt/shame, or depression/burnout.

3. Ask each group to fill out the chart together in Handout 19 for their assigned emotion. Ask them to come up with as many reasons as they can to explain why they might be experiencing that emotion and what the emotion might be signaling, and then record their responses on a flipchart.

Original material by Karl Mulle, © 2016 Association for Talent Development (ATD). Used with permission.

EMOTIONAL INTELLIGENCE training   1

Learning Activity 10: The E-Motion Chart, *continued*

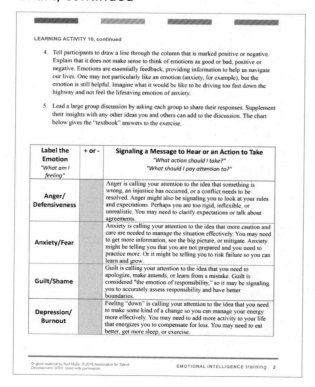

LEARNING ACTIVITY 10, continued

4. Tell participants to draw a line through the column that is marked positive or negative. Explain that it does not make sense to think of emotions as good or bad, positive or negative. Emotions are essentially feedback, providing information to help us navigate our lives. One may not particularly like an emotion (anxiety, for example), but the emotion is still helpful. Imagine what it would be like to be driving too fast down the highway and not feel the lifesaving emotion of anxiety.

5. Lead a large group discussion by asking each group to share their responses. Supplement their insights with any other ideas you and others can add to the discussion. The chart below gives the "textbook" answers to the exercise.

Label the Emotion *"What am I feeling"*	+ or -	Signaling a Message to Hear or an Action to Take *"What action should I take?"* *"What should I pay attention to?"*
Anger/ Defensiveness		Anger is calling your attention to the idea that something is wrong, an injustice has occurred, or a conflict needs to be resolved. Anger might also be signaling you to look at your rules and expectations. Perhaps you are too rigid, inflexible, or unrealistic. You may need to clarify expectations or talk about agreements.
Anxiety/Fear		Anxiety is calling your attention to the idea that more caution and care are needed to manage the situation effectively. You may need to get more information, see the big picture, or mitigate. Anxiety might be telling you that you are not prepared and you need to practice more. Or it might be telling you to risk failure so you can learn and grow.
Guilt/Shame		Guilt is calling your attention to the idea that you need to apologize, make amends, or learn from a mistake. Guilt is considered "the emotion of responsibility," so it may be signaling you to accurately assess responsibility and have better boundaries.
Depression/ Burnout		Feeling "down" is calling your attention to the idea that you need to make some kind of a change so you can manage your energy more effectively. You may need to add more activity to your life that energizes you to compensate for loss. You may need to eat better, get more sleep, or exercise.

Original material by Karl Mulle, © 2016 Association for Talent Development (ATD). Used with permission.

EMOTIONAL INTELLIGENCE training   2

Learning Activity 11: Self-Awareness Competencies

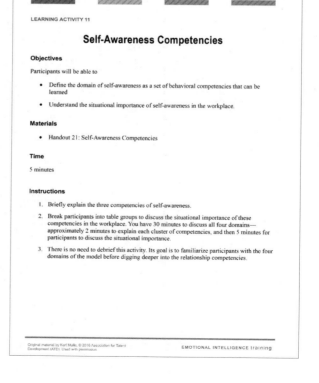

LEARNING ACTIVITY 11

Self-Awareness Competencies

Objectives

Participants will be able to

- Define the domain of self-awareness as a set of behavioral competencies that can be learned
- Understand the situational importance of self-awareness in the workplace.

Materials

- Handout 21: Self-Awareness Competencies

Time

5 minutes

Instructions

1. Briefly explain the three competencies of self-awareness.

2. Break participants into table groups to discuss the situational importance of these competencies in the workplace. You have 30 minutes to discuss all four domains—approximately 2 minutes to explain each cluster of competencies, and then 5 minutes for participants to discuss the situational importance.

3. There is no need to debrief this activity. Its goal is to familiarize participants with the four domains of the model before digging deeper into the relationship competencies.

Original material by Karl Mulle, © 2016 Association for Talent Development (ATD). Used with permission.

EMOTIONAL INTELLIGENCE training

EMOTIONAL INTELLIGENCE training

Learning Activity 12: Self-Management Competencies

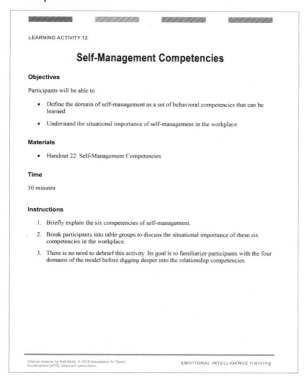

Self-Management Competencies

Objectives

Participants will be able to

- Define the domain of self-management as a set of behavioral competencies that can be learned
- Understand the situational importance of self-management in the workplace.

Materials

- Handout 22: Self-Management Competencies

Time

10 minutes

Instructions

1. Briefly explain the six competencies of self-management.
2. Break participants into table groups to discuss the situational importance of these six competencies in the workplace.
3. There is no need to debrief this activity. Its goal is to familiarize participants with the four domains of the model before digging deeper into the relationship competencies.

Original material by Karl Mulle. © 2016 Association for Talent Development (ATD). Used with permission.   EMOTIONAL INTELLIGENCE training

Learning Activity 13: Social Awareness Competencies

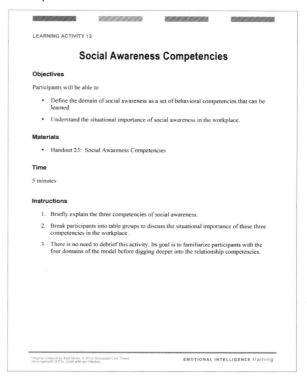

Social Awareness Competencies

Objectives

Participants will be able to

- Define the domain of social awareness as a set of behavioral competencies that can be learned
- Understand the situational importance of social awareness in the workplace.

Materials

- Handout 23: Social Awareness Competencies

Time

5 minutes

Instructions

1. Briefly explain the three competencies of social awareness.
2. Break participants into table groups to discuss the situational importance of these three competencies in the workplace.
3. There is no need to debrief this activity. Its goal is to familiarize participants with the four domains of the model before digging deeper into the relationship competencies.

Original material by Karl Mulle. © 2016 Association for Talent Development (ATD). Used with permission.   EMOTIONAL INTELLIGENCE training

Learning Activity 14: Relationship Management Competencies

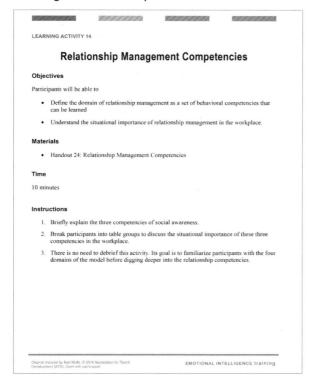

Relationship Management Competencies

Objectives

Participants will be able to

- Define the domain of relationship management as a set of behavioral competencies that can be learned
- Understand the situational importance of relationship management in the workplace.

Materials

- Handout 24: Relationship Management Competencies

Time

10 minutes

Instructions

1. Briefly explain the three competencies of social awareness.
2. Break participants into table groups to discuss the situational importance of these three competencies in the workplace.
3. There is no need to debrief this activity. Its goal is to familiarize participants with the four domains of the model before digging deeper into the relationship competencies.

Original material by Karl Mulle. © 2016 Association for Talent Development (ATD). Used with permission.   EMOTIONAL INTELLIGENCE training

Learning Activity 15: The Emotional Competency of Empathy

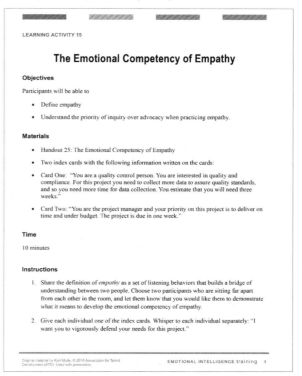

The Emotional Competency of Empathy

Objectives

Participants will be able to

- Define empathy
- Understand the priority of inquiry over advocacy when practicing empathy.

Materials

- Handout 25: The Emotional Competency of Empathy
- Two index cards with the following information written on the cards:
- Card One: "You are a quality control person. You are interested in quality and compliance. For this project you need to collect more data to assure quality standards, and so you need more time for data collection. You estimate that you will need three weeks."
- Card Two: "You are the project manager and your priority on this project is to deliver on time and under budget. The project is due in one week."

Time

10 minutes

Instructions

1. Share the definition of *empathy* as a set of listening behaviors that builds a bridge of understanding between two people. Choose two participants who are sitting far apart from each other in the room, and let them know that you would like them to demonstrate what it means to develop the emotional competency of empathy.
2. Give each individual one of the index cards. Whisper to each individual separately: "I want you to vigorously defend your needs for this project."

Original material by Karl Mulle. © 2016 Association for Talent Development (ATD). Used with permission.   EMOTIONAL INTELLIGENCE training   1

Learning Activity 15: The Emotional Competency of Empathy, *continued*

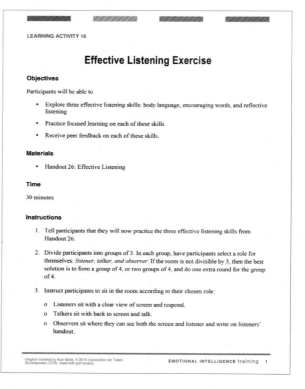

3. Begin with either of the two individuals, and ask them to take turns responding to each other for 3 or 4 rounds.

4. After 3 or 4 rounds, thank them and tell them they can take their seats.

5. Use the actual physical distance that separates these two participants from each other to explain that *empathy* is a set of listening skills that builds a bridge (gesture a large arc from one individual to the other) of understanding between two or more individuals. In this example you have two people standing on different sides of a situation, each with different concerns, interests, perspectives, and points of view.

6. Conduct a large group discussion to debrief the activity using the questions that follow.

7. End the activity by quoting Stephen Covey's Habit 5 from his book *The 7 Habits of Highly Effective People*: "Seek first to understand and then to be understood."

Discussion Questions for Debriefing

- Whose side of the bridge did [*participant name*] start on to build the bridge of understanding?

- Whose side of the bridge did [*other participant name*] start on to build the bridge of understanding?

- Did the bridge ever get built?

- And here is the key question: Whose side of the bridge should you start on to build the bridge of understanding?

- Tell the room that you purposely instructed each person in the role play to be defensive instead of understanding. Then ask the two volunteers what they could have done differently to build the bridge of understanding?

Learning Activity 16: Effective Listening Exercise

Effective Listening Exercise

Objectives

Participants will be able to

- Explore three effective listening skills: body language, encouraging words, and reflective listening

- Practice focused learning on each of these skills

- Receive peer feedback on each of these skills.

Materials

- Handout 26: Effective Listening

Time

30 minutes

Instructions

1. Tell participants that they will now practice the three effective listening skills from Handout 26.

2. Divide participants into groups of 3. In each group, have participants select a role for themselves: *listener, talker, and observer*. If the room is not divisible by 3, then the best solution is to form a group of 4, or two groups of 4, and do one extra round for the group of 4.

3. Instruct participants to sit in the room according to their chosen role:

   o Listeners sit with a clear view of screen and respond.

   o Talkers sit with back to screen and talk.

   o Observers sit where they can see both the screen and listener and write on listeners' handout.

Learning Activity 16: Effective Listening Exercise, *continued*

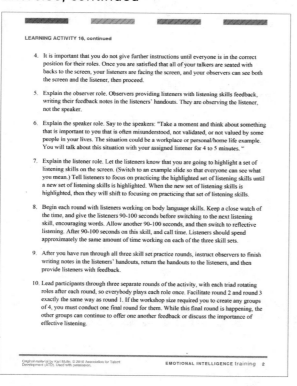

4. It is important that you do not give further instructions until everyone is in the correct position for their roles. Once you are satisfied that all of your talkers are seated with backs to the screen, your listeners are facing the screen, and your observers can see both the screen and the listener, then proceed.

5. Explain the observer role. Observers providing listeners with listening skills feedback, writing their feedback notes in the listeners' handouts. They are observing the listener, not the speaker.

6. Explain the speaker role. Say to the speakers: "Take a moment and think about something that is important to you that is often misunderstood, not validated, or not valued by some people in your lives. The situation could be a workplace or personal/home life example. You will talk about this situation with your assigned listener for 4 to 5 minutes."

7. Explain the listener role. Let the listeners know that you are going to highlight a set of listening skills on the screen. (Switch to an example slide so that everyone can see what you mean.) Tell listeners to focus on practicing the highlighted set of listening skills until a new set of listening skills is highlighted. When the new set of listening skills is highlighted, then they will shift to focusing on practicing that set of listening skills.

8. Begin each round with listeners working on body language skills. Keep a close watch of the time, and give the listeners 90-100 seconds before switching to the next listening skill, encouraging words. Allow another 90-100 seconds, and then switch to reflective listening. After 90-100 seconds on this skill, and call time. Listeners should spend approximately the same amount of time working on each of the three skill sets.

9. After you have run through all three skill set practice rounds, instruct observers to finish writing notes in the listeners' handouts, return the handouts to the listeners, and then provide listeners with feedback.

10. Lead participants through three separate rounds of the activity, with each triad rotating roles after each round, so everybody plays each role once. Facilitate round 2 and round 3 exactly the same way as round 1. If the workshop size required you to create any groups of 4, you must conduct one final round for them. While this final round is happening, the other groups can continue to offer one another feedback or discuss the importance of effective listening.

Learning Activity 16: Effective Listening Exercise, *continued*

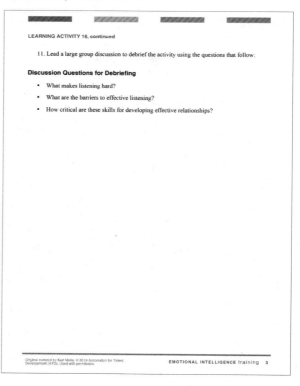

11. Lead a large group discussion to debrief the activity using the questions that follow:

Discussion Questions for Debriefing

- What makes listening hard?

- What are the barriers to effective listening?

- How critical are these skills for developing effective relationships?

Learning Activity 17: Collaborative Intention Self-Assessment

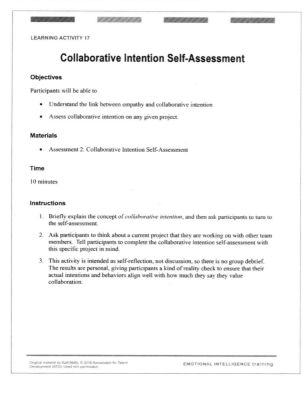

Learning Activity 18: Empathy and Feeling Blockers

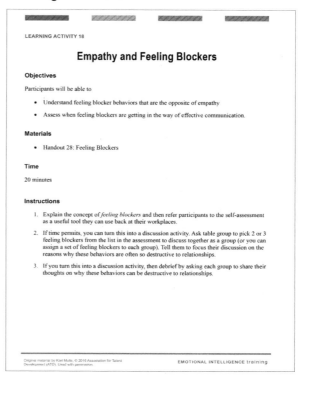

Learning Activity 19: Discretionary Emotional Energy

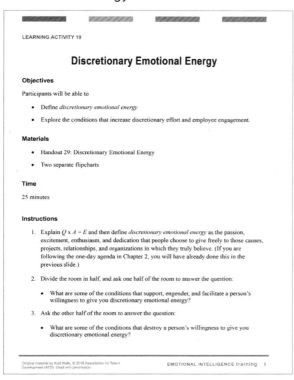

Learning Activity 19: Discretionary Emotional Energy, *continued*

LEARNING ACTIVITY 19, continued

4. Ask participants to share their answers to the two questions and then write them on two separate flipcharts. List the positive, supportive conditions on one chart and the negative, destructive conditions on the other. Post charts in the room as reminder of how to foster discretionary emotional energy and employment engagement.

5. Transition from this discussion to application points that support these answers. Explain that anytime you show a slide or turn to a section of the handout that begins with the title: "EQuip Yourself for Success" that you transitioning to application points. You will be sharing three application points for increasing the emotional competencies of influence, teamwork, and collaboration.

Learning Activity 20: Map Your Personal Influence Network

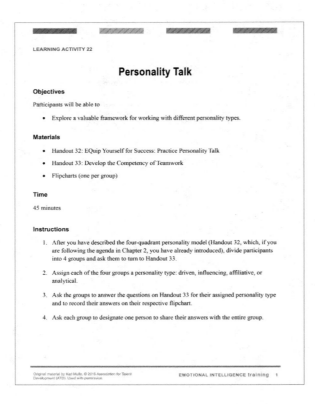

LEARNING ACTIVITY 20

Map Your Personal Influence Network

Objectives

Participants will be able to

- Understand the importance of building a robust, diverse influence network
- Map out their personal influence networks.

Materials

- Handout 30: EQuip Yourself for Success: Map Your Personal Influence Network

Time

10 minutes

Instructions

1. Explain that this activity will help participants explore the importance of cultivating a broad network of relationships with people inside and outside their companies whose support they need to carry out their initiatives.

2. Ask participants to turn to Handout 30. Give them 7 minutes to create their personal influence maps on the second page of the handout, using the example on the first page as a model. Advise them to consider all their connections, including their close inner circle of friends, people they naturally turn to for support, and other associates. The handout also provides questions to help trigger their thinking as they create their maps.

3. The debrief for this activity will occur in Learning Activity 21, so move directly into that activity.

EMOTIONAL INTELLIGENCE training

Learning Activity 21: Evaluate Your Personal Influence Network

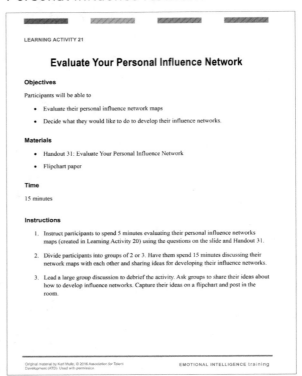

LEARNING ACTIVITY 21

Evaluate Your Personal Influence Network

Objectives

Participants will be able to

- Evaluate their personal influence network maps
- Decide what they would like to do to develop their influence networks.

Materials

- Handout 31: Evaluate Your Personal Influence Network
- Flipchart paper

Time

15 minutes

Instructions

1. Instruct participants to spend 5 minutes evaluating their personal influence networks maps (created in Learning Activity 20) using the questions on the slide and Handout 31.

2. Divide participants into groups of 2 or 3. Have them spend 15 minutes discussing their network maps with each other and sharing ideas for developing their influence networks.

3. Lead a large group discussion to debrief the activity. Ask groups to share their ideas about how to develop influence networks. Capture their ideas on a flipchart and post in the room.

EMOTIONAL INTELLIGENCE training

Learning Activity 22: Personality Talk

LEARNING ACTIVITY 22

Personality Talk

Objectives

Participants will be able to

- Explore a valuable framework for working with different personality types.

Materials

- Handout 32: EQuip Yourself for Success: Practice Personality Talk
- Handout 33: Develop the Competency of Teamwork
- Flipcharts (one per group)

Time

45 minutes

Instructions

1. After you have described the four-quadrant personality model (Handout 32, which, if you are following the agenda in Chapter 2, you have already introduced), divide participants into 4 groups and ask them to turn to Handout 33.

2. Assign each of the four groups a personality type: driven, influencing, affiliative, or analytical.

3. Ask the groups to answer the questions on Handout 33 for their assigned personality type and to record their answers on their respective flipchart.

4. Ask each group to designate one person to share their answers with the entire group.

EMOTIONAL INTELLIGENCE training 1

Learning Activity 22: Personality Talk, *continued*

LEARNING ACTIVITY 22, continued

5. Debrief by asking other participants to share additional insights. Encourage those who identify with a particular type to share their thoughts. Supplement the information shared with any additional tips or insights that you have.

6. Close activity by referring participants to the chart on the second page of Handout 33. It provides a valuable framework for working successfully with the different personality styles.

EMOTIONAL INTELLIGENCE training 2

EMOTIONAL INTELLIGENCE training

Learning Activity 23: Teaming and Collaboration Action Plan

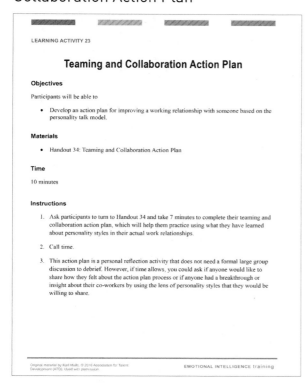

LEARNING ACTIVITY 23

Teaming and Collaboration Action Plan

Objectives

Participants will be able to

- Develop an action plan for improving a working relationship with someone based on the personality talk model.

Materials

- Handout 34: Teaming and Collaboration Action Plan

Time

10 minutes

Instructions

1. Ask participants to turn to Handout 34 and take 7 minutes to complete their teaming and collaboration action plan, which will help them practice using what they have learned about personality styles in their actual work relationships.

2. Call time.

3. This action plan is a personal reflection activity that does not need a formal large group discussion to debrief. However, if time allows, you could ask if anyone would like to share how they felt about the action plan process or if anyone had a breakthrough or insight about their co-workers by using the lens of personality styles that they would be willing to share.

EMOTIONAL INTELLIGENCE training

Learning Activity 24: The Two Messages

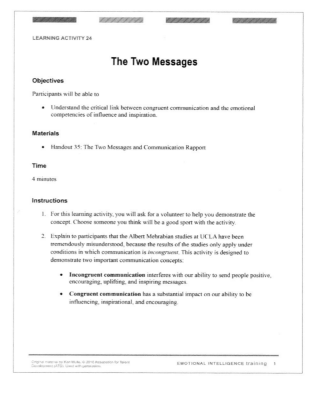

LEARNING ACTIVITY 24

The Two Messages

Objectives

Participants will be able to

- Understand the critical link between congruent communication and the emotional competencies of influence and inspiration.

Materials

- Handout 35: The Two Messages and Communication Rapport

Time

4 minutes

Instructions

1. For this learning activity, you will ask for a volunteer to help you demonstrate the concept. Choose someone you think will be a good sport with the activity.

2. Explain to participants that the Albert Mehrabian studies at UCLA have been tremendously misunderstood, because the results of the studies only apply under conditions in which communication is *incongruent*. This activity is designed to demonstrate two important communication concepts:

   - **Incongruent communication** interferes with our ability to send people positive, encouraging, uplifting, and inspiring messages.

   - **Congruent communication** has a substantial impact on our ability to be influencing, inspirational, and encouraging.

EMOTIONAL INTELLIGENCE training   1

Learning Activity 24: The Two Messages, *continued*

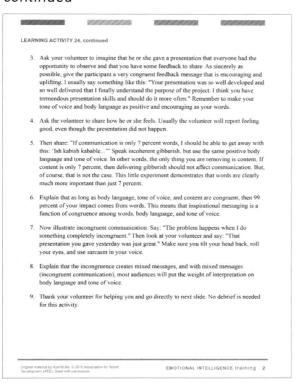

LEARNING ACTIVITY 24, continued

3. Ask your volunteer to imagine that he or she gave a presentation that everyone had the opportunity to observe and that you have some feedback to share. As sincerely as possible, give the participant a very congruent feedback message that is encouraging and uplifting. I usually say something like this: "Your presentation was so well developed and so well delivered that I finally understand the purpose of the project. I think you have tremendous presentation skills and should do it more often." Remember to make your tone of voice and body language as positive and encouraging as your words.

4. Ask the volunteer to share how he or she feels. Usually the volunteer will report feeling good, even though the presentation did not happen.

5. Then share: "If communication is only 7 percent words, I should be able to get away with this: 'Ish kabish kabable...'" Speak incoherent gibberish, but use the same positive body language and tone of voice. In other words, the only thing you are removing is content. If content is only 7 percent, then delivering gibberish should not affect communication. But, of course, that is not the case. This little experiment demonstrates that words are clearly much more important than just 7 percent.

6. Explain that as long as body language, tone of voice, and content are congruent, then 99 percent of your impact comes from words. This means that inspirational messaging is a function of congruence among words, body language, and tone of voice.

7. Now illustrate incongruent communication. Say: "The problem happens when I do something completely incongruent." Then look at your volunteer and say: "That presentation you gave yesterday was just great." Make sure you tilt your head back, roll your eyes, and use sarcasm in your voice.

8. Explain that the incongruence creates mixed messages, and with mixed messages (incongruent communication), most audiences will put the weight of interpretation on body language and tone of voice.

9. Thank your volunteer for helping you and go directly to next slide. No debrief is needed for this activity.

EMOTIONAL INTELLIGENCE training   2

Learning Activity 25: Building Rapport

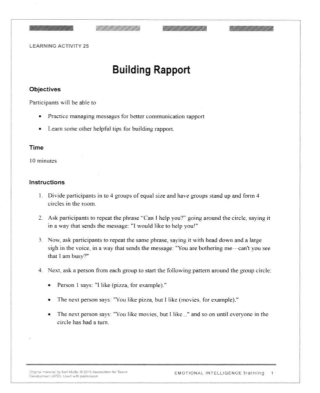

LEARNING ACTIVITY 25

Building Rapport

Objectives

Participants will be able to

- Practice managing messages for better communication rapport
- Learn some other helpful tips for building rapport

Time

10 minutes

Instructions

1. Divide participants in to 4 groups of equal size and have groups stand up and form 4 circles in the room.

2. Ask participants to repeat the phrase "Can I help you?" going around the circle, saying it in a way that sends the message: "I would like to help you!"

3. Now, ask participants to repeat the same phrase, saying it with head down and a large sigh in the voice, in a way that sends the message: "You are bothering me—can't you see that I am busy?"

4. Next, ask a person from each group to start the following pattern around the group circle:

   - Person 1 says: "I like (pizza, for example)."

   - The next person says: "You like pizza, but I like (movies, for example)."

   - The next person says: "You like movies, but I like..." and so on until everyone in the circle has had a turn.

EMOTIONAL INTELLIGENCE training   1

Learning Activity 25: Building Rapport, *continued*

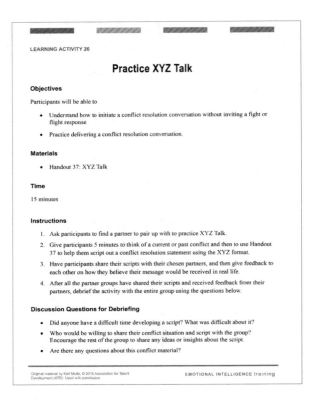

LEARNING ACTIVITY 25, continued

5. Now do the exact same activity again, but change the pattern. This time instead of using the word but, you are going to insert the word and. The pattern will go like this:

    - Person 1 says: "I like *(pizza for example)*."
    - The next person says: "You like pizza, and I like *(movies, for example)*."
    - The next person says: "You like movies, and I like..." and so on until everyone in the circle has had a turn.

6. Ask participants to explain the difference in feeling messages between using the word *but* and using the word *and*.

7. Tell participants they can sit down and then ask them to explain the difference in feeling messages between *"Why ... you ...?"* vs. *"What can I ...?"* or *"How can I ...?"*

8. Talk through the rest of the points on Slide 55 by sharing with participants some other examples and tips for building rapport.

    - When delivering both reinforcing and redirecting feedback in the same conversation, instead of saying "You did this really well, but..." replace but with an if/then statement: "Your presentation was so well developed. If you provide a link to your research, then it will be even more impactful."
    - Talk about a common interest.
    - Use metaphorical language that aligns with a person's interests. For example, if you know someone loves gardening, you might say: "We did our best to plant the seed. Now let's see if it grows!"
    - Use their sensory language. People will often use phrases such as "I think" or "I see" or "I feel." Use the same phrasing to help build rapport.
    - Mirror body language. People tend to feel more comfortable around people who are like them, so when you mirror their body language, you create a sense of likeness and commonality.

9. Debrief by asking participants to share any techniques or tips for building rapport from their experiences.

Original material by Karl Mulle, © 2016 Association for Talent Development (ATD). Used with permission.   EMOTIONAL INTELLIGENCE training   2

Learning Activity 26: Practice XYZ Talk

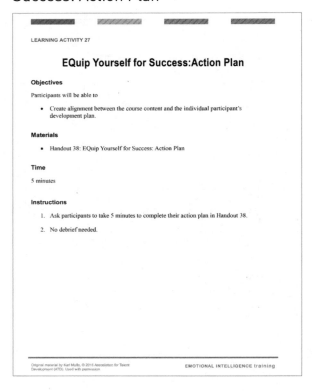

LEARNING ACTIVITY 26

Practice XYZ Talk

Objectives

Participants will be able to

- Understand how to initiate a conflict resolution conversation without inviting a fight or flight response
- Practice delivering a conflict resolution conversation.

Materials

- Handout 37: XYZ Talk

Time

15 minutes

Instructions

1. Ask participants to find a partner to pair up with to practice XYZ Talk.
2. Give participants 5 minutes to think of a current or past conflict and then to use Handout 37 to help them script out a conflict resolution statement using the XYZ format.
3. Have participants share their scripts with their chosen partners, and then give feedback to each other on how they believe their message would be received in real life.
4. After all the partner groups have shared their scripts and received feedback from their partners, debrief the activity with the entire group using the questions below.

Discussion Questions for Debriefing

- Did anyone have a difficult time developing a script? What was difficult about it?
- Who would be willing to share their conflict situation and script with the group? Encourage the rest of the group to share any ideas or insights about the script.
- Are there any questions about this conflict material?

Original material by Karl Mulle, © 2016 Association for Talent Development (ATD). Used with permission.   EMOTIONAL INTELLIGENCE training

Learning Activity 27: EQuip Yourself for Success: Action Plan

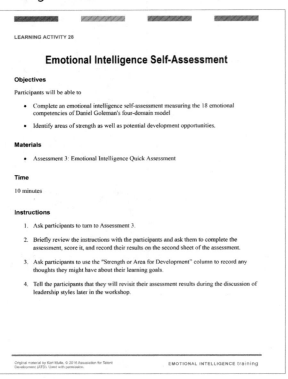

LEARNING ACTIVITY 27

EQuip Yourself for Success: Action Plan

Objectives

Participants will be able to

- Create alignment between the course content and the individual participant's development plan.

Materials

- Handout 38: EQuip Yourself for Success: Action Plan

Time

5 minutes

Instructions

1. Ask participants to take 5 minutes to complete their action plan in Handout 38.
2. No debrief needed.

Original material by Karl Mulle, © 2016 Association for Talent Development (ATD). Used with permission.   EMOTIONAL INTELLIGENCE training

Learning Activity 28: Emotional Intelligence Self-Assessment

LEARNING ACTIVITY 28

Emotional Intelligence Self-Assessment

Objectives

Participants will be able to

- Complete an emotional intelligence self-assessment measuring the 18 emotional competencies of Daniel Goleman's four-domain model
- Identify areas of strength as well as potential development opportunities.

Materials

- Assessment 3: Emotional Intelligence Quick Assessment

Time

10 minutes

Instructions

1. Ask participants to turn to Assessment 3.
2. Briefly review the instructions with the participants and ask them to complete the assessment, score it, and record their results on the second sheet of the assessment.
3. Ask participants to use the "Strength or Area for Development" column to record any thoughts they might have about their learning goals.
4. Tell the participants that they will revisit their assessment results during the discussion of leadership styles later in the workshop.

Original material by Karl Mulle, © 2016 Association for Talent Development (ATD). Used with permission.   EMOTIONAL INTELLIGENCE training

Learning Activity 29: Emotional Contagion

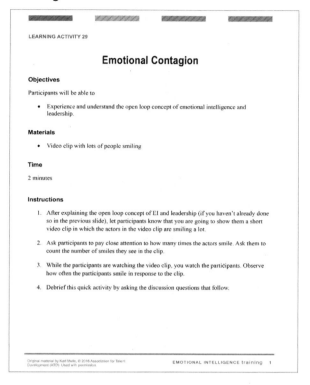

LEARNING ACTIVITY 29

Emotional Contagion

Objectives

Participants will be able to

- Experience and understand the open loop concept of emotional intelligence and leadership.

Materials

- Video clip with lots of people smiling

Time

2 minutes

Instructions

1. After explaining the open loop concept of EI and leadership (if you haven't already done so in the previous slide), let participants know that you are going to show them a short video clip in which the actors in the video clip are smiling a lot.

2. Ask participants to pay close attention to how many times the actors smile. Ask them to count the number of smiles they see in the clip.

3. While the participants are watching the video clip, you watch the participants. Observe how often the participants smile in response to the clip.

4. Debrief this quick activity by asking the discussion questions that follow.

Original material by Karl Mulle, © 2016 Association for Talent Development (ATD). Used with permission. EMOTIONAL INTELLIGENCE training 1

Learning Activity 29: Emotional Contagion, *continued*

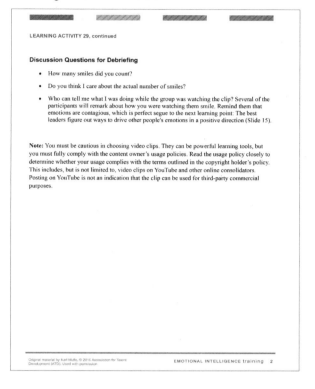

LEARNING ACTIVITY 29, continued

Discussion Questions for Debriefing

- How many smiles did you count?
- Do you think I care about the actual number of smiles?
- Who can tell me what I was doing while the group was watching the clip? Several of the participants will remark about how you were watching them smile. Remind them that emotions are contagious, which is perfect segue to the next learning point: The best leaders figure out ways to drive other people's emotions in a positive direction (Slide 15).

Note: You must be cautious in choosing video clips. They can be powerful learning tools, but you must fully comply with the content owner's usage policies. Read the usage policy closely to determine whether your usage complies with the terms outlined in the copyright holder's policy. This includes, but is not limited to, video clips on YouTube and other online consolidators. Posting on YouTube is not an indication that the clip can be used for third-party commercial purposes.

Original material by Karl Mulle, © 2016 Association for Talent Development (ATD). Used with permission. EMOTIONAL INTELLIGENCE training 2

Learning Activity 30: A Person Who Has Made a Difference in My Life

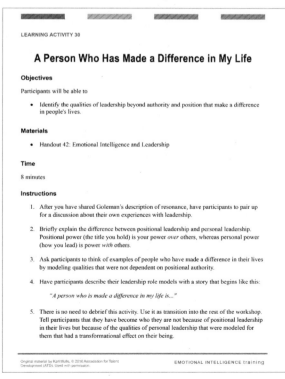

LEARNING ACTIVITY 30

A Person Who Has Made a Difference in My Life

Objectives

Participants will be able to

- Identify the qualities of leadership beyond authority and position that make a difference in people's lives.

Materials

- Handout 42: Emotional Intelligence and Leadership

Time

8 minutes

Instructions

1. After you have shared Goleman's description of resonance, have participants to pair up for a discussion about their own experiences with leadership.

2. Briefly explain the difference between positional leadership and personal leadership. Positional power (the title you hold) is your power *over* others, whereas personal power (how you lead) is power *with* others.

3. Ask participants to think of examples of people who have made a difference in their lives by modeling qualities that were not dependent on positional authority.

4. Have participants describe their leadership role models with a story that begins like this:

    "A person who is made a difference in my life is..."

5. There is no need to debrief this activity. Use it as transition into the rest of the workshop. Tell participants that they have become who they are not because of positional leadership in their lives but because of the qualities of personal leadership that were modeled for them that had a transformational effect on their being.

Original material by Karl Mulle, © 2016 Association for Talent Development (ATD). Used with permission. EMOTIONAL INTELLIGENCE training

Learning Activity 31: Resonant vs. Dissonant Leadership

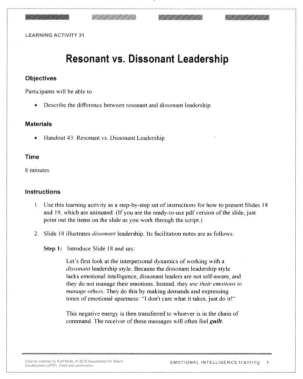

LEARNING ACTIVITY 31

Resonant vs. Dissonant Leadership

Objectives

Participants will be able to

- Describe the difference between resonant and dissonant leadership.

Materials

- Handout 43: Resonant vs. Dissonant Leadership

Time

8 minutes

Instructions

1. Use this learning activity as a step-by-step set of instructions for how to present Slides 18 and 19, which are animated. (If you are the ready-to-use pdf version of the slide, just point out the items on the slide as you work through the script.)

2. Slide 18 illustrates *dissonant* leadership. Its facilitation notes are as follows:

    Step 1: Introduce Slide 18 and say:

    Let's first look at the interpersonal dynamics of working with a *dissonant* leadership style. Because the dissonant leadership style lacks emotional intelligence, dissonant leaders are not self-aware, and they do not manage their emotions. Instead, they *use their emotions to manage others*. They do this by making demands and expressing tones of emotional upsetness: "I don't care what it takes, just do it!"

    This negative energy is then transferred to whoever is in the chain of command. The receiver of these messages will often feel **guilt**.

Original material by Karl Mulle, © 2016 Association for Talent Development (ATD). Used with permission. EMOTIONAL INTELLIGENCE training 1

Learning Activity 31: Resonant vs. Dissonant Leadership, *continued*

LEARNING ACTIVITY 31, continued

Step 2: Introduce the word *guilt*:

Guilt is often called the emotion of responsibility. In other words, the receiver feels responsible for the emotional upset of the leader.

An interesting double bind happens to the person feeling guilt. There is a natural kindness in most people that has learned to respond to aggression with compliance and helpfulness. This part of us gives in and says yes to the dissonant leader.

Step 3: Introduce the animated word *yes*:

There is another authentic voice in most people that wants to say *no*.

Step 4: Introduce the animated word *no*:

And so the people feeling guilty are in a double bind. If they say yes, they feel guilty about not saying no, and if they say no, they feel guilty about not saying yes. Either way they feel guilty, and so they give in.

Step 5: Introduce the animated word *give in*:

Interestingly, giving in provides some immediate relief from the guilt. When receivers give in, they are rewarded with approval.

Step 6: Introduce the animated word *approval*:

The approval brings immediate relief from the guilt, but at what cost? The continual tendency to give in to all of the demands and negative energy creates a resentment that causes receivers to no longer respect or even like the dissonant leader. As resentment grows, so does the guilt of not liking the leader.

And where will people go to get rid of this guilt? Right back to the leader who has the power to give them the approval they need to gain relief from the guilt.

So it is a vicious cycle. Notice that this pattern of leadership can produce results, but the results always come at a cost to the relationship.

Original material by Karl Mulle. © 2016 Association for Talent Development (ATD). Used with permission. EMOTIONAL INTELLIGENCE training **2**

Learning Activity 31: Resonant vs. Dissonant Leadership, *continued*

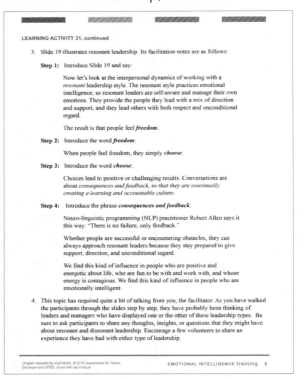

LEARNING ACTIVITY 31, continued

3. Slide 19 illustrates resonant leadership. Its facilitation notes are as follows:

Step 1: Introduce Slide 19 and say:

Now let's look at the interpersonal dynamics of working with a *resonant* leadership style. The resonant style practices emotional intelligence, so resonant leaders are self-aware and manage their own emotions. They provide the people they lead with a mix of direction and support, and they lead others with both respect and unconditional regard.

The result is that people feel *freedom*.

Step 2: Introduce the word *freedom*:

When people feel freedom, they simply *choose*.

Step 3: Introduce the word *choose*:

Choices lead to positive or challenging results. Conversations are about *consequences and feedback*, so that they are continually creating a learning and accountable culture.

Step 4: Introduce the phrase *consequences and feedback*:

Neuro-linguistic programming (NLP) practitioner Robert Allen says it this way: "There is no failure, only feedback."

Whether people are successful or encountering obstacles, they can always approach conversations because they stay prepared to give support, direction, and unconditional regard.

We find this kind of influence in people who are positive and energetic about life, who are fun to be with and work with, and whose energy is contagious. We find this kind of influence in people who are emotionally intelligent.

4. This topic has required quite a bit of talking from you, the facilitator. As you have walked the participants through the slides step by step, they have probably been thinking of leaders and managers who have displayed one or the other of these leadership types. Be sure to ask participants to share any thoughts, insights, or questions that they might have about resonant and dissonant leadership. Encourage a few volunteers to share an experience they have had with either type of leadership.

Original material by Karl Mulle. © 2016 Association for Talent Development (ATD). Used with permission. EMOTIONAL INTELLIGENCE training **3**

Learning Activity 32: Goleman's Six Styles of Leadership

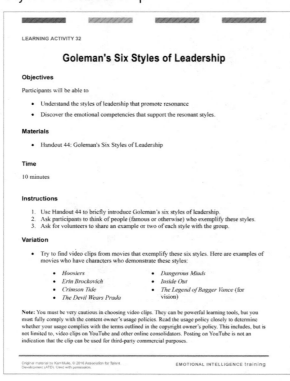

LEARNING ACTIVITY 32

Goleman's Six Styles of Leadership

Objectives

Participants will be able to

- Understand the styles of leadership that promote resonance
- Discover the emotional competencies that support the resonant styles.

Materials

- Handout 44: Goleman's Six Styles of Leadership

Time

10 minutes

Instructions

1. Use Handout 44 to briefly introduce Goleman's six styles of leadership.
2. Ask participants to think of people (famous or otherwise) who exemplify these styles.
3. Ask for volunteers to share an example or two of each style with the group.

Variation

- Try to find video clips from movies that exemplify these six styles. Here are examples of movies who have characters who demonstrate these styles:

  - *Hoosiers*
  - *Erin Brockovich*
  - *Crimson Tide*
  - *The Devil Wears Prada*

  - *Dangerous Minds*
  - *Inside Out*
  - *The Legend of Bagger Vance* (for vision)

Note: You must be very cautious in choosing video clips. They can be powerful learning tools, but you must fully comply with the content owner's usage policies. Read the usage policy closely to determine whether your usage complies with the terms outlined in the copyright owner's policy. This includes, but is not limited to, video clips on YouTube and other online consolidators. Posting on YouTube is not an indication that the clip can be used for third-party commercial purposes.

Original material by Karl Mulle. © 2016 Association for Talent Development (ATD). Used with permission. EMOTIONAL INTELLIGENCE training

Learning Activity 33: My Leadership Style

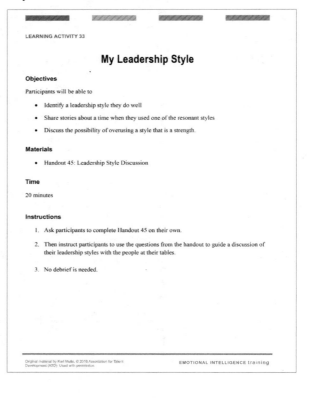

LEARNING ACTIVITY 33

My Leadership Style

Objectives

Participants will be able to

- Identify a leadership style they do well
- Share stories about a time when they used one of the resonant styles
- Discuss the possibility of overusing a style that is a strength.

Materials

- Handout 45: Leadership Style Discussion

Time

20 minutes

Instructions

1. Ask participants to complete Handout 45 on their own.

2. Then instruct participants to use the questions from the handout to guide a discussion of their leadership styles with the people at their tables.

3. No debrief is needed.

Original material by Karl Mulle. © 2016 Association for Talent Development (ATD). Used with permission. EMOTIONAL INTELLIGENCE training

Learning Activity 34: Leadership Style Action Plan

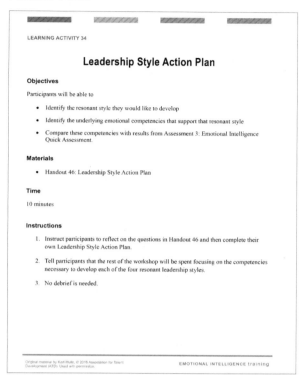

LEARNING ACTIVITY 34

Leadership Style Action Plan

Objectives

Participants will be able to

- Identify the resonant style they would like to develop
- Identify the underlying emotional competencies that support that resonant style
- Compare these competencies with results from Assessment 3: Emotional Intelligence Quick Assessment.

Materials

- Handout 46: Leadership Style Action Plan

Time

10 minutes

Instructions

1. Instruct participants to reflect on the questions in Handout 46 and then complete their own Leadership Style Action Plan.

2. Tell participants that the rest of the workshop will be spent focusing on the competencies necessary to develop each of the four resonant leadership styles.

3. No debrief is needed.

Original material by Karl Mulle, © 2016 Association for Talent Development (ATD). Used with permission.   EMOTIONAL INTELLIGENCE training

Learning Activity 35: The Indispensable Competency of Empathy

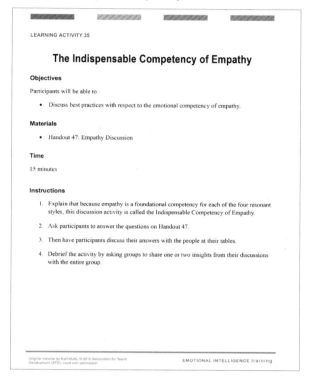

LEARNING ACTIVITY 35

The Indispensable Competency of Empathy

Objectives

Participants will be able to

- Discuss best practices with respect to the emotional competency of empathy.

Materials

- Handout 47: Empathy Discussion

Time

15 minutes

Instructions

1. Explain that because empathy is a foundational competency for each of the four resonant styles, this discussion activity is called the Indispensable Competency of Empathy.

2. Ask participants to answer the questions on Handout 47.

3. Then have participants discuss their answers with the people at their tables.

4. Debrief the activity by asking groups to share one or two insights from their discussions with the entire group.

Original material by Karl Mulle, © 2016 Association for Talent Development (ATD). Used with permission.   EMOTIONAL INTELLIGENCE training

Learning Activity 36: Managing Defensiveness

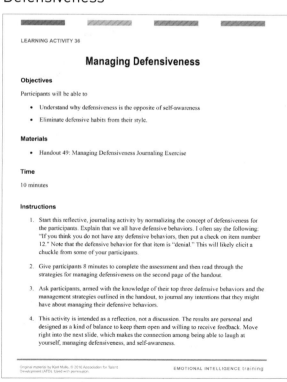

LEARNING ACTIVITY 36

Managing Defensiveness

Objectives

Participants will be able to

- Understand why defensiveness is the opposite of self-awareness
- Eliminate defensive habits from their style.

Materials

- Handout 49: Managing Defensiveness Journaling Exercise

Time

10 minutes

Instructions

1. Start this reflective, journaling activity by normalizing the concept of defensiveness for the participants. Explain that we all have defensive behaviors. I often say the following: "If you think you do not have any defensive behaviors, then put a check on item number 12." Note that the defensive behavior for that item is "denial." This will likely elicit a chuckle from some of your participants.

2. Give participants 8 minutes to complete the assessment and then read through the strategies for managing defensiveness on the second page of the handout.

3. Ask participants, armed with the knowledge of their top three defensive behaviors and the management strategies outlined in the handout, to journal any intentions that they might have about managing their defensive behaviors.

4. This activity is intended as a reflection, not a discussion. The results are personal and designed as a kind of balance to keep them open and willing to receive feedback. Move right into the next slide, which makes the connection among being able to laugh at yourself, managing defensiveness, and self-awareness.

Original material by Karl Mulle, © 2016 Association for Talent Development (ATD). Used with permission.   EMOTIONAL INTELLIGENCE training

Learning Activity 37: Keep Your Eye on the Grand Marshmallow

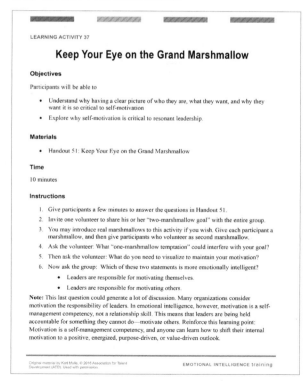

LEARNING ACTIVITY 37

Keep Your Eye on the Grand Marshmallow

Objectives

Participants will be able to

- Understand why having a clear picture of who they are, what they want, and why they want it is so critical to self-motivation
- Explore why self-motivation is critical to resonant leadership.

Materials

- Handout 51: Keep Your Eye on the Grand Marshmallow

Time

10 minutes

Instructions

1. Give participants a few minutes to answer the questions in Handout 51.

2. Invite one volunteer to share his or her "two-marshmallow goal" with the entire group.

3. You may introduce real marshmallows to this activity if you wish. Give each participant a marshmallow, and then give participants who volunteer as second marshmallow.

4. Ask the volunteer: What "one-marshmallow temptation" could interfere with your goal?

5. Then ask the volunteer: What do you need to visualize to maintain your motivation?

6. Now ask the group: Which of these two statements is more emotionally intelligent?

   - Leaders are responsible for motivating themselves.
   - Leaders are responsible for motivating others.

Note: This last question could generate a lot of discussion. Many organizations consider motivation the responsibility of leaders. In emotional intelligence, however, motivation is a self-management competency, not a relationship skill. This means that leaders are being held accountable for something they cannot do—motivate others. Reinforce this learning point: Motivation is a self-management competency, and anyone can learn how to shift their internal motivation to a positive, energized, purpose-driven, or value-driven outlook.

Original material by Karl Mulle, © 2016 Association for Talent Development (ATD). Used with permission.   EMOTIONAL INTELLIGENCE training

Learning Activity 38: The Riddle: The Competency of Self-Confidence

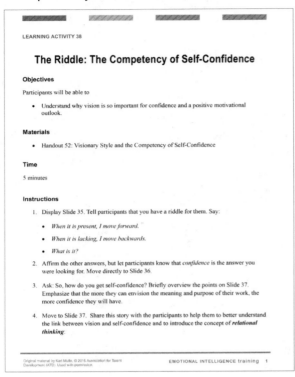

The Riddle: The Competency of Self-Confidence

Objectives

Participants will be able to

- Understand why vision is so important for confidence and a positive motivational outlook.

Materials

- Handout 52: Visionary Style and the Competency of Self-Confidence

Time

5 minutes

Instructions

1. Display Slide 35. Tell participants that you have a riddle for them. Say:

    - *When it is present, I move forward.*

    - *When it is lacking, I move backwards.*

    - *What is it?*

2. Affirm the other answers, but let participants know that *confidence* is the answer you were looking for. Move directly to Slide 36.

3. Ask: So, how do you get self-confidence? Briefly overview the points on Slide 37. Emphasize that the more they can envision the meaning and purpose of their work, the more confidence they will have.

4. Move to Slide 37. Share this story with the participants to help them to better understand the link between vision and self-confidence and to introduce the concept of *relational thinking*:

EMOTIONAL INTELLIGENCE training   1

Learning Activity 38: The Riddle: The Competency of Self-Confidence, *continued*

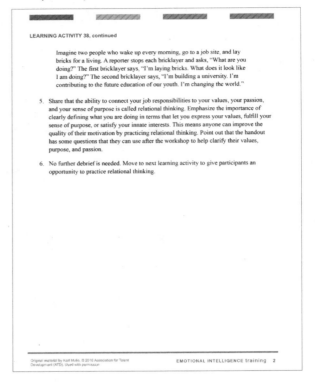

Imagine two people who wake up every morning, go to a job site, and lay bricks for a living. A reporter stops each bricklayer and asks, "What are you doing?" The first bricklayer says, "I'm laying bricks. What does it look like I am doing?" The second bricklayer says, "I'm building a university. I'm contributing to the future education of our youth. I'm changing the world."

5. Share that the ability to connect your job responsibilities to your values, your passion, and your sense of purpose is called relational thinking. Emphasize the importance of clearly defining what you are doing in terms that let you express your values, fulfill your sense of purpose, or satisfy your innate interests. This means anyone can improve the quality of their motivation by practicing relational thinking. Point out that the handout has some questions that they can use after the workshop to help clarify their values, purpose, and passion.

6. No further debrief is needed. Move to next learning activity to give participants an opportunity to practice relational thinking.

EMOTIONAL INTELLIGENCE training   2

Learning Activity 39: Practice Relational Thinking

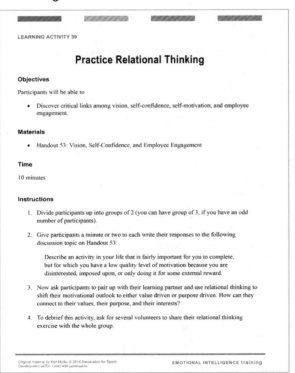

Practice Relational Thinking

Objectives

Participants will be able to

- Discover critical links among vision, self-confidence, self-motivation, and employee engagement.

Materials

- Handout 53: Vision, Self-Confidence, and Employee Engagement

Time

10 minutes

Instructions

1. Divide participants up into groups of 2 (you can have group of 3, if you have an odd number of participants).

2. Give participants a minute or two to each write their responses to the following discussion topic on Handout 53:

    Describe an activity in your life that is fairly important for you to complete, but for which you have a low quality level of motivation because you are disinterested, imposed upon, or only doing it for some external reward.

3. Now ask participants to pair up with their learning partner and use relational thinking to shift their motivational outlook to either value driven or purpose driven. How can they connect to their values, their purpose, and their interests?

4. To debrief this activity, ask for several volunteers to share their relational thinking exercise with the whole group.

EMOTIONAL INTELLIGENCE training

Learning Activity 40: Visionary Style and Managing Transition

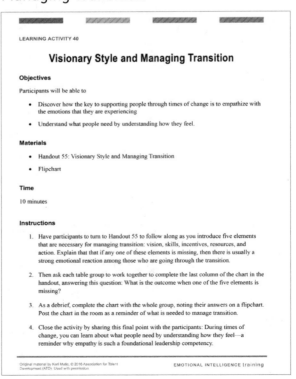

Visionary Style and Managing Transition

Objectives

Participants will be able to

- Discover how the key to supporting people through times of change is to empathize with the emotions that they are experiencing

- Understand what people need by understanding how they feel.

Materials

- Handout 55: Visionary Style and Managing Transition

- Flipchart

Time

10 minutes

Instructions

1. Have participants to turn to Handout 55 to follow along as you introduce five elements that are necessary for managing transition: vision, skills, incentives, resources, and action. Explain that that if any one of these elements is missing, then there is usually a strong emotional reaction among those who are going through the transition.

2. Then ask each table group to work together to complete the last column of the chart in the handout, answering this question: What is the outcome when one of the five elements is missing?

3. As a debrief, complete the chart with the whole group, noting their answers on a flipchart. Post the chart in the room as a reminder of what is needed to manage transition.

4. Close the activity by sharing this final point with the participants: During times of change, you can learn about what people need by understanding how they feel—a reminder why empathy is such a foundational leadership competency.

EMOTIONAL INTELLIGENCE training

Learning Activity 41: Communicating Your Vision

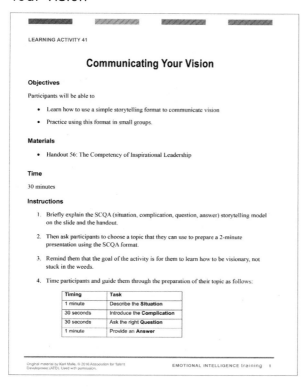

Learning Activity 41: Communicating Your Vision, *continued*

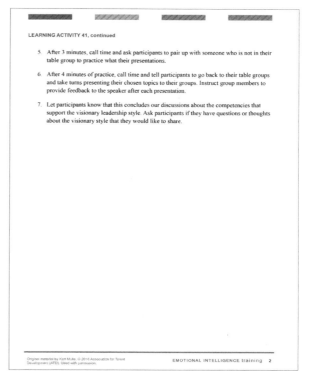

Learning Activity 42: Judger–Learner Questions

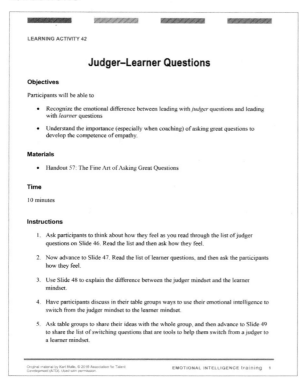

Learning Activity 42: Judger–Learner Questions, *continued*

LEARNING ACTIVITY 42, continued

Variation

- You may want to supplement this discussion, with thoughts about how many of the workshop's learning points are beginning to integrate quite nicely with one another. You could easily add System 1 thinking, unconscious bias, single-marshmallow goals, and impulsive behaviors to the judger mindset. You can add System 2 thinking, mindfulness, mental agility, intentionality, reframe, the ABCs of Life, two-marshmallow goals, and relational thinking to the learner mindset. Make a simple flipchart with two columns. Bring up workshop topics and ask participants which column you should write it in.

Source: I am indebted to Marilee Adams and her excellent book for the ideas in this learning activity. M. Adams, *Change Your Questions, Change Your Life*, 3rd ed. (San Francisco: Berrett-Koehler, 2016).

Learning Activity 43: Coaching Dialogue

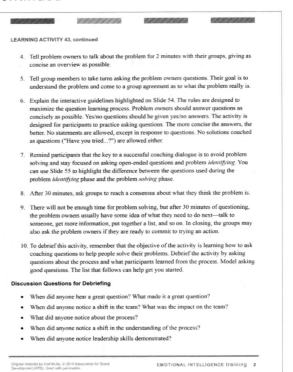

LEARNING ACTIVITY 43

Coaching Dialogue

Objectives

Participants will be able to

- Understand the importance of asking powerful questions when problem identifying and problem solving
- Practice asking questions to help coach someone.

Materials

- Handout 60: Coaching Dialogue Job Aid

Time

40 minutes

Instructions

1. Choose one the three different ways to conduct this activity:
   - Fishbowl: One group practices the coaching dialogue and other participants observe
   - Large Group: All participants sit in one large circle
   - Small Group: Participants work in table groups of 4 to 8 people
2. Once you have chosen the activity design, ask problem solving groups to choose one person to be their problem owner. If you are going to give table groups an opportunity to lead their own coaching dialogues, then they must also identify a person who will be responsible for enforcing the rules and managing the process.
3. Give problem owners a minute to choose a challenge, situation, or problem to talk about. The problem should not be easily solved—the more complex the better.

EMOTIONAL INTELLIGENCE training 1

Learning Activity 43: Coaching Dialogue, *continued*

LEARNING ACTIVITY 43, continued

4. Tell problem owners to talk about the problem for 2 minutes with their groups, giving as concise an overview as possible.
5. Tell group members to take turns asking the problem owners questions. Their goal is to understand the problem and come to a group agreement as to what the problem really is.
6. Explain the interactive guidelines highlighted on Slide 54. The rules are designed to maximize the question learning process. Problem owners should answer questions as concisely as possible. Yes/no questions should be given yes/no answers. The activity is designed for participants to practice asking questions. The more concise the answers, the better. No statements are allowed, except in response to questions. No solutions couched as questions ("Have you tried...?") are allowed either.
7. Remind participants that the key to a successful coaching dialogue is to avoid problem solving and stay focused on asking open-ended questions and problem *identifying*. You can use Slide 55 to highlight the difference between the questions used during the problem *identifying* phase and the problem *solving* phase.
8. After 30 minutes, ask groups to reach a consensus about what they think the problem is.
9. There will not be enough time for problem solving, but after 30 minutes of questioning, the problem owners usually have some idea of what they need to do next—talk to someone, get more information, put together a list, and so on. In closing, the groups may also ask the problem owners if they are ready to commit to trying an action.
10. To debrief this activity, remember that the objective of the activity is learning how to ask coaching questions to help people solve their problems. Debrief the activity by asking questions about the process and what participants learned from the process. Model asking good questions. The list that follows can help get you started.

Discussion Questions for Debriefing

- When did anyone hear a great question? What made it a great question?
- When did anyone notice a shift in the team? What was the impact on the team?
- What did anyone notice about the process?
- When did anyone notice a shift in the understanding of the process?
- When did anyone notice leadership skills demonstrated?

EMOTIONAL INTELLIGENCE training 2

Learning Activity 43: Coaching Dialogue, *continued*

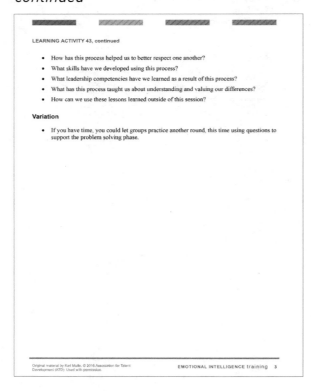

LEARNING ACTIVITY 43, continued

- How has this process helped us to better respect one another?
- What skills have we developed using this process?
- What leadership competencies have we learned as a result of this process?
- What has this process taught us about understanding and valuing our differences?
- How can we use these lessons learned outside of this session?

Variation

- If you have time, you could let groups practice another round, this time using questions to support the problem solving phase.

EMOTIONAL INTELLIGENCE training 3

Learning Activity 44: The Competency of Developing Others

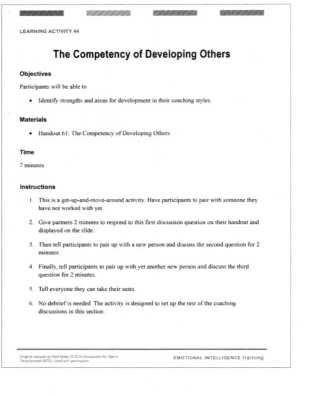

LEARNING ACTIVITY 44

The Competency of Developing Others

Objectives

Participants will be able to

- Identify strengths and areas for development in their coaching styles.

Materials

- Handout 61: The Competency of Developing Others

Time

7 minutes

Instructions

1. This is a get-up-and-move-around activity. Have participants to pair with someone they have not worked with yet.
2. Give partners 2 minutes to respond to this first discussion question on their handout and displayed on the slide.
3. Then tell participants to pair up with a new person and discuss the second question for 2 minutes.
4. Finally, tell participants to pair up with yet another new person and discuss the third question for 2 minutes.
5. Tell everyone they can take their seats.
6. No debrief is needed. The activity is designed to set up the rest of the coaching discussions in this section.

EMOTIONAL INTELLIGENCE training

EMOTIONAL INTELLIGENCE training

Learning Activity 45: The Hot/Cold Game

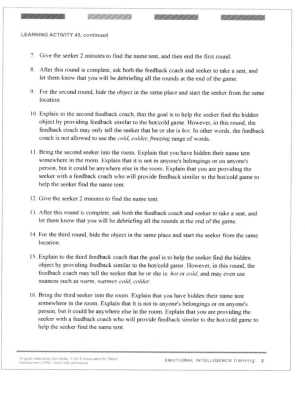

LEARNING ACTIVITY 45

The Hot/Cold Game

Objectives

Participants will be able to

- Discover the importance of providing both reinforcing and redirecting feedback when creating a learning culture.

Time

30 minutes

Instructions

1. Ask participants if they have ever played the hot/cold game when they were children. Explain that they will be playing a variation of this game.

2. Ask for three volunteers to play the role of seekers (looking for a hidden article). Ask them to wait outside while you give instructions to the feedback coaches.

3. Ask for three more volunteers to play the role of feedback coaches. They will be giving the seekers feedback similar to the hot/cold game. The rest of the participants will be observers, observing the seekers and coaches.

4. Choose a simple item, such a participant's name tent, and hide it somewhere in the room. Do not hide it on anyone's person or in anyone's belongings.

5. Explain to the first feedback coach that the goal is to help the seeker find the hidden object by providing feedback similar to the hot/cold game. In this round, the feedback coach may only tell the seeker that he or she is *cold*. In other words, the feedback coach is not allowed to use the *warm, warmer, hot* range of words.

6. Bring the first seeker into the room. Explain that you have hidden his or her name tent somewhere in the room. Explain that it is not in anyone's belongings or on anyone's person, but it could be anywhere else in the room. Explain that you are providing the seeker with a feedback coach who will provide feedback similar to the hot/cold game to help the seeker find the name tent.

Original material by Karl Mulle, © 2016 Association for Talent Development (ATD). Used with permission.

EMOTIONAL INTELLIGENCE training   1

Learning Activity 45: The Hot/Cold Game, *continued*

LEARNING ACTIVITY 45, continued

7. Give the seeker 2 minutes to find the name tent, and then end the first round.

8. After this round is complete, ask both the feedback coach and seeker to take a seat, and let them know that you will be debriefing all the rounds at the end of the game.

9. For the second round, hide the object in the same place and start the seeker from the same location.

10. Explain to the second feedback coach, that the goal is to help the seeker find the hidden object by providing feedback similar to the hot/cold game. However, in this round, the feedback coach may only tell the seeker that he or she is *hot*. In other words, the feedback coach is not allowed to use the *cold, colder, freezing* range of words.

11. Bring the second seeker into the room. Explain that you have hidden their name tent somewhere in the room. Explain that it is not in anyone's belongings or on anyone's person, but it could be anywhere else in the room. Explain that you are providing the seeker with a feedback coach who will provide feedback similar to the hot/cold game to help the seeker find the name tent.

12. Give the seeker 2 minutes to find the name tent.

13. After this round is complete, ask both the feedback coach and seeker to take a seat, and let them know that you will be debriefing all the rounds at the end of the game.

14. For the third round, hide the object in the same place and start the seeker from the same location.

15. Explain to the third feedback coach that the goal is to help the seeker find the hidden object by providing feedback similar to the hot/cold game. However, in this round, the feedback coach may tell the seeker that he or she is: *hot or cold*, and may even use nuances such as *warm, warmer, cold, colder*.

16. Bring the third seeker into the room. Explain that you have hidden their name tent somewhere in the room. Explain that it is not in anyone's belongings or on anyone's person, but it could be anywhere else in the room. Explain that you are providing the seeker with a feedback coach who will provide feedback similar to the hot/cold game to help the seeker find the name tent.

Original material by Karl Mulle, © 2016 Association for Talent Development (ATD). Used with permission.

EMOTIONAL INTELLIGENCE training   2

Learning Activity 45: The Hot/Cold Game, *continued*

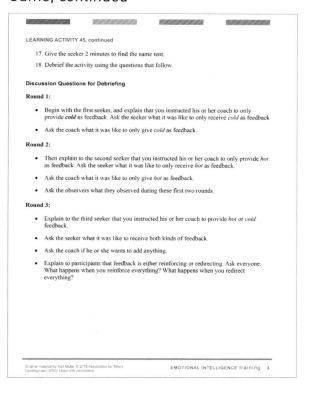

LEARNING ACTIVITY 45, continued

17. Give the seeker 2 minutes to find the name tent.

18. Debrief the activity using the questions that follow.

Discussion Questions for Debriefing

Round 1:

- Begin with the first seeker, and explain that you instructed his or her coach to only provide *cold* as feedback. Ask the seeker what it was like to only receive *cold* as feedback.

- Ask the coach what it was like to only give *cold* as feedback.

Round 2:

- Then explain to the second seeker that you instructed his or her coach to only provide *hot* as feedback. Ask the seeker what it was like to only receive *hot* as feedback.

- Ask the coach what it was like to only give *hot* as feedback.

- Ask the observers what they observed during these first two rounds.

Round 3:

- Explain to the third seeker that you instructed his or her coach to provide *hot or cold* feedback.

- Ask the seeker what it was like to receive both kinds of feedback.

- Ask the coach if he or she wants to add anything.

- Explain to participants that feedback is either reinforcing or redirecting. Ask everyone: What happens when you reinforce everything? What happens when you redirect everything?

Original material by Karl Mulle, © 2016 Association for Talent Development (ATD). Used with permission.

EMOTIONAL INTELLIGENCE training   3

Learning Activity 46: SBI Practice

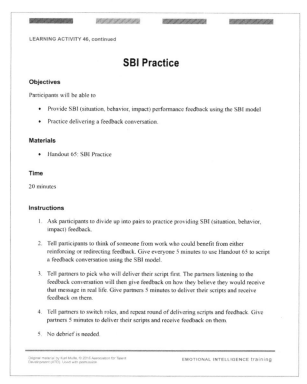

LEARNING ACTIVITY 46, continued

SBI Practice

Objectives

Participants will be able to

- Provide SBI (situation, behavior, impact) performance feedback using the SBI model

- Practice delivering a feedback conversation.

Materials

- Handout 65: SBI Practice

Time

20 minutes

Instructions

1. Ask participants to divide up into pairs to practice providing SBI (situation, behavior, impact) feedback.

2. Tell participants to think of someone from work who could benefit from either reinforcing or redirecting feedback. Give everyone 5 minutes to use Handout 65 to script a feedback conversation using the SBI model.

3. Tell partners to pick who will deliver their script first. The partners listening to the feedback conversation will then give feedback on how they believe they would receive that message in real life. Give partners 5 minutes to deliver their scripts and receive feedback on them.

4. Tell partners to switch roles, and repeat round of delivering scripts and feedback. Give partners 5 minutes to deliver their scripts and receive feedback on them.

5. No debrief is needed.

Original material by Karl Mulle, © 2016 Association for Talent Development (ATD). Used with permission.

EMOTIONAL INTELLIGENCE training

Learning Activity 47: Coaching Action Plan and Closing

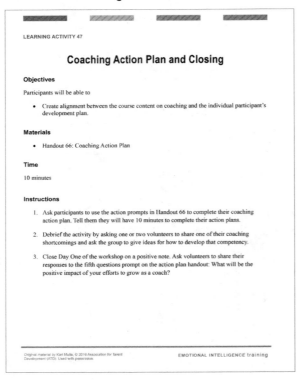

Coaching Action Plan and Closing

Objectives

Participants will be able to

- Create alignment between the course content on coaching and the individual participant's development plan.

Materials

- Handout 66: Coaching Action Plan

Time

10 minutes

Instructions

1. Ask participants to use the action prompts in Handout 66 to complete their coaching action plan. Tell them they will have 10 minutes to complete their action plans.

2. Debrief the activity by asking one or two volunteers to share one of their coaching shortcomings and ask the group to give ideas for how to develop that competency.

3. Close Day One of the workshop on a positive note. Ask volunteers to share their responses to the fifth questions prompt on the action plan handout: What will be the positive impact of your efforts to grow as a coach?

Learning Activity 48: Welcome and Lessons Learned

Welcome and Lessons Learned

Objectives

Participants will be able to

- Reinforce lessons learned from Day One and get energized for Day Two.

Materials

- Koosh ball or a other soft object that can be tossed from person to person

Time

10 minutes

Instructions

1. Have participants form a large circle. Tell them that they will be sharing lessons learned or other key learning points from Day One of the workshop.

2. Hold the ball and start by sharing something you learned from the workshop. Then toss the Koosh ball (or other soft throwing object) to a participant and ask him or her to share a key learning point from Day One's workshop.

3. When the participant is done sharing, tell him or her to toss the ball to someone else who will share another key learning point. Continue this pattern until everyone has had a chance to share.

4. Tell everyone they can take their seats and move directly into the next slide on learning objectives for Day Two.

Learning Activity 49: Discussion of the Meta-Model for Working Effectively With Others

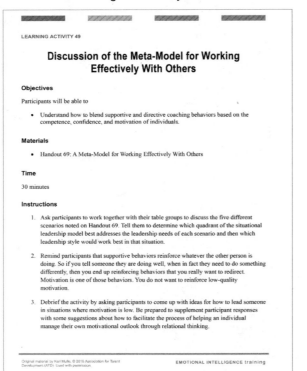

Discussion of the Meta-Model for Working Effectively With Others

Objectives

Participants will be able to

- Understand how to blend supportive and directive coaching behaviors based on the competence, confidence, and motivation of individuals.

Materials

- Handout 69: A Meta-Model for Working Effectively With Others

Time

30 minutes

Instructions

1. Ask participants to work together with their table groups to discuss the five different scenarios noted on Handout 69. Tell them to determine which quadrant of the situational leadership model best addresses the leadership needs of each scenario and then which leadership style would work best in that situation.

2. Remind participants that supportive behaviors reinforce whatever the other person is doing. So if you tell someone they are doing well, when in fact they need to do something differently, then you end up reinforcing behaviors that you really want to redirect. Motivation is one of those behaviors. You do not want to reinforce low-quality motivation.

3. Debrief the activity by asking participants to come up with ideas for how to lead someone in situations where motivation is low. Be prepared to supplement participant responses with some suggestions about how to facilitate the process of helping an individual manage their own motivational outlook through relational thinking.

Learning Activity 50: The Tallest Freestanding Dot Tower

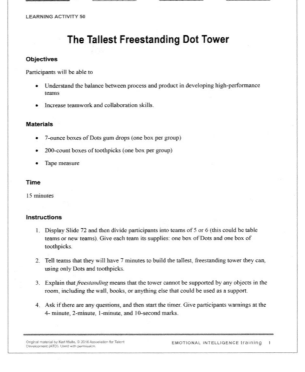

The Tallest Freestanding Dot Tower

Objectives

Participants will be able to

- Understand the balance between process and product in developing high-performance teams

- Increase teamwork and collaboration skills.

Materials

- 7-ounce boxes of Dots gum drops (one box per group)

- 200-count boxes of toothpicks (one box per group)

- Tape measure

Time

15 minutes

Instructions

1. Display Slide 72 and then divide participants into teams of 5 or 6 (this could be table teams or new teams). Give each team its supplies: one box of Dots and one box of toothpicks.

2. Tell teams that they will have 7 minutes to build the tallest, freestanding tower they can, using only Dots and toothpicks.

3. Explain that *freestanding* means that the tower cannot be supported by any objects in the room, including the wall, books, or anything else that could be used as a support.

4. Ask if there are any questions, and then start the timer. Give participants warnings at the 4- minute, 2-minute, 1-minute, and 10-second marks.

Learning Activity 50: The Tallest Freestanding Dot Tower, *continued*

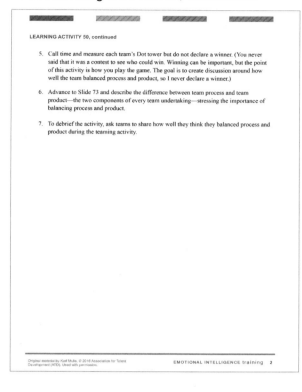

LEARNING ACTIVITY 50, continued

5. Call time and measure each team's Dot tower but do not declare a winner. (You never said that it was a contest to see who could win. Winning can be important, but the point of this activity is how you play the game. The goal is to create discussion around how well the team balanced process and product, so I never declare a winner.)

6. Advance to Slide 73 and describe the difference between team process and team product—the two components of every team undertaking—stressing the importance of balancing process and product.

7. To debrief the activity, ask teams to share how well they think they balanced process and product during the teaming activity.

Original material by Karl Mulle, © 2016 Association for Talent Development (ATD). Used with permission. — EMOTIONAL INTELLIGENCE training 2

Learning Activity 51: The Elements of Effective Team Process

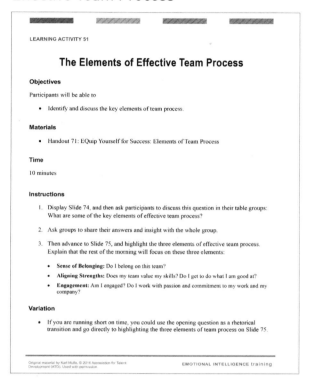

LEARNING ACTIVITY 51

The Elements of Effective Team Process

Objectives

Participants will be able to

- Identify and discuss the key elements of team process.

Materials

- Handout 71: EQuip Yourself for Success: Elements of Team Process

Time

10 minutes

Instructions

1. Display Slide 74, and then ask participants to discuss this question in their table groups: What are some of the key elements of effective team process?

2. Ask groups to share their answers and insight with the whole group.

3. Then advance to Slide 75, and highlight the three elements of effective team process. Explain that the rest of the morning will focus on these three elements:

   - **Sense of Belonging:** Do I belong on this team?
   - **Aligning Strengths:** Does my team value my skills? Do I get to do what I am good at?
   - **Engagement:** Am I engaged? Do I work with passion and commitment to my work and my company?

Variation

- If you are running short on time, you could use the opening question as a rhetorical transition and go directly to highlighting the three elements of team process on Slide 75.

Original material by Karl Mulle, © 2016 Association for Talent Development (ATD). Used with permission. — EMOTIONAL INTELLIGENCE training

Learning Activity 52: The Uniqueness–Belonging Model

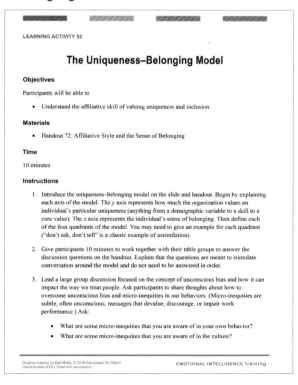

LEARNING ACTIVITY 52

The Uniqueness–Belonging Model

Objectives

Participants will be able to

- Understand the affiliative skill of valuing uniqueness and inclusion.

Materials

- Handout 72: Affiliative Style and the Sense of Belonging

Time

10 minutes

Instructions

1. Introduce the uniqueness–belonging model on the slide and handout. Begin by explaining each axis of the model. The *y* axis represents how much the organization values an individual's particular uniqueness (anything from a demographic variable to a skill to a core value). The *x* axis represents the individual's sense of belonging. Then define each of the four quadrants of the model. You may need to give an example for each quadrant ("don't ask, don't tell" is a classic example of assimilation).

2. Give participants 10 minutes to work together with their table groups to answer the discussion questions on the handout. Explain that the questions are meant to stimulate conversation around the model and do not need to be answered in order.

3. Lead a large group discussion focused on the concept of unconscious bias and how it can impact the way we treat people. Ask participants to share thoughts about how to overcome unconscious bias and micro-inequities in our behaviors. (Micro-inequities are subtle, often unconscious, messages that devalue, discourage, or impair work performance.) Ask:

   - What are some micro-inequities that you are aware of in your own behavior?
   - What are some micro-inequities that you are aware of in the culture?

Original material by Karl Mulle, © 2016 Association for Talent Development (ATD). Used with permission. — EMOTIONAL INTELLIGENCE training

Learning Activity 53: Motivation 3.0

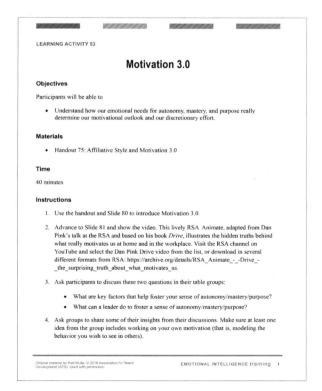

LEARNING ACTIVITY 53

Motivation 3.0

Objectives

Participants will be able to

- Understand how our emotional needs for autonomy, mastery, and purpose really determine our motivational outlook and our discretionary effort.

Materials

- Handout 75: Affiliative Style and Motivation 3.0

Time

40 minutes

Instructions

1. Use the handout and Slide 80 to introduce Motivation 3.0.

2. Advance to Slide 81 and show the video. This lively RSA Animate, adapted from Dan Pink's talk at the RSA and based on his book *Drive*, illustrates the hidden truths behind what really motivates us at home and in the workplace. Visit the RSA channel on YouTube and select the Dan Pink Drive video from the list, or download in several different formats from RSA: https://archive.org/details/RSA_Animate_-_-Drive_-_the_surprising_truth_about_what_motivates_us.

3. Ask participants to discuss these two questions in their table groups:

   - What are key factors that help foster your sense of autonomy/mastery/purpose?
   - What can a leader do to foster a sense of autonomy/mastery/purpose?

4. Ask groups to share some of their insights from their discussions. Make sure at least one idea from the group includes working on your own motivation (that is, modeling the behavior you wish to see in others).

Original material by Karl Mulle, © 2016 Association for Talent Development (ATD). Used with permission. — EMOTIONAL INTELLIGENCE training 1

Learning Activity 53: Motivation 3.0, *continued*

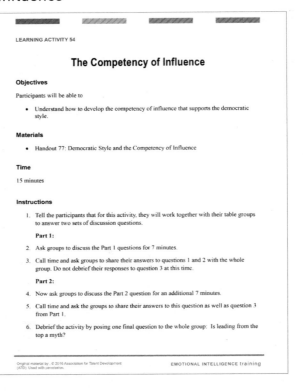

LEARNING ACTIVITY 53, continued

5. Advance to Slide 82 and share the big idea here: Engagement and motivation are internally activated whenever your emotional needs for autonomy, master, and purpose are met. Emphasize that motivation is a skill. It falls under the domain of self-management, so we need to engage System 2 thinking to motivate ourselves.

6. Advance to Slide 83 to make clear the links among leadership, motivation, and engagement.

Discussion Questions for Debriefing

- Do you believe that people are self-directed and that optimal motivation is activated when our basic psychological needs are met? If so, why do think that is?

- Are there any other core needs besides autonomy, mastery, and purpose? What might they be?

Note: Video clip is courtesy of RSA, The Royal Society for the Encouragement of Arts, Manufactures, and Commerce, which has granted permission to use the clip in the workshops in this book provided that you give full credit to RSA, www.TheRSA.org

Learning Activity 54: The Competency of Influence

LEARNING ACTIVITY 54

The Competency of Influence

Objectives

Participants will be able to

- Understand how to develop the competency of influence that supports the democratic style.

Materials

- Handout 77: Democratic Style and the Competency of Influence

Time

15 minutes

Instructions

1. Tell the participants that for this activity, they will work together with their table groups to answer two sets of discussion questions.

   Part 1:

2. Ask groups to discuss the Part 1 questions for 7 minutes.

3. Call time and ask groups to share their answers to questions 1 and 2 with the whole group. Do not debrief their responses to question 3 at this time.

   Part 2:

4. Now ask groups to discuss the Part 2 question for an additional 7 minutes.

5. Call time and ask the groups to share their answers to this question as well as question 3 from Part 1.

6. Debrief the activity by posing one final question to the whole group: Is leading from the top a myth?

Learning Activity 55: The Six Principles of Influence

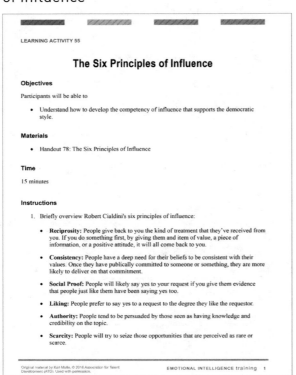

LEARNING ACTIVITY 55

The Six Principles of Influence

Objectives

Participants will be able to

- Understand how to develop the competency of influence that supports the democratic style.

Materials

- Handout 78: The Six Principles of Influence

Time

15 minutes

Instructions

1. Briefly overview Robert Cialdini's six principles of influence:

   - **Reciprosity:** People give back to you the kind of treatment that they've received from you. If you do something first, by giving them and item of value, a piece of information, or a positive attitude, it will all come back to you.

   - **Consistency:** People have a deep need for their beliefs to be consistent with their values. Once they have publically committed to someone or something, they are more likely to deliver on that commitment.

   - **Social Proof:** People will likely say yes to your request if you give them evidence that people just like them have been saying yes too.

   - **Liking:** People prefer to say yes to a request to the degree they like the requestor.

   - **Authority:** People tend to be persuaded by those seen as having knowledge and credibility on the topic.

   - **Scarcity:** People will try to seize those opportunities that are perceived as rare or scarce.

Learning Activity 55: The Six Principles of Influence, *continued*

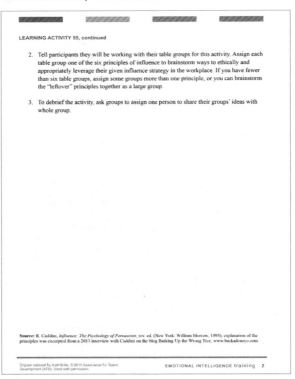

LEARNING ACTIVITY 55, continued

2. Tell participants they will be working with their table groups for this activity. Assign each table group one of the six principles of influence to brainstorm ways to ethically and appropriately leverage their given influence strategy in the workplace. If you have fewer than six table groups, assign some groups more than one principle, or you can brainstorm the "leftover" principles together as a large group.

3. To debrief the activity, ask groups to assign one person to share their groups' ideas with whole group.

Source: R. Cialdini, *Influence: The Psychology of Persuasion*, rev. ed. (New York: William Morrow, 1995); explanation of the principles was excerpted from a 2013 interview with Cialdini on the blog Barking Up the Wrong Tree, www.bakadesuyo.com

Learning Activity 56: Case Studies in Conflict

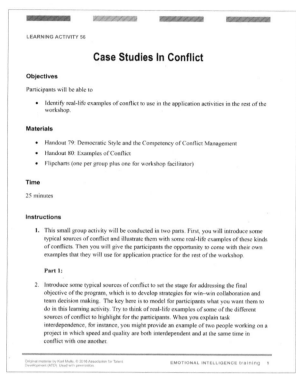

LEARNING ACTIVITY 56

Case Studies In Conflict

Objectives

Participants will be able to

- Identify real-life examples of conflict to use in the application activities in the rest of the workshop.

Materials

- Handout 79: Democratic Style and the Competency of Conflict Management
- Handout 80: Examples of Conflict
- Flipcharts (one per group plus one for workshop facilitator)

Time

25 minutes

Instructions

1. This small group activity will be conducted in two parts. First, you will introduce some typical sources of conflict and illustrate them with some real-life examples of these kinds of conflicts. Then you will give the participants the opportunity to come with their own examples that they will use for application practice for the rest of the workshop.

    Part 1:

2. Introduce some typical sources of conflict to set the stage for addressing the final objective of the program, which is to develop strategies for win–win collaboration and team decision making. The key here is to model for participants what you want them to do in this learning activity. Try to think of real-life examples of some of the different sources of conflict to highlight for the participants. When you explain task interdependence, for instance, you might provide an example of two people working on a project in which speed and quality are both interdependent and at the same time in conflict with one another.

Original material by Karl Mulle, © 2016 Association for Talent Development (ATD). Used with permission.
EMOTIONAL INTELLIGENCE training   1

Learning Activity 56: Case Studies in Conflict, *continued*

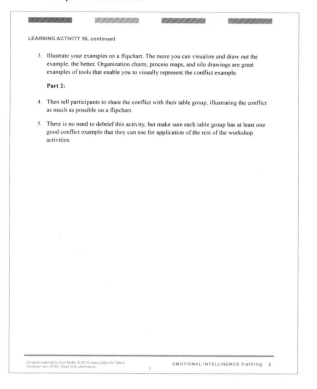

LEARNING ACTIVITY 56, continued

3. Illustrate your examples on a flipchart. The more you can visualize and draw out the example, the better. Organization charts, process maps, and silo drawings are great examples of tools that enable you to visually represent the conflict example.

    Part 2:

4. Then tell participants to share the conflict with their table group, illustrating the conflict as much as possible on a flipchart.

5. There is no need to debrief this activity, but make sure each table group has at least one good conflict example that they can use for application of the rest of the workshop activities.

Original material by Karl Mulle, © 2016 Association for Talent Development (ATD). Used with permission.
EMOTIONAL INTELLIGENCE training   2

Learning Activity 57: Step 1 Practice: Identify and Collaborate

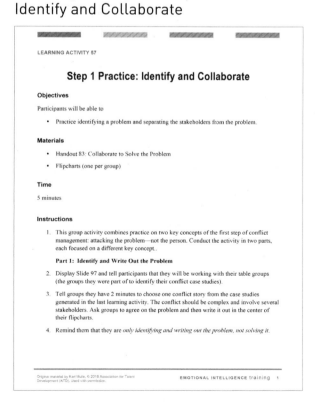

LEARNING ACTIVITY 57

Step 1 Practice: Identify and Collaborate

Objectives

Participants will be able to

- Practice identifying a problem and separating the stakeholders from the problem.

Materials

- Handout 83: Collaborate to Solve the Problem
- Flipcharts (one per group)

Time

5 minutes

Instructions

1. This group activity combines practice on two key concepts of the first step of conflict management: attacking the problem—not the person. Conduct the activity in two parts, each focused on a different key concept.

    Part 1: Identify and Write Out the Problem

2. Display Slide 97 and tell participants that they will be working with their table groups (the groups they were part of to identify their conflict case studies).

3. Tell groups they have 2 minutes to choose one conflict story from the case studies generated in the last learning activity. The conflict should be complex and involve several stakeholders. Ask groups to agree on the problem and then write it out in the center of their flipcharts.

4. Remind them that they are *only identifying and writing out the problem, not solving it.*

Original material by Karl Mulle, © 2016 Association for Talent Development (ATD). Used with permission.
EMOTIONAL INTELLIGENCE training   1

Learning Activity 57: Step 1 Practice: Identify and Collaborate, *continued*

LEARNING ACTIVITY 57, continued

5. Call time and check in with all the groups to make sure they have identified an intractable problem.

    Part 2: Collaborate to Solve the Problem

6. Now display Slide 98 and ask them to turn to their Handout 83.

7. Tell groups they have 2 minutes to identify all of the stakeholders the problem owner needs to collaborate with and then write the stakeholders on their flipcharts. Refer them to the handout template as an example of how to list the stakeholders.

8. Emphasize that they are only *identifying stakeholders, not solving the problem.*

9. No debrief is need for this activity. It will provide the basis for the next learning activity.

Original material by Karl Mulle, © 2016 Association for Talent Development (ATD). Used with permission.
EMOTIONAL INTELLIGENCE training   2

Learning Activity 58: Step 2 Practice: Inputs, Outputs, and Managing the Process

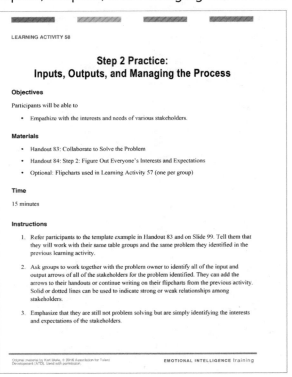

LEARNING ACTIVITY 58

Step 2 Practice:
Inputs, Outputs, and Managing the Process

Objectives

Participants will be able to

- Empathize with the interests and needs of various stakeholders.

Materials

- Handout 83: Collaborate to Solve the Problem
- Handout 84: Step 2: Figure Out Everyone's Interests and Expectations
- Optional: Flipcharts used in Learning Activity 57 (one per group)

Time

15 minutes

Instructions

1. Refer participants to the template example in Handout 83 and on Slide 99. Tell them that they will work with their same table groups and the same problem they identified in the previous learning activity.

2. Ask groups to work together with the problem owner to identify all of the input and output arrows of all of the stakeholders for the problem identified. They can add the arrows to their handouts or continue writing on their flipcharts from the previous activity. Solid or dotted lines can be used to indicate strong or weak relationships among stakeholders.

3. Emphasize that they are still not problem solving but are simply identifying the interests and expectations of the stakeholders.

Original material by Karl Mulle, © 2016 Association for Talent Development (ATD). Used with permission.　　　EMOTIONAL INTELLIGENCE training

Learning Activity 59: Step 3 Practice: Brainstorm

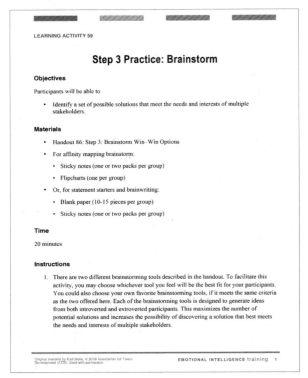

LEARNING ACTIVITY 59

Step 3 Practice: Brainstorm

Objectives

Participants will be able to

- Identify a set of possible solutions that meet the needs and interests of multiple stakeholders.

Materials

- Handout 86: Step 3: Brainstorm Win–Win Options
- For affinity mapping brainstorm:
  - Sticky notes (one or two packs per group)
  - Flipcharts (one per group)
- Or, for statement starters and brainwriting:
  - Blank paper (10-15 pieces per group)
  - Sticky notes (one or two packs per group)

Time

20 minutes

Instructions

1. There are two different brainstorming tools described in the handout. To facilitate this activity, you may choose whichever tool you feel will be the best fit for your participants. You could also choose your own favorite brainstorming tools, if it meets the same criteria as the two offered here. Each of the brainstorming tools is designed to generate ideas from both introverted and extroverted participants. This maximizes the number of potential solutions and increases the possibility of discovering a solution that best meets the needs and interests of multiple stakeholders.

Original material by Karl Mulle, © 2016 Association for Talent Development (ATD). Used with permission.　　　EMOTIONAL INTELLIGENCE training　1

Learning Activity 59: Step 3 Practice: Brainstorm, *continued*

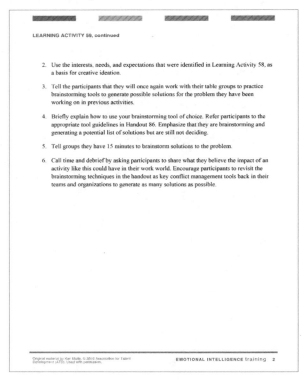

LEARNING ACTIVITY 59, continued

2. Use the interests, needs, and expectations that were identified in Learning Activity 58, as a basis for creative ideation.

3. Tell the participants that they will once again work with their table groups to practice brainstorming tools to generate possible solutions for the problem they have been working on in previous activities.

4. Briefly explain how to use your brainstorming tool of choice. Refer participants to the appropriate tool guidelines in Handout 86. Emphasize that they are brainstorming and generating a potential list of solutions but are still not deciding.

5. Tell groups they have 15 minutes to brainstorm solutions to the problem.

6. Call time and debrief by asking participants to share what they believe the impact of an activity like this could have in their work world. Encourage participants to revisit the brainstorming techniques in the handout as key conflict management tools back in their teams and organizations to generate as many solutions as possible.

Original material by Karl Mulle, © 2016 Association for Talent Development (ATD). Used with permission.　　　EMOTIONAL INTELLIGENCE training　2

Learning Activity 60: Step 4 Practice: Rock, Paper, Scissors

LEARNING ACTIVITY 60

Step 4 Practice: Rock, Paper, Scissors

Objectives

Participants will be able to

- Discover why yielding to principle instead of pressure preserves both collaborative intention and relationship effectiveness.

Time

5 minutes

Instructions

1. Lead the entire group in a game of rock, paper, scissors.

2. Now ask participants to find a playing partner. If you have an uneven number of participants, you will need to partner with one of the participants.

3. Tell teams that on your signal, each matchup must play a best-of-three game of rock, paper, scissors.

4. When all teams have finished the game, tell the winners to move on to the next round and the losers to cheer the winners on in the next round.

5. The winners of the second round move on to the third round, and the losers of the second round cheer on the winners in the next round.

6. Continue for as many rounds as necessary to end up with a final pairing of two winners. Each of the winners should have half of the class cheering for him or her.

7. The finalists will play one final best-of-three game of rock, paper, scissors.

Original material by Karl Mulle, © 2016 Association for Talent Development (ATD). Used with permission.　　　EMOTIONAL INTELLIGENCE training　1

Learning Activity 60: Step 4 Practice: Rock, Paper, Scissors, *continued*

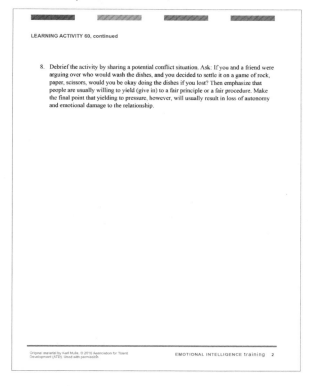

8. Debrief the activity by sharing a potential conflict situation. Ask: If you and a friend were arguing over who would wash the dishes, and you decided to settle it on a game of rock, paper, scissors, would you be okay doing the dishes if you lost? Then emphasize that people are usually willing to yield (give in) to a fair principle or a fair procedure. Make the final point that yielding to pressure, however, will usually result in loss of autonomy and emotional damage to the relationship.

Learning Activity 61: Step 4 Practice: Decision Matrix Exercise

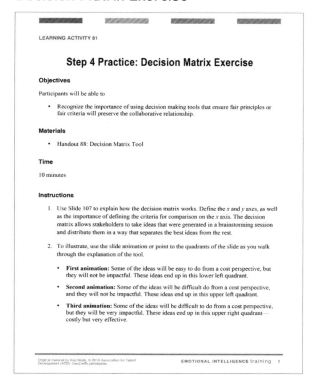

Step 4 Practice: Decision Matrix Exercise

Objectives

Participants will be able to

- Recognize the importance of using decision making tools that ensure fair principles or fair criteria will preserve the collaborative relationship.

Materials

- Handout 88: Decision Matrix Tool

Time

10 minutes

Instructions

1. Use Slide 107 to explain how the decision matrix works. Define the x and y axes, as well as the importance of defining the criteria for comparison on the x axis. The decision matrix allows stakeholders to take ideas that were generated in a brainstorming session and distribute them in a way that separates the best ideas from the rest.

2. To illustrate, use the slide animation or point to the quadrants of the slide as you walk through the explanation of the tool.

   - **First animation:** Some of the ideas will be easy to do from a cost perspective, but they will not be impactful. These ideas end up in this lower left quadrant.
   - **Second animation:** Some of the ideas will be difficult do from a cost perspective, and they will not be impactful. These ideas end up in this upper left quadrant.
   - **Third animation:** Some of the ideas will be difficult to do from a cost perspective, but they will be very impactful. These ideas end up in this upper right quadrant—costly but very effective.

Learning Activity 61: Step 4 Practice: Decision Matrix Exercise, *continued*

- **Fourth animation:** And finally, some of the ideas will be easy to do from a cost perspective, and they will be very impactful. These ideas end up in this lower right quadrant.
- **Fifth animation:** The ideas in the lower right quadrant are probably the best options that most stakeholders would collaboratively agree to implement.

3. After explaining the tool, give groups 5 minutes to use the tool to separate the ideas they generated during their brainstorming session by placing the sticky notes in the appropriate quadrant.

4. Debrief the activity by emphasizing that yielding to pressure is costly, while yielding to principle preserves the relationship. Refocus participants on the idea that the democratic leadership style uses tool like these because they facilitate effective decisions with maximum buy-in.

Discussion Questions for Debriefing

- Debrief the activity by emphasizing that yielding pressure is costly, while yielding to principle preserves the relationship.

Learning Activity 62: EQuip Yourself for Success: Action Plan

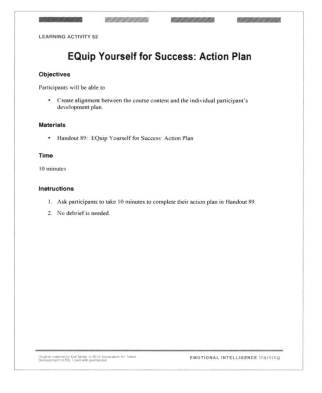

EQuip Yourself for Success: Action Plan

Objectives

Participants will be able to

- Create alignment between the course content and the individual participant's development plan.

Materials

- Handout 89: EQuip Yourself for Success: Action Plan

Time

10 minutes

Instructions

1. Ask participants to take 10 minutes to complete their action plan in Handout 89.
2. No debrief is needed.

Chapter 12

Assessments

What's in This Chapter

- Four assessments to use in workshop sessions
- Instructions on how to fill out, score, and interpret the assessments

---

Assessments and evaluations are essential components of any workshop—before it begins, as it goes on, and when it concludes. To prepare an effective workshop for participants, you have to assess their needs and those of their organization. Although a formal needs assessment is outside the scope of this book, Chapter 5 will provide information on how you can identify participant needs.

Assessments, evaluations, and surveys used after the workshop are vital both for the organization and for you as the facilitator. Assessment 1 provides a workshop evaluation to help you discover if you and the workshop have met the goals and expectations of your participants. Although negative comments can be tough to read, ultimately they allow you to continually learn and improve your skills as a learning facilitator. Assessment 4: Facilitator Competencies provides an instrument to help you manage your professional development and increase the effectiveness of your training sessions. You can use this tool in a number of ways: self-assessment, end-of-course feedback, observer feedback, or as a gauge for tracking professional growth with repeated ratings.

Assessments 2 and 3 are learning tools you can use during a workshop to help participants identify areas of strength and potential development opportunities. When used at the beginning of a workshop, they can help the participants and the facilitator decide how to focus workshop time around potential learning goals. When used at the end of a workshop or as a takeaway tool, they can help participants create an action plan that builds on strengths and targets developmental goals.

Assessment 3 is not intended to replace more research-based assessment tools. It is, however, designed as a tool for participants to use their own emotional intelligence to measure their emotional intelligence. Given the reliability of self-awareness, the ideal way for participants to use this assessment is to answer each statement using a combination of self-awareness and feedback from others. In other words, the value of this assessment as a guide for personal development will be maximized if participants solicit the feedback of others, especially on those statements in which they may be somewhat uncertain about how to rate themselves. As participants rate themselves on each statement, they should ideally take a moment to reflect on whether or not their rating could benefit from someone else's feedback. Each statement is a potential opportunity to open up a conversation with someone to gain valuable feedback.

Assessments Included in *Emotional Intelligence Training*

Assessment 1: Workshop Evaluation

Assessment 2: Collaborative Intention Self-Assessment

Assessment 3: Emotional Intelligence Quick Assessment

Assessment 4: Facilitator Competencies

Assessment 1: Workshop Evaluation

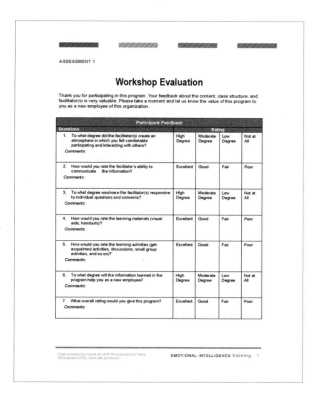

Assessment 1: Workshop Evaluation, *continued*

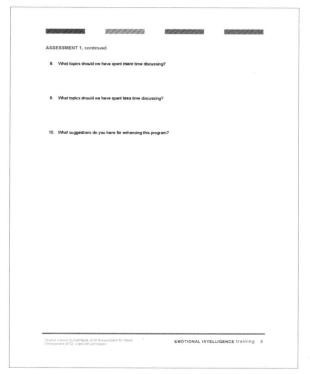

Assessment 2: Collaborative Intention Self-Assessment

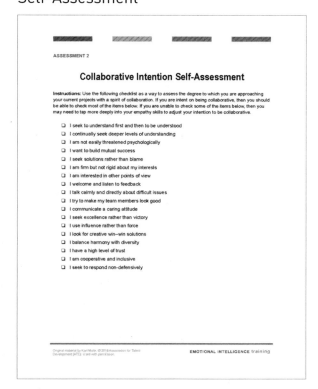

Assessment 3: Emotional Intelligence Quick Assessment

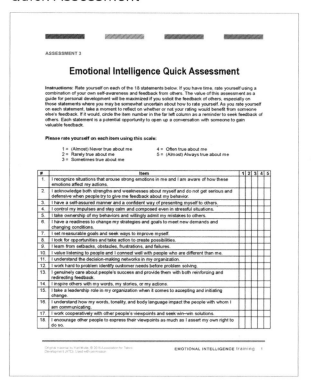

Assessment 3: Emotional Intelligence Quick Assessment, *continued*

ASSESSMENT 3, continued

Scoring the Emotional Intelligence Quick Assessment

Each of the 18 statements relates to one of the emotional competencies of Goleman's four-domain model. If you rated yourself 4 or higher on the statement, then you can consider the corresponding emotional competency to be a strength. If you rated yourself 2 or lower on a statement, then you can consider the corresponding emotional competency an area where you might need development.

	Rating	Emotional Competency	Strength or Area for Development?
1.		Emotional Self-Awareness	
2.		Accurate Self-Assessment	
3.		Self-Confidence	
4.		Emotional Self-Control	
5.		Transparency	
6.		Adaptability	
7.		Achievement Orientation	
8.		Initiative	
9.		Optimism	
10.		Empathy	
11.		Organizational Awareness	
12.		Service	
13.		Developing Others	
14.		Inspirational Leadership	
15.		Change Catalyst	
16.		Influence	
17.		Conflict Management	
18.		Teamwork and Collaboration	

Original material by Karl Mulle, © 2016 Association for Talent Development (ATD). Used with permission.

EMOTIONAL INTELLIGENCE training 2

Assessment 4: Facilitator Competencies

ASSESSMENT 4

Facilitator Competencies

This assessment instrument will help you as the facilitator manage your professional development and increase the effectiveness of your training sessions. You can use this instrument in the following ways:

Self-assessment. Use the assessment to rate yourself on the five-point scale, which will generate an overall profile and help determine the competency areas that are in the greatest need of improvement.

End-of-course feedback. Honest feedback from the training participants can lessen the possibility that facilitators deceive themselves about the 12 competencies. Trainees may not be able to rate the facilitator on all 12, so it may be necessary to ask the participants to rate only those they consider themselves qualified to address.

Observer feedback. Facilitators may observe each other's training sessions and provide highly useful information on the 12 competencies that are crucial to be effective in conducting training.

Repeat ratings. This assessment can be the basis for tracking professional growth on the competencies needed to be an effective facilitator. The repeat measure may be obtained as often as needed to gauge progress on action plans for improvement.

The Competencies

Facilitators are faced with challenges anytime they lead a training session. Many skills are necessary to help participants meet their learning needs and to ensure that the organization achieves its desired results for the training. This assessment contains a set of 12 important competencies that effective training requires. Not all seasoned facilitators have expertise in all of these competencies, but they may represent learning and growth areas for almost any facilitator.

Here is a detailed explanation of the importance of each of the dozen crucial elements of facilitator competence:

Original material by Karl Mulle, © 2016 Association for Talent Development (ATD). Used with permission.

EMOTIONAL INTELLIGENCE training 1

Assessment 4: Facilitator Competencies, *continued*

ASSESSMENT 4, continued

Understanding adult learners: Uses knowledge of the principles of adult learning in both designing and delivering training.

Effective facilitators are able to draw on the experiences of the learners in a training session and then give them the applicable content and tools to engage them fully and help them see the value of the learning. It is also important to address the participants' various learning styles and provide them with opportunities to solve problems and think critically so they can work through real business issues and develop additional skills.

Presentation skills: Presents content clearly to achieve the desired outcomes of the training. Encourages learners to generate their own answers through effectively leading group discussions.

Of all the competencies a facilitator uses during a training session, none may be more obvious than the need to have exceptional presentation skills. The facilitator's ability to present content effectively and in an entertaining way is one of the first things learners notice and is a large part of a successful workshop. The nature of adult learning makes it equally important that the facilitator is not just a talking head but is also adept at initiating, drawing out, guiding, and summarizing information gleaned from large-group discussions during a training session. The facilitator's role is not to feed answers to learners as if they are empty vessels waiting to be filled. Rather, it is the facilitator's primary task to generate learning on the part of the participants through their own process of discovery.

Communication skills: Expresses self well, both verbally and in writing. Understands nonverbal communication and listens effectively.

Beyond presenting information and leading discussions, it is vital for a facilitator to be highly skilled in all aspects of communication. He or she should use language that learners can understand; give clear directions for activities; involve trainees through appropriate humor, anecdotes, and examples; and build on the ideas of others. This will lead to training sessions that are engaging and highly valuable for the participants. Facilitators must also be able to listen well and attend to learners' nonverbal communication to create common meaning and mutual understanding.

Original material by Karl Mulle, © 2016 Association for Talent Development (ATD). Used with permission.

EMOTIONAL INTELLIGENCE training 2

Assessment 4: Facilitator Competencies, *continued*

ASSESSMENT 4, continued

Emotional intelligence: Respects learners' viewpoints, knowledge, and experience. Recognizes and responds appropriately to others' feelings, attitudes, and concerns.

Because learners may have many different backgrounds, experience levels, and opinions in the same training sessions, facilitators must be able to handle a variety of situations and conversations well, and be sensitive to others' emotions. They must pay close attention to the dynamics in the room, be flexible enough to make immediate changes to activities during training to meet the needs of learners, and create an open and trusting learning environment. Attendees should feel comfortable expressing their opinions, asking questions, and participating in activities without fear of repercussion or disapproval. Monitoring learners' emotions during a training session also helps the facilitator gauge when it may be time to change gears if conflict arises, if discussion needs to be refocused on desired outcomes, or if there is a need to delve deeper into a topic to encourage further learning.

Training methods: Varies instructional approaches to address different learning styles and hold learners' interest.

All learners have preferred learning styles, and one of the keys to effective training facilitation is to use a variety of methods to address them. Some people are more visual ("see it") learners, and others are more auditory ("hear it") or kinesthetic ("do it") learners. An effective facilitator must be familiar with a variety of training methods to tap into each participant's style(s) and maintain interest during the training session. These methods may include such activities as small group activities, individual exercises, case studies, role plays, simulations, and games.

Subject matter expertise: Possesses deep knowledge of training content and applicable experience to draw upon.

Facilitators must have solid background knowledge of the training topic at hand and be able to share related experience to help learners connect theory to real-world scenarios. Anecdotes and other examples to illustrate how the training content relates to participants' circumstances and work can enhance the learning experience and encourage learners to apply the information and also to use the tools they have been given. It is also crucial that facilitators know their topics inside and out, so they can answer the trainees' questions and guide them toward problem-solving and skill development.

Original material by Karl Mulle, © 2016 Association for Talent Development (ATD). Used with permission.

EMOTIONAL INTELLIGENCE training 3

Assessment 4: Facilitator Competencies, *continued*

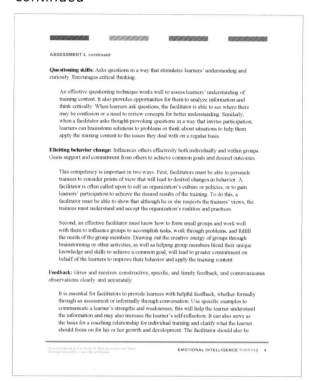

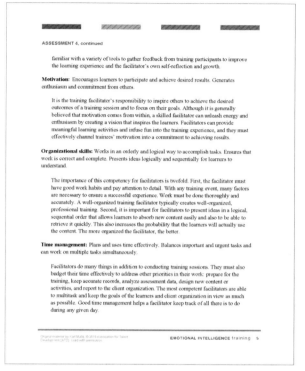

Assessment 4: Facilitator Competencies, *continued*

Assessment 4: Facilitator Competencies, *continued*

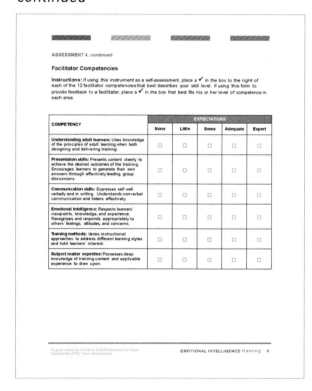

Chapter 13
Handouts

What's in This Chapter

- Eighty-nine handouts to use in your workshops
- Complete instructions for how to use to handouts

Handouts comprise the various materials you will provide to the learners throughout the course of the workshop. In some cases, the handouts simply provide information and notes on the content, worksheets to complete, and so forth. In other cases, they offer tools that provide important and practical materials for use in and out of the workshop, such as reference materials, tip sheets, samples of completed forms, flowcharts, and so forth. The definitions of handout and tool are somewhat fluid.

The workshop agendas in Chapters 1–3 and the learning activities in Chapter 11 will provide instructions for how and when to use the handouts within the context of the workshop.

Handouts Included in *Emotional Intelligence Training*

Half-Day Workshop: The New Science of Success

Handout 1: Half-Day Workshop Learning Objectives: The New Science of Success

Handout 2: The Anatomy of an Emotion

Handout 3: When Emotions Get the Best of Us

Handout 4: Two Brain Systems That Control Your Attention

Handout 5: System 1 vs. System 2 Thinking

One-Day Workshop: The New Science of Relationships

Handout 29: Discretionary Emotional Energy

Handout 30: EQuip Yourself for Success: Map Your Personal Influence Network

Handout 31: EQuip Yourself for Success: Evaluate Your Personal Influence Network

Handout 32: EQuip Yourself for Success: Practice Personality Talk

Handout 33: Develop the Competency of Teamwork

Handout 34: Teaming and Collaboration Action Plan

Handout 35: EQuip Yourself for Success: The Two Messages and Communication Rapport

Handout 36: The Competency of Conflict Management

Handout 37: XYZ Talk

Handout 38: EQuip Yourself for Success: Action Plan

Two-Day Workshop: The New Science of Leadership

Handout 39: Two-Day Workshop Learning Objectives: The New Science of Leadership

Handout 40: The Anatomy of an Emotion

Handout 41: Emotional Intelligence Defined

Handout 42: Emotional Intelligence and Leadership

Handout 43: Resonant vs. Dissonant Leadership

Handout 44: Goleman's Six Styles of Leadership

Handout 45: Leadership Style Discussion

Handout 46: Leadership Style Action Plan

Handout 47: Empathy Discussion

Handout 48: The Johari Window

Handout 49: Managing Defensiveness Journaling Exercise

Handout 50: Visionary Style and the Competency of Self-Awareness

Handout 51: Keep Your Eye on the Grand Marshmallow

Handout 76: Using Employment Engagement Surveys

Handout 77: Democratic Style and the Competency of Influence

Handout 78: The Six Principles of Influence

Handout 79: Democratic Style and the Competency of Conflict Management

Handout 80: Examples of Conflict Worksheet

Handout 81: EQuip Yourself for Success: Four Steps of Conflict Management

Handout 82: Step 1: Attack the Problem, Not the Person

Handout 83: Collaborate to Solve the Problem

Handout 84: Step 2: Figure Out Everyone's Interests and Expectations

Handout 85: Know Your BATNA

Handout 86: Step 3: Brainstorm Win–Win Options

Handout 87: Step 4: Insist on Using Fair Procedures and Principles

Handout 88: Decision Matrix Tool

Handout 89: EQuip Yourself for Success: Action Plan

Handout 1: Half-Day Workshop Learning Objectives: The New Science of Success

Half-Day Workshop Learning Objectives: The New Science of Success

Upon successful completion of this workshop, you will be able to accomplish the following objectives:

- Learn about the anatomy of an emotion and how emotions and thoughts work together to influence behaviors
- Understand the link between emotional intelligence and success in life
- Discern the difference between automatic limbic decisions and intentional, conscious decisions
- Discover when your automatic processes serve you well, and when they need to be better managed
- Practice agile thinking, increasing self-awareness and intentional thinking
- Leverage both due diligence and intuition to make effective decisions
- Develop cognitive and behavioral strategies to *manage emotions intelligently.*

Handout 2: The Anatomy of an Emotion

The Anatomy of an Emotion

The Original Story of Your Emotions

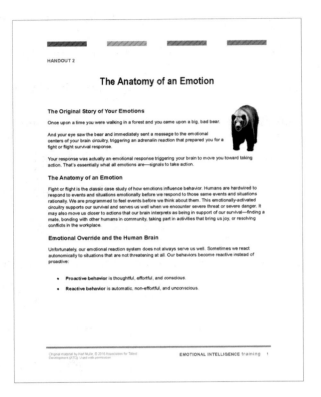

Once upon a time you were walking in a forest and you came upon a big, bad bear.

And your eye saw the bear and immediately sent a message to the emotional centers of your brain circuitry, triggering an adrenalin reaction that prepared you for a fight or flight survival response.

Your response was actually an emotional response triggering your brain to move you toward taking action. That's essentially what all emotions are—signals to take action.

The Anatomy of an Emotion

Fight or flight is the classic case study of how emotions influence behavior. Humans are hardwired to respond to events and situations emotionally before we respond to those same events and situations rationally. We are programmed to feel events before we think about them. This emotionally-activated circuitry supports our survival and serves us well when we encounter severe threat or severe danger. It may also move us closer to actions that our brain interprets as being in support of our survival—finding a mate, bonding with other humans in community, taking part in activities that bring us joy, or resolving conflicts in the workplace.

Emotional Override and the Human Brain

Unfortunately, our emotional reaction system does not always serve us well. Sometimes we react autonomically to situations that are not threatening at all. Our behaviors become reactive instead of proactive:

- **Proactive behavior** is thoughtful, effortful, and conscious.
- **Reactive behavior** is automatic, non-effortful, and unconscious.

Handout 2: The Anatomy of an Emotion, *continued*

Sometimes our emotional reactions take over when a better response would be a rational, effortful, intentional response. To understand our human potential to be undermined by our emotional responses, we need to get to know our brain a little better:

- **The Human Brain.** The neocortex is the part of our brain that controls rational thinking including the higher brain functions of awareness, reasoning, voluntary movement, conscious, intentional thought, and language skills. We call this part of the brain the human brain.
- **The Reptilian Brain.** The original story of our emotions introduces us to a more primal part of our brain. All vertebrate animals have a mass of cells situated at the top of their spinal cord comprising the brainstem. The cells of the brainstem coordinate most of our involuntary functions, such as blood circulation, and govern our most automatic instincts, such as fight or flight. Sometimes referred to as the reptilian brain, this primitive brain has the power to override the rational thinking functions of the neocortex and take control of our actions when it perceives a threat.
- **The Mammalian Brain.** Tucked in beneath the neocortex and wrapping around the brainstem in something of a horseshoe configuration is a series of structures comprising the limbic area of the brain. Our emotions originate here. The limbic area, sometimes called the mammalian brain, stores our emotionally linked learned emotional responses to particular circumstances. The reference to mammals with regard to this part of our brain has to do with the learning capacity of the limbic system that is shared by all warm-blooded mammals. Over the course of our experiences in life, we each accumulate and store literally thousands of emotional memories in our mammalian brains. These memories comprise the total of our emotional experiences and serve as activation points for emotional responses whenever we encounter current situations that are reminiscent of these stored memories. In other words, our emotions are taking their cues from memories stored in our limbic systems and are triggering us to behave accordingly.

When Emotions Get the Best of Us

All of this means that our emotional brain has the power to influence our behaviors *before* our rational brain knows what is happening. When the part of our brain that is emotional *overrides* the part of our brain that is rational, it can result in inappropriate reactions that can sabotage our success. We find ourselves wishing that we had taken a moment to think about these emotions *before* responding. This capacity to think about emotions, to manage them, to choose an appropriate response, and to relate effectively with other emotional people is called *emotional intelligence.*

The New Science of Success

It is as if a kind of tug-of-war is being waged between our emotionally charged brain and our rational brain. We could call this *reactive* side of the tug-of-war *emotional un-intelligence,* because we are allowing our emotional impulses to manage our behaviors instead of using our rational intelligence to manage both our emotions and our behaviors. Indeed, if we are able to delay our emotional reaction long enough to mindfully, intentionally, consciously engage our rational brain, we will discover a new list of behavioral options that could lead us to handle the situation in a more intelligent and successful way. We call this *proactive* side of the tug-of-war *emotional intelligence—the new science of success.*

Handout 3: When Emotions Get the Best of Us

When Emotions Get the Best of Us

Instructions: Think of a real-life example in which your emotions took control of your behaviors and caused you to do something that you later regretted. Briefly answer the questions below about that situation. Then share your answers with your triad.

1. What was the situation?

2. What were you feeling?

3. What did you do?

4. What were the consequences?

Handout 4: Two Brain Systems That Control Your Attention

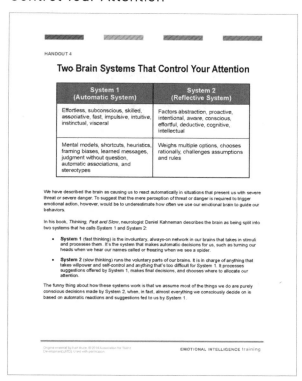

Handout 5: System 1 vs. System 2 Thinking

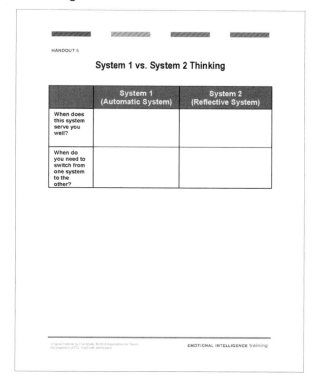

Handout 6: Mental Agility

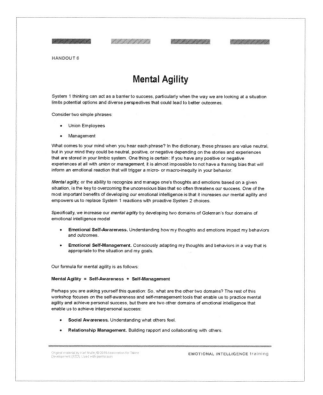

Handout 7: Emotions, Thoughts, and Behaviors

Emotions, Thoughts, and Behaviors

Disruptive Emotions and Reactive Behavior

Consider the following list of emotions:

- Anger or Defensiveness
- Fear or Anxiety
- Guilt or Shame
- Feeling "down"
- Insecurity
- Embarrassment

What do all these emotions have in common? They tend to get the best of us in certain situations. We call these emotions *disruptive emotions*, because they so often threaten to override rational thoughts and take *disruptive* control of behaviors. When we are aware of these emotions and take personal responsibility for managing them, we can maintain a sense of control or composure. When we lack awareness and avoid personal responsibility, then we often lose composure and end up looking foolish. All of these disruptive emotions have the power to trigger reactive behaviors that are inappropriate in many human interactions. We lose our tempers, intimidate others, surrender under pressure, sulk and complain because we didn't get what we wanted, and so on.

Such behaviors risk sabotaging personal and professional success. But this does not mean that these disruptive emotions are bad or even negative. Each one of these emotions is a signal that can point us in the right direction. When managed well, these emotions can provide tremendous amounts of information and energy to help us navigate through difficult situations and proactively choose the right response. Anxiety before a presentation, for example, could simply be a signal indicating that more preparation is necessary. Indeed, the anxiety will spur on the appropriate amounts of preparation and rehearsal, as long as it is managed well.

Handout 7: Emotions, Thoughts, and Behaviors, *continued*

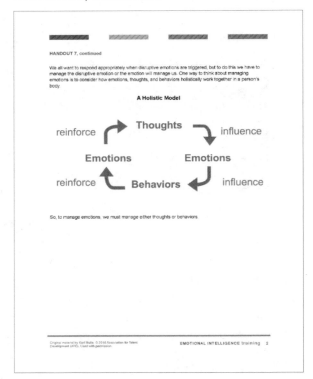

Handout 8: Behavioral Strategies for Managing Your Emotions

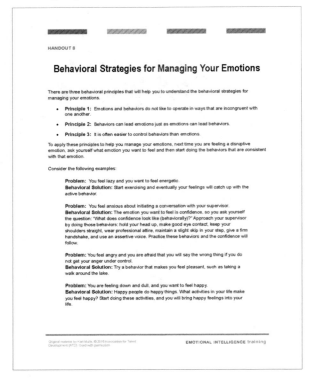

Handout 9: Cognitive Strategies and the ABCs of Life

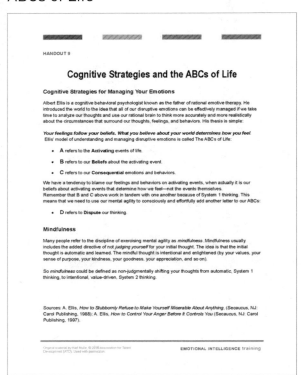

Handout 10: Emotional Triggers Exercise

HANDOUT 10

Emotional Triggers Exercise

Instructions: Fill out this chart using an example of when your emotions got the best of you.

Emotional Trigger	Underlying Belief or Value	Impact When Triggered	What Can I Do (Cognitive or Behavioral Strategies)?
Example: *Being unfairly judged or treated.*	*All people should be treated and evaluated equally and based on objective criteria.*	*I become defensive or argumentative and angry. People stop listening, feel threatened and shut down, or lash out.*	*Recognize value of subjective judgment (and the fact that I cannot eliminate it!) Seek to understand the other person's true intentions and feelings. Take away information that is valuable for me and discard what is not—without becoming angry or defending my position. Remember to balance my desire for life to be fair with my interest in preserving the relationship.*

Top 5 Emotional Triggers in the Workplace:

1. Condescension and lack of respect.
2. Being treated unfairly.
3. Being unappreciated.
4. Feeling that you're not being listened to or heard.
5. Being held to unrealistic deadlines.

Handout 11: EQuip Yourself for Success: Manage Expectations

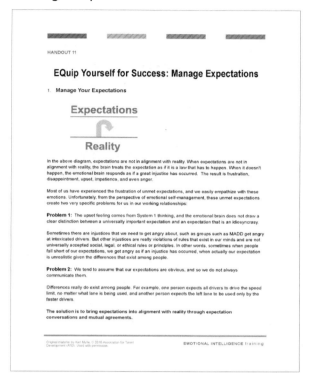

Handout 12: EQuip Yourself for Success: Manage Expectations Discussion

Handout 12: EQuip Yourself for Success: Manage Expectations Discussion, *continued*

Handout 13: EQuip Yourself for Success: Choose Your Battles

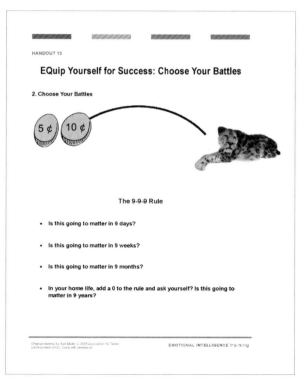

Handout 14: EQuip Yourself for Success: Practice Asking System 2 Questions

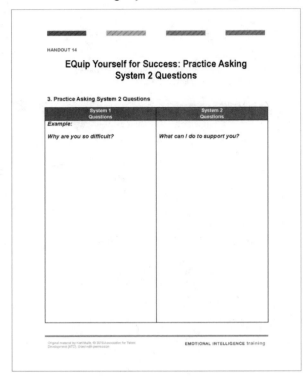

Handout 15: EQuip Yourself for Success: The Power of Reframes

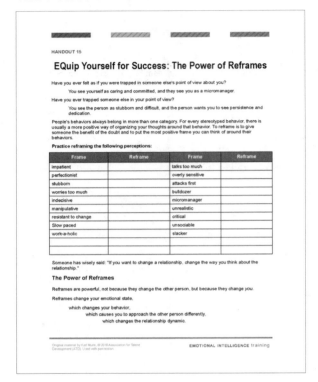

Handout 16: EQuip Yourself for Success: Action Plan

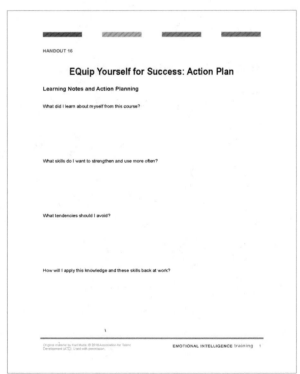

Handout 16: EQuip Yourself for Success: Action Plan, *continued*

What do I want to develop or improve?	Why is it important?
How will I do it?	**What values will motivate me to do it?**

Dates Applied	I did...	Discoveries

EMOTIONAL INTELLIGENCE training   2

Handout 17: One-Day Workshop Learning Objectives: The New Science of Relationships

HANDOUT 17

One-Day Workshop Learning Objectives: The New Science of Relationships

Upon successful completion of this workshop, you will be able to accomplish the following objectives:

- Learn about the anatomy of an emotion and how emotions and thoughts work together to influence behaviors
- Explore the four-domain model of emotional intelligence
- Define *emotional intelligence* as a set of competencies that can be learned
- Explore the competencies related to social awareness and relationship effectiveness
- Practice how to build rapport and demonstrate empathy
- Manage defensiveness and develop collaborative intention
- Understand discretionary emotional energy and explore the conditions that increase employee engagement
- Develop strategies for increasing teamwork and collaboration among team members with different emotional triggers
- Increase confidence in managing conflict and difficult emotional conversations.

Original material by Karl Mulle. © 2016 Association for Talent Development (ATD). Used with permission.

EMOTIONAL INTELLIGENCE training

Handout 18: The Anatomy of an Emotion

HANDOUT 18

The Anatomy of an Emotion

The Original Story of Your Emotions

Once upon a time you were walking in a forest and you came upon a big, bad bear.

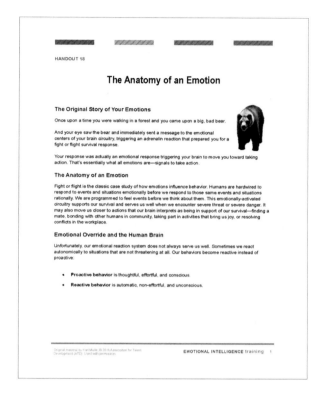

And your eye saw the bear and immediately sent a message to the emotional centers of your brain circuitry, triggering an adrenalin reaction that prepared you for a fight or flight survival response.

Your response was actually an emotional response triggering your brain to move you toward taking action. That's essentially what all emotions are—signals to take action.

The Anatomy of an Emotion

Fight or flight is the classic case study of how emotions influence behavior. Humans are hardwired to respond to events and situations emotionally before we respond to those same events and situations rationally. We are programmed to feel events before we think about them. This emotionally-activated circuitry supports our survival and serves us well when we encounter severe threat or severe danger. It may also move us closer to actions that our brain interprets as being in support of our survival—finding a mate, bonding with other humans in community, taking part in activities that bring us joy, or resolving conflicts in the workplace.

Emotional Override and the Human Brain

Unfortunately, our emotional reaction system does not always serve us well. Sometimes we react autonomically to situations that are not threatening at all. Our behaviors become reactive instead of proactive.

- **Proactive behavior** is thoughtful, effortful, and conscious.
- **Reactive behavior** is automatic, non-effortful, and unconscious.

Original material by Karl Mulle. © 2016 Association for Talent Development (ATD). Used with permission.

EMOTIONAL INTELLIGENCE training   1

Handout 18: The Anatomy of an Emotion, *continued*

HANDOUT 18, continued

Sometimes our emotional reactions take over when a better response would be a rational, effortful, intentional response. To understand our human potential to be undermined by our emotional responses, we need to get to know our brain a little better.

- **The Human Brain.** The neocortex is the part of our brain that controls rational thinking including the higher brain functions of awareness, reasoning, voluntary movement, conscious, intentional thought, and language skills. We call this part of the brain the human brain.
- **The Reptilian Brain.** The original story of our emotions introduces us to a more primal part of our brain. All vertebrate animals have a mass of cells situated at the top of their spinal cord comprising the brainstem. The cells of the brainstem coordinate most of our involuntary functions, such as blood circulation, and govern our most automatic instincts, such as fight or flight. Sometimes referred to as the reptilian brain, this primitive brain has the power to override the rational thinking functions of the neocortex and take control of our actions when it perceives a threat.
- **The Mammalian Brain.** Tucked in beneath the neocortex and wrapping around the brainstem in something of a horseshoe configuration is a series of structures comprising the limbic area of the brain. Our emotions originate there. The limbic area, sometimes called the mammalian brain, stores our emotionally linked memories. It is this area of the brain that triggers learned emotional responses to particular circumstances. The reference to mammals with regard to this part of our brain has to do with the learning capacity of the limbic system that is shared by all warm-blooded mammals. Over the course of our experiences in life, we each accumulate and store literally thousands of emotional memories in our mammalian brains. These memories comprise the total of our emotional experiences and serve as activation points for emotional responses whenever we encounter current situations that are reminiscent of these stored memories. In other words, our emotions are taking their cues from memories stored in our limbic systems and are triggering us to behave accordingly.

When Emotions Get the Best of Us

All of this means that our emotional brain has the power to influence our behaviors *before* our rational brain knows what is happening. When the part of our brain that is emotional *overrides* the part of our brain that is rational, it can result in inappropriate reactions that can sabotage our success. We find ourselves wishing that we had taken a moment to think about these emotions *before* responding. This capacity to think about emotions, to manage them, to choose an appropriate response, and to relate effectively with other emotional people is called *emotional intelligence*.

The New Science of Relationships

The tug-of-war that is being waged between our emotionally charged brain and our rational brain can have a profound impact on the success of our interpersonal relationships. We call the reactive side of the tug-of-war emotional *un-intelligence*, because we are allowing our emotional impulses to manage our behaviors instead of using our rational intelligence to manage both our emotions and our behaviors. Indeed, if we are able to delay our emotional reactions long enough to mindfully and intentionally engage our rational brains, we will discover a new set of behavioral options that will help us avoid dysfunction, and manage the relationships of our lives in a more intelligent and effective way. We call this proactive side of the tug-of-war emotional intelligence—*the new science of relationships.*

Original material by Karl Mulle. © 2016 Association for Talent Development (ATD). Used with permission.

EMOTIONAL INTELLIGENCE training   2

Handout 19: The E-Motion Chart

HANDOUT 19

The E-Motion Chart

Most people don't really *listen* to their feelings. That is, they don't see their feelings as what they really are: signals for taking action. Many people simply see their feelings as something to be avoided or something to become overwhelmed by. They either drown in their feelings or they depress them. Choose, instead, to see your feelings as an internal guidance system that can signal you to pay attention and take action. Remember, it is an *e-motion.*

Instructions: Fill out the chart by answering the questions for each emotion.

Label the Emotion *"What am I feeling?"*	+ or -	Signaling a Message to Hear or an Action to Take *"What action should I take?"* *"What should I pay attention to?"*	When the Emotion Controls Me *"What happens when the emotion gets the best of me?"*
Anger/ Defensiveness			
Anxiety/Fear			
Guilt/Shame			
Depression/ Burnout			

Original material by Karl Mulle. © 2016 Association for Talent Development (ATD). Used with permission.

EMOTIONAL INTELLIGENCE training

Handout 20: Emotional Intelligence Defined

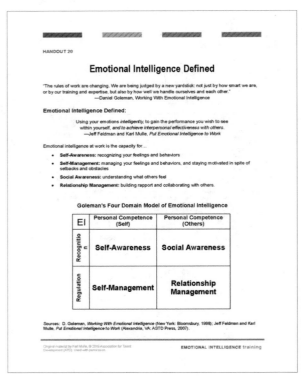

HANDOUT 20

Emotional Intelligence Defined

"The rules of work are changing. We are being judged by a new yardstick: not just by how smart we are, or by our training and expertise, but also by how well we handle ourselves and each other."
—Daniel Goleman, *Working With Emotional Intelligence*

Emotional Intelligence Defined:

Using your emotions *intelligently*, to gain the performance you wish to see within yourself, *and to achieve interpersonal effectiveness with others.*
—Jeff Feldman and Karl Mulle, *Put Emotional Intelligence to Work*

Emotional intelligence at work is the capacity for...

- **Self-Awareness:** recognizing your feelings and behaviors
- **Self-Management:** managing your feelings and behaviors, and staying motivated in spite of setbacks and obstacles
- **Social Awareness:** understanding what others feel
- **Relationship Management:** building rapport and collaborating with others.

Goleman's Four Domain Model of Emotional Intelligence

EI	Personal Competence (Self)	Personal Competence (Others)
Recognition	Self-Awareness	Social Awareness
Regulation	Self-Management	Relationship Management

Sources: D. Goleman, *Working With Emotional Intelligence* (New York: Bloomsbury, 1998); Jeff Feldman and Karl Mulle, *Put Emotional Intelligence to Work* (Alexandria, VA: ASTD Press, 2007).

Original material by Karl Mulle, © 2016 Association for Talent Development (ATD). Used with permission. EMOTIONAL INTELLIGENCE training

Handout 21: Self-Awareness Competencies

HANDOUT 21

Self-Awareness Competencies

Instructions: In your small group, discuss the situational importance of each of the self-awareness competencies in the workplace.

People are often given the feedback that they need to work on their emotional intelligence. The problem with such feedback is that it is like telling people they need to work on their knowledge of history or on their cooking skills. The categories are too broad to provide the receivers with any meaningful information that they can use for personal growth.

In this workshop, we have attempted a simple definition of emotional intelligence and delineated it into the four-domain model. These four domains are then further delineated into 18 competencies.

A competency, by definition, is a set of behaviors that people can learn. This is good news! By defining emotional intelligence behaviorally, not only are we able to give one another effective feedback, but we can develop our emotional intelligence by developing the underlying competencies.

Three competencies support the emotional intelligence domain of **self-awareness**.

Self-Awareness Competencies	
Emotional Self-Awareness	Reading one's own emotions and recognizing their impact
Accurate Self-Assessment	Knowing one's strengths and limits
Self-Confidence	A sound sense of one's self-worth and capabilities

Situational Importance:

Original material by Karl Mulle, © 2016 Association for Talent Development (ATD). Used with permission. EMOTIONAL INTELLIGENCE training

Handout 22: Self-Management Competencies

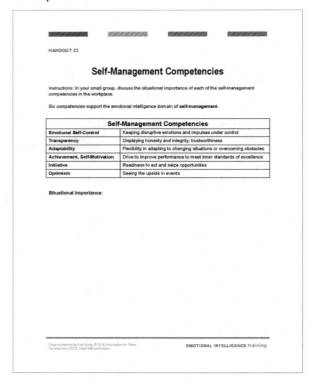

HANDOUT 22

Self-Management Competencies

Instructions: In your small group, discuss the situational importance of each of the self-management competencies in the workplace.

Six competencies support the emotional intelligence domain of **self-management**.

Self-Management Competencies	
Emotional Self-Control	Keeping disruptive emotions and impulses under control
Transparency	Displaying honesty and integrity; trustworthiness
Adaptability	Flexibility in adapting to changing situations or overcoming obstacles
Achievement, Self-Motivation	Drive to improve performance to meet inner standards of excellence
Initiative	Readiness to act and seize opportunities
Optimism	Seeing the upside in events

Situational Importance:

Original material by Karl Mulle, © 2016 Association for Talent Development (ATD). Used with permission. EMOTIONAL INTELLIGENCE training

Handout 23: Social Awareness Competencies

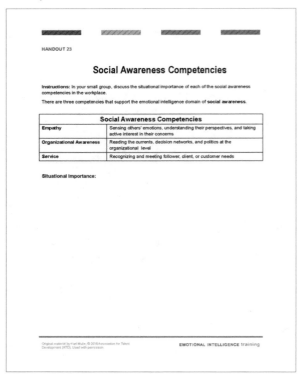

HANDOUT 23

Social Awareness Competencies

Instructions: In your small group, discuss the situational importance of each of the social awareness competencies in the workplace.

There are three competencies that support the emotional intelligence domain of **social awareness**.

Social Awareness Competencies	
Empathy	Sensing others' emotions, understanding their perspectives, and taking active interest in their concerns
Organizational Awareness	Reading the currents, decision networks, and politics at the organizational level
Service	Recognizing and meeting follower, client, or customer needs

Situational Importance:

Original material by Karl Mulle, © 2016 Association for Talent Development (ATD). Used with permission. EMOTIONAL INTELLIGENCE training

Handout 24: Relationship Management Competencies

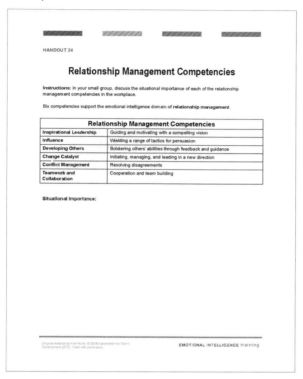

Handout 25: The Emotional Competency of Empathy

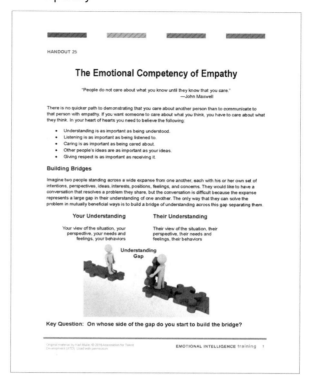

Handout 25: The Emotional Competency of Empathy, *continued*

Handout 26: Effective Listening

Handout 27: Collaborative Intention

Handout 28: Empathy and Feeling Blockers Checklist

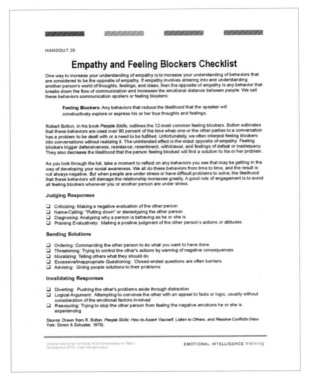

Handout 29: Discretionary Emotional Energy

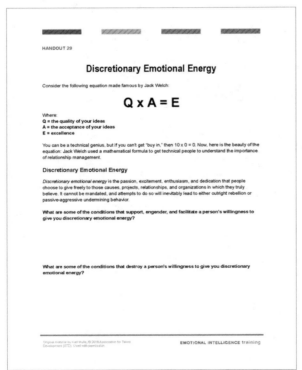

Handout 30: EQuip Yourself for Success: Map Your Personal Influence Network

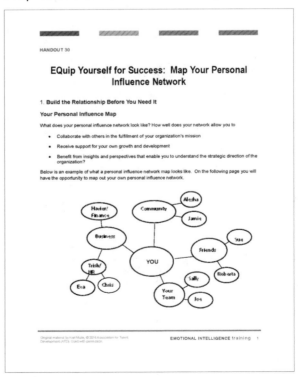

Handout 30: EQuip Yourself for Success: Map Your Personal Influence Network, *continued*

Handout 31: EQuip Yourself for Success: Evaluate Your Personal Influence Network

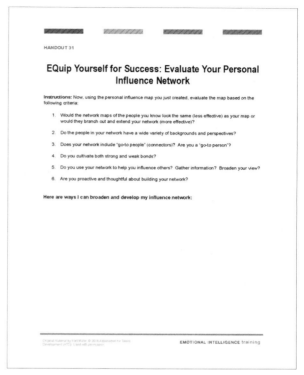

Handout 32: EQuip Yourself for Success: Practice Personality Talk

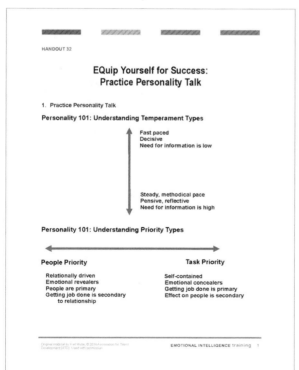

Handout 32: EQuip Yourself for Success: Practice Personality Talk, *continued*

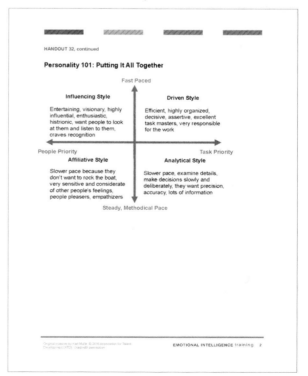

Handout 33: Develop the Competency of Teamwork

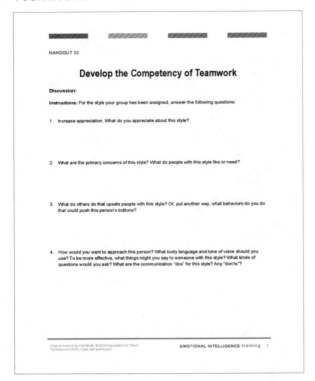

Handout 33: Develop the Competency of Teamwork, *continued*

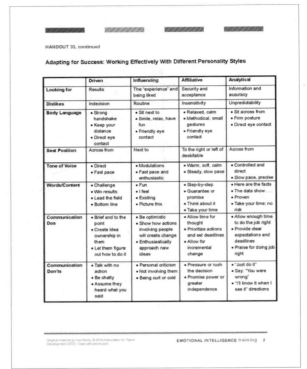

Handout 34: Teaming and Collaboration Action Plan

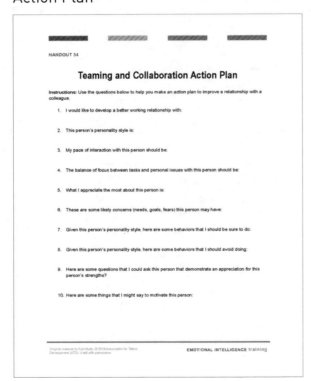

Handout 35: EQuip Yourself for Success: The Two Messages and Communication Rapport

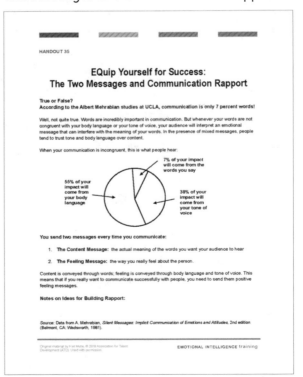

Handout 36: The Competency of Conflict Management

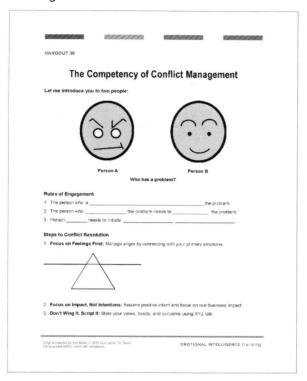

Handout 37: XYZ Talk

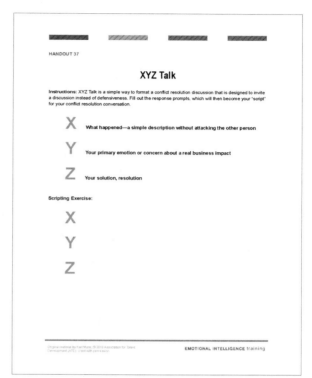

Handout 38: EQuip Yourself for Success: Action Plan

Handout 38: EQuip Yourself for Success: Action Plan, *continued*

HANDOUT 38, continued

What do I want to develop or improve?	Why is it important?
How will I do it?	**What values will motivate me to do it?**

Dates Applied	I did...	Discoveries

Original material by Karl Mulle, © 2016 Association for Talent Development (ATD). Used with permission.   EMOTIONAL INTELLIGENCE training   2

Handout 39: Two-Day Workshop Learning Objectives: The New Science of Leadership

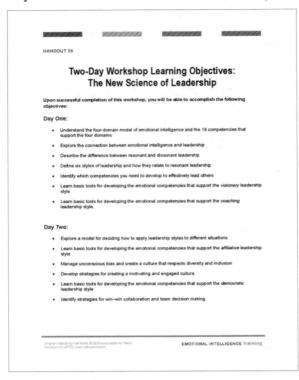

HANDOUT 39

Two-Day Workshop Learning Objectives: The New Science of Leadership

Upon successful completion of this workshop, you will be able to accomplish the following objectives:

Day One:

- Understand the four-domain model of emotional intelligence and the 18 competencies that support the four domains
- Explore the connection between emotional intelligence and leadership
- Describe the difference between resonant and dissonant leadership
- Define six styles of leadership and how they relate to resonant leadership
- Identify which competencies you need to develop to effectively lead others
- Learn basic tools for developing the emotional competencies that support the *visionary leadership* style
- Learn basic tools for developing the emotional competencies that support the *coaching* leadership style

Day Two:

- Explore a model for deciding how to apply leadership styles to different situations
- Learn basic tools for developing the emotional competencies that support the *affiliative leadership* style
- Manage unconscious bias and create a culture that respects diversity and inclusion
- Develop strategies for creating a motivating and engaged culture
- Learn basic tools for developing the emotional competencies that support the *democratic* leadership style
- Identify strategies for win–win collaboration and team decision making.

Original material by Karl Mulle, © 2016 Association for Talent Development (ATD). Used with permission. **EMOTIONAL INTELLIGENCE** training

---

Handout 40: The Anatomy of an Emotion

HANDOUT 40

The Anatomy of an Emotion

The Original Story of Your Emotions

Once upon a time you were walking in a forest and you came upon a big, bad bear.

And your eye saw the bear and immediately sent a message to the emotional centers of your brain circuitry, triggering an adrenalin reaction that prepared you for a fight or flight survival response.

Your response was actually an emotional response triggering your brain to move you toward taking action. That's essentially what all emotions are—signals to take action.

The Anatomy of an Emotion

Fight or flight is the classic case study of how emotions influence behavior. Humans are hardwired to respond to events and situations emotionally before we respond to those same events and situations rationally. We are programmed to feel events before we think about them. This emotionally-activated circuitry supports our survival and serves us well when we encounter severe threat or severe danger. It may also move us closer to actions that our brain interprets as being in support of our survival—finding a mate, bonding with other humans in community, taking part in activities that bring us joy, or resolving conflicts in the workplace.

Emotional Override and the Human Brain

Unfortunately, our emotional reaction system does not always serve us well. Sometimes we react autonomically to situations that are not threatening at all. Our behaviors become reactive instead of proactive:

- **Proactive behavior** is thoughtful, effortful, and conscious.
- **Reactive behavior** is automatic, non-effortful, and unconscious.

Original material by Karl Mulle, © 2016 Association for Talent Development (ATD). Used with permission. **EMOTIONAL INTELLIGENCE** training 1

Handout 40: The Anatomy of an Emotion, *continued*

HANDOUT 40, continued

Sometimes our emotional reactions take over when a better response would be a rational, effortful, intentional response. To understand our human potential to be undermined by our emotional responses, we need to get to know our brain a little better:

- **The Human Brain.** The neocortex is the part of our brain that controls rational thinking including the higher brain functions of awareness, reasoning, voluntary movement, conscious, intentional thought, and language skills. We call this part of the brain the human brain.

- **The Reptilian Brain.** The original story of our emotions introduces us to a more primal part of our brain. All vertebrate animals have a mass of cells situated at the top of their spinal cord comprising the brainstem. The cells of the brainstem coordinate most of our involuntary functions, such as blood circulation, and govern our most automatic instincts, such as fight or flight. Sometimes referred to as the reptilian brain, this primitive brain has the power to override the rational thinking functions of the neocortex and take control of our actions when it perceives a threat.

- **The Mammalian Brain.** Tucked in beneath the neocortex and wrapping around the brainstem in something of a horseshoe configuration is a series of structures comprising the limbic area of the brain. Our emotions originate here. The limbic area, sometimes called the mammalian brain, stores our emotionally linked memories. It is this area of the brain that triggers learned emotional responses to particular circumstances. The reference to mammals with regard to this part of our brain has to do with the learning capacity of the limbic system that is shared by all warm-blooded mammals. Over the course of our experiences in life, we each accumulate and store literally thousands of emotional memories in our mammalian brains. These memories comprise the total of our emotional experiences and serve as activation points for emotional responses whenever we encounter current situations that are reminiscent of these stored memories. In other words, our emotions are taking their cues from memories stored in our limbic systems and are triggering us to behave accordingly.

When Emotions Get the Best of Us

All of this means that our emotional brain has the power to influence our behaviors *before* our rational brain knows what is happening. When the part of our brain that is emotional *overrides* the part of our brain that is rational, it can result in inappropriate reactions that can sabotage our success. We find ourselves wishing that we had taken a moment to think about these emotions before responding. This capacity to think about emotions, to manage them, to choose an appropriate response, and to relate effectively with other emotional people is called *emotional intelligence.*

The New Science of Leadership

The tug-of-war that is being waged between our emotionally charged brain and our rational brain can have a profound impact on the success of our interpersonal relationships. We call the reactive side of the tug-of-war emotional *un-intelligence* because we are allowing our emotional impulses to manage our behaviors instead of using our rational intelligence to manage both our emotions and our behaviors. Indeed, if we are able to delay our emotional reactions long enough to mindfully and intentionally engage our rational brains, we will discover a new set of behavioral options that will help us avoid dysfunction, and manage the relationships of our lives in a more intelligent and effective way. We call this *proactive* side of the tug-of-war *emotional intelligence—the new science of leadership.*

Original material by Karl Mulle, © 2016 Association for Talent Development (ATD). Used with permission. **EMOTIONAL INTELLIGENCE** training 2

Handout 41: Emotional Intelligence Defined

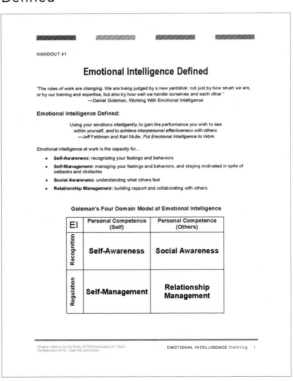

HANDOUT 41

Emotional Intelligence Defined

"The rules of work are changing. We are being judged by a new yardstick: not just by how smart we are, or by our training and expertise, but also by how well we handle ourselves and each other."
—Daniel Goleman, Working With Emotional Intelligence

Emotional Intelligence Defined:

Using your emotions *intelligently,* to gain the performance you wish to see within yourself, *and to achieve interpersonal effectiveness with others.*
—Jeff Feldman and Karl Mulle, *Put Emotional Intelligence to Work*

Emotional intelligence at work is the capacity for...

- **Self-Awareness:** recognizing your feelings and behaviors
- **Self-Management:** managing your feelings and behaviors, and staying motivated in spite of setbacks and obstacles
- **Social Awareness:** understanding what others feel
- **Relationship Management:** building rapport and collaborating with others.

Goleman's Four Domain Model of Emotional Intelligence

EI	Personal Competence (Self)	Personal Competence (Others)
Recognition	Self-Awareness	Social Awareness
Regulation	Self-Management	Relationship Management

Original material by Karl Mulle, © 2016 Association for Talent Development (ATD). Used with permission. **EMOTIONAL INTELLIGENCE** training 1

EMOTIONAL INTELLIGENCE training

Handout 41: Emotional Intelligence Defined, *continued*

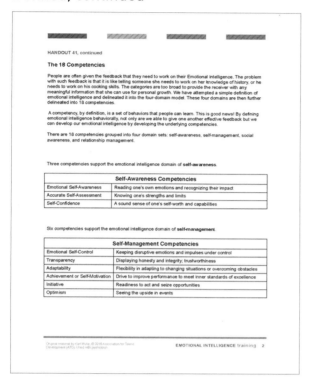

Handout 41: Emotional Intelligence Defined, *continued*

Handout 42: Emotional Intelligence and Leadership

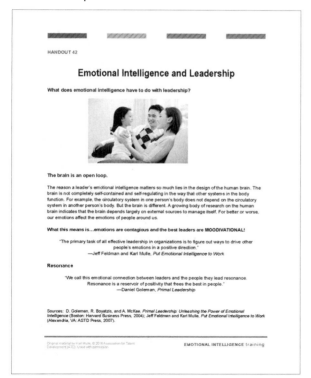

Handout 43: Resonant vs. Dissonant Leadership

Handout 44: Goleman's Six Styles of Leadership

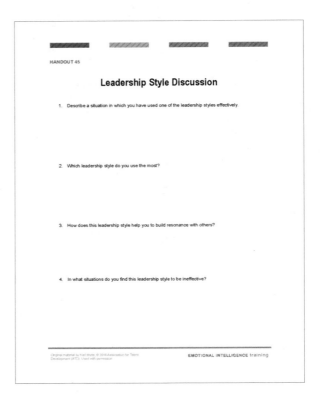

HANDOUT 44

Goleman's Six Styles of Leadership

Style and Supporting Competencies	How It Builds Resonance	Impact on Climate	When Appropriate
Visionary Inspirational leadership, self-confidence, self-awareness, empathy, change catalyst, transparency	Moves people toward shared dreams	Most strongly positive	When changes require a new vision, or when a clear direction is needed
Coaching Developing others, emotional self-awareness, empathy	Connects what a person wants with the organization's goals	Highly positive	To help an employee improve performance by building long-term capabilities
Affiliative Teamwork and collaboration, empathy	Creates harmony by connecting people to each other	Positive	To heal rifts in a team, motivate during stressful times, or strengthen connections
Democratic Teamwork and collaboration, conflict management, influence, empathy	Values people's input and gets commitment through participation	Positive	To build buy-in or consensus, or get valuable input from employees
Pacesetting* Achievement, initiative	Meets challenging and exciting goals	Because too frequently poorly executed, often highly negative	To get high-quality results from a motivated and competent team
Commanding* Influence, achievement, initiative	Soothes fears by giving clear direction in an emergency	Because so often misused, highly negative	In a crisis, to kick-start a turnaround, or with problem employees

*Pacesetting and command both lack empathy.

Source: D. Goleman, R. Boyatzis, and A. McKee, *Primal Leadership: Realizing the Power of Emotional Intelligence* (Boston: Harvard Business Press, 2002).

Original material by Karl Mulle, © 2016 Association for Talent Development (ATD). Used with permission.

EMOTIONAL INTELLIGENCE training

Handout 45: Leadership Style Discussion

HANDOUT 45

Leadership Style Discussion

1. Describe a situation in which you have used one of the leadership styles effectively.

2. Which leadership style do you use the most?

3. How does this leadership style help you to build resonance with others?

4. In what situations do you find this leadership style to be ineffective?

Original material by Karl Mulle, © 2016 Association for Talent Development (ATD). Used with permission.

EMOTIONAL INTELLIGENCE training

Handout 46: Leadership Style Action Plan

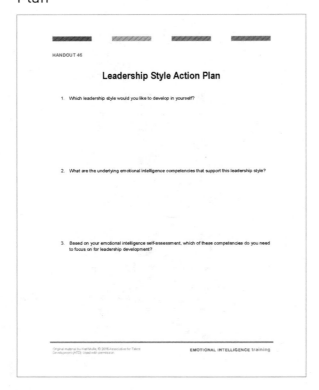

HANDOUT 46

Leadership Style Action Plan

1. Which leadership style would you like to develop in yourself?

2. What are the underlying emotional intelligence competencies that support this leadership style?

3. Based on your emotional intelligence self-assessment, which of these competencies do you need to focus on for leadership development?

Original material by Karl Mulle, © 2016 Association for Talent Development (ATD). Used with permission.

EMOTIONAL INTELLIGENCE training

Handout 47: Empathy Discussion

HANDOUT 47

Empathy Discussion

Instructions: Think of a time when someone showed you great empathy, and then answer the questions that follow.

What specifically did they do?

How did their expression of empathy affect you?

Original material by Karl Mulle, © 2016 Association for Talent Development (ATD). Used with permission.

EMOTIONAL INTELLIGENCE training

Handout 48: The Johari Window

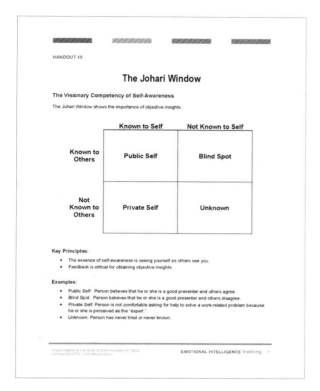

Handout 48: The Johari Window, *continued*

HANDOUT 48, continued

Private-Self Issues:

- If you are competent in some area, why don't others see it?
- Is there a cost to you and others for maintaining private-self characteristics?
- If you were to demonstrate this competency so that others could see it, how would you do this?

Blind Spot Issues:

- Do other people see you differently than you see yourself?
- Are you open to feedback about that?

Key Question: What is the value of increasing the public self?

Handout 49: Managing Defensiveness Journaling Exercise

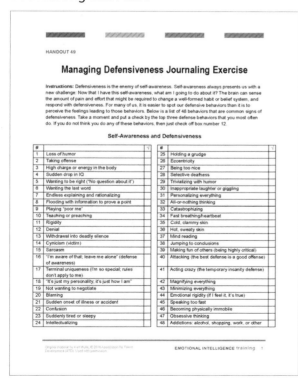

Handout 49: Managing Defensiveness Journaling Exercise, *continued*

HANDOUT 49, continued

Managing Defensiveness

Successfully reducing your defensiveness involves increasing your self-awareness of your own defensive behaviors and then managing those behaviors. Your top three signs of defensiveness are now your personal early warning system that you are becoming fearful or protective of something and are beginning to get defensive. This defensiveness will ultimately hinder your effectiveness in knowing who you are, having clarity, and therefore developing the visionary style. Here are strategies that can help you manage these defensive responses.

1. **Take Responsibility:** Acknowledge that you are becoming defensive and that you have a responsibility to maintain a collaborative spirit and intention when working with others.

2. **Slow Down:** Relax, take a deep breath, slow down physically, take a short walk, go to the restroom, splash some water on your face, take a time out, reschedule the rest of the meeting, and so on. Do whatever is necessary to center yourself.

3. **Confront Your Negative Self-Talk and Assumptions:** Change any negative self-talk into a more supportive frame of mind.

4. **Go to the Balcony:** This is a negotiation technique that implies psychologically removing yourself from the scene of your physical reality and seeing yourself as if looking down from a balcony over a stage. From this vantage point, you are able to be a momentary observer of what is happening both around you and within you. A few quick questions can help you connect, tune in, and choose appropriate action: What's the situation down there? What am I feeling about that situation? What is important to me? How are my feelings supporting or getting in the way of what I want in this situation?

5. **Increase Your Appreciation:** While you are on the balcony, try to increase your appreciation of the people you need to work with. What are their strengths? What is important to them? How are they feeling about this situation?

6. **Start Over and Choose a Non-defensive Response.**

Journaling Exercise

Instructions: Take a moment to journal any intentions you might have about managing your defensive behaviors.

Handout 50: Visionary Style and the Competency of Self-Awareness

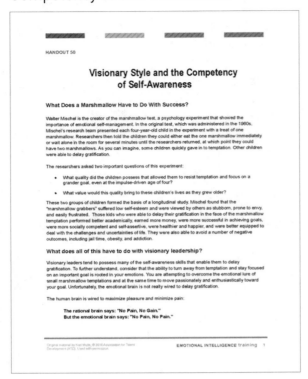

Visionary Style and the Competency of Self-Awareness

What Does a Marshmallow Have to Do With Success?

Walter Mischel is the creator of the marshmallow test, a psychology experiment that showed the importance of emotional self-management. In the original test, which was administered in the 1960s, Mischel's research team presented each four-year-old child in the experiment with a treat of one marshmallow. Researchers then told the children they could either eat the one marshmallow immediately or wait alone in the room for several minutes until the researchers returned, at which point they could have two marshmallows. As you can imagine, some children quickly gave in to temptation. Other children were able to delay gratification.

The researchers asked two important questions of this experiment:

- What quality did the children possess that allowed them to resist temptation and focus on a grander goal, even at the impulse-driven age of four?
- What value would this quality bring to these children's lives as they grew older?

These two groups of children formed the basis of a longitudinal study. Mischel found that the "marshmallow grabbers" suffered low self-esteem and were viewed by others as stubborn, prone to envy, and easily frustrated. Those kids who were able to delay their gratification in the face of the marshmallow temptation performed better academically, earned more money, were more successful in achieving goals, were more socially competent and self-assertive, were healthier and happier, and were better equipped to deal with the challenges and uncertainties of life. They were also able to avoid a number of negative outcomes, including jail time, obesity, and addiction.

What does all of this have to do with visionary leadership?

Visionary leaders tend to possess many of the self-awareness skills that enable them to delay gratification. To further understand, consider that the ability to turn away from temptation and stay focused on an important goal is rooted in your emotions. You are attempting to overcome the emotional lure of small marshmallow temptations and at the same time to move passionately and enthusiastically toward your goal. Unfortunately, the emotional brain is not really wired to delay gratification.

The human brain is wired to maximize pleasure and minimize pain:

The rational brain says: "No Pain, No Gain."
But the emotional brain says: "No Pain, No Pain."

Handout 50: Visionary Style and the Competency of Self-Awareness, *continued*

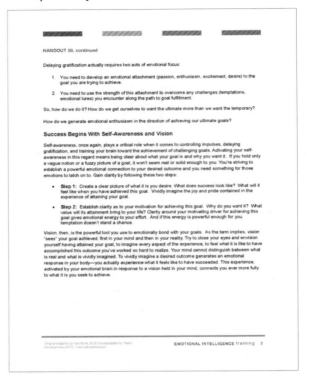

Delaying gratification actually requires two acts of emotional focus:

1. You need to develop an emotional attachment (passion, enthusiasm, excitement, desire) to the goal you are trying to achieve.

2. You need to use the strength of this attachment to overcome any challenges (temptations, emotional lures) you encounter along the path to goal fulfillment.

So, how do we do it? How do we get ourselves to want the ultimate more than we want the temporary?

How do we generate emotional enthusiasm in the direction of achieving our ultimate goals?

Success Begins With Self-Awareness and Vision

Self-awareness, once again, plays a critical role when it comes to controlling impulses, delaying gratification, and training your brain toward the achievement of challenging goals. Activating your self-awareness in this regard means being clear about what your goal is and why you want it. If you hold only a vague notion or a fuzzy picture of a goal, it won't seem real or solid enough to you. You're striving to establish a powerful emotional connection to your desired outcome and you need something for those emotions to latch on to. Gain clarity by following these two steps:

- **Step 1:** Create a clear picture of what it is you desire. What does success look like? What will it feel like when you have achieved this goal. Vividly imagine the joy and pride contained in the experience of attaining your goal.

- **Step 2:** Establish clarity as to your motivation for achieving this goal. Why do you want it? What value will its attainment bring to your life? Clarity around your motivating driver for achieving this goal gives emotional energy to your effort. And if this energy is powerful enough for you, temptation doesn't stand a chance.

Vision, then, is the powerful tool you use to emotionally bond with your goals. As the term implies, vision "sees" your goal achieved, first in your mind and then in your reality. Try to close your eyes and envision yourself having attained your goal, to imagine every aspect of the experience, to feel what it is like to have accomplished this outcome you've worked so hard to realize. Your mind cannot distinguish between what is real and what is vividly imagined. To vividly imagine a desired outcome generates an emotional response in your body—you actually experience what it feels like to have succeeded. This experience, activated by your emotional brain in response to a vision held in your mind, connects you ever more fully to what it is you seek to achieve.

Handout 50: Visionary Style and the Competency of Self-Awareness, *continued*

Introducing Your Reticular Activating System

Critical to your success is fixing your attention on the things you really want to achieve, not on the obstacles and temptations that you are trying to avoid. As great golfers say...

Never look where you don't want to go.

There is an important scientific reason why vision works. Have you ever purchased a car, driven off of the car lot, down the highway, and then suddenly started noticing other cars that are the same as the car you just purchased? Why does your brain notice the brand you purchased, and even the color, and ignore the billions of other data points that are just as easily available for observation? Your brain is noticing because of a filter system in your brain called the reticular activating system, which is the part of your brain that takes in external stimuli and decides where to focus your attention.

How does your reticular activating system decide?

The filter system works on the basis of want and don't want. In other words, your clarity around what you want or what you don't want programs your filter system to see opportunities that align with what you hope to attract and what you hope to avoid. Unfortunately, many people are clearer about what they don't want than they are about what they want. Their attention is focused in the wrong direction. This is where self-awareness and clarifying what you want plays a critical role.

Source: W. Mischel, The Marshmallow Test: Mastering Self-Control (New York: Little, Brown, 2014).

Handout 51: Keep Your Eye on the Grand Marshmallow

Keep Your Eye on the Grand Marshmallow

What Are Your Grand Marshmallow Goals?

You have goals you're striving to attain. You're working hard for a promotion or perhaps to finish law school. You're saving for your dream house or putting money away for retirement. You're sweating to shed a few pounds or putting miles underfoot as you work up to running a marathon. To stick with the marshmallow metaphor, you might call such goals your Grand Marshmallow Goals. You can imagine how it will feel to realize your goals, how these achievements will benefit your life. You can imagine how wonderful it will be to take a big puffy bite out of the Grand Marshmallow.

Whatever achievements you seek to realize, however, there are temptations along the way that try to lure you off the path. Distractions, diversions, and doubts are the small marshmallows you must resist in pursuit of your Grand Marshmallow. The small marshmallows certainly taste good, and it is tempting to eat just one or two. But deep inside, you know that the satisfaction they would bring would be fleeting and that giving in to these small marshmallow temptations ultimately undermines the pursuit of your grander goal.

Keep Your Eye on the Grand Marshmallow

1. What is a two-marshmallow goal in your life? Create a clear picture of what it is you desire.

2. What is your motivation for achieving this goal? Why do you want it? What value will its attainment bring to your life?

Handout 52: Visionary Style and the Competency of Self-Confidence

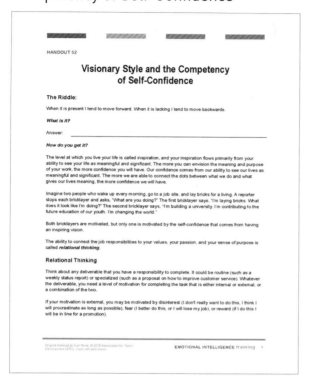

Handout 52: Visionary Style and the Competency of Self-Confidence, *continued*

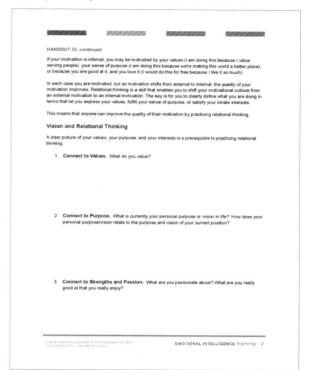

Handout 53: Vision, Self-Confidence, and Employee Engagement

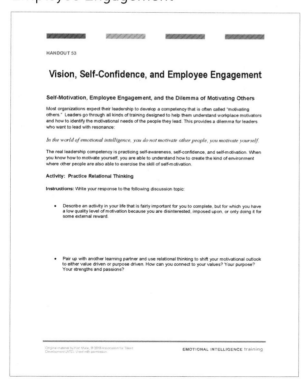

Handout 54: Visionary Style and the Competency of Change Catalyst

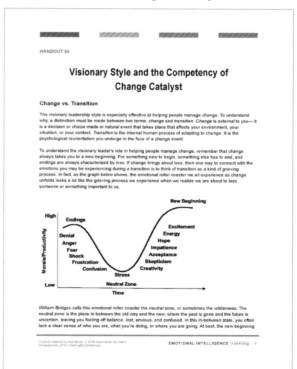

Handout 54: Visionary Style and the Competency of Change Catalyst, *continued*

may seem like a shining beacon in the far off distance, but the darkness of the neutral zone makes it impossible for you to really know what the "new way" is going to be like until you arrive at its threshold. Given these realities, one can see why the visionary style of leadership is so effective.

The Visionary Style and Leading Change

Leading change is a true relationship management issue. If navigating change individually is difficult, you can only imagine the challenge associated with guiding others through the uncertainty of change and its associated transitional journey. We have sometimes described it as akin to the process of herding cats.

In the workplace, the process of change and transition often creates a human drama with the players acting out two different roles. One role is enacted by those who are initiating or driving the change. These initiators of change are often perceived as being seated at the higher levels of authority within the organization. It has been said that organizations are great at creating change but bad at managing transition. This is because when those in authority initiate change, they often expect growth to be linear, moving from high productivity to even higher productivity as demonstrated on the graph above.

This expectation fails to take into account the other role in the human drama—those driven by the change into transition. Those in this role are expected to be good followers of change, good transitioners if you will, but they often feel victim to decisions made from on high. People do not resist change, they resist *being changed*. Those who wish to lead change will quickly learn that it is not easy to drive others into transition. More realistically, productivity and even morale often hit a low point before moving up the learning curve to that place where performance and morale exceeds the conditions that were in place before change was initiated.

During times of change and transition, visionary leaders understand both the depths and the heights of performance, morale, and productivity, so they are uniquely positioned to guide others.

Think About This . . .

- Consider a change you have experienced in your life. Choose something significant, something dramatic, or perhaps something even traumatic. Reflect on your journey through that change.
- What event or decision brought the change about?
- What did you have to let go of or allow to come to an end in order to move forward?
- How long did the journey take before you arrived at some new sense of a new beginning?
- What was it like when you were in the middle, having let go of the old but not yet arrived at the new?
- What emotions did you experience along the way and how did your emotional intelligence come into play?

Original material by Karl Mulle, © 2016 Association for Talent Development (ATD). Used with permission. EMOTIONAL INTELLIGENCE training 2

Handout 55: Visionary Style and Managing Transition

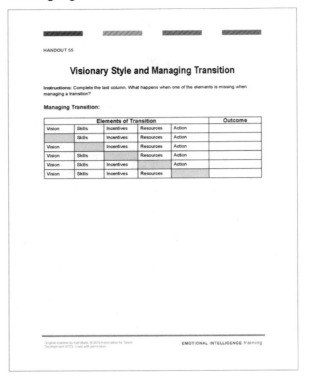

Visionary Style and Managing Transition

Instructions: Complete the last column. What happens when one of the elements is missing when managing a transition?

Managing Transition:

Elements of Transition					Outcome
Vision	Skills	Incentives	Resources	Action	
	Skills	Incentives	Resources	Action	
Vision		Incentives	Resources	Action	
Vision	Skills		Resources	Action	
Vision	Skills	Incentives		Action	
Vision	Skills	Incentives	Resources		

Original material by Karl Mulle, © 2016 Association for Talent Development (ATD). Used with permission. EMOTIONAL INTELLIGENCE training

Handout 56: The Competency of Inspirational Leadership

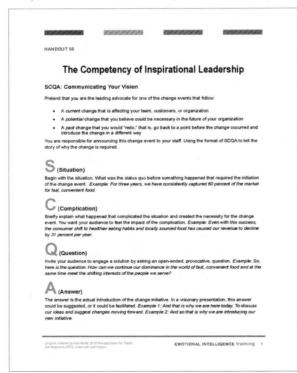

The Competency of Inspirational Leadership

SCQA: Communicating Your Vision

Pretend that you are the leading advocate for one of the change events that follow:

- A *current* change that is affecting your team, customers, or organization
- A *potential* change that you believe could be necessary in the future of your organization
- A *past* change that you would "redo," that is, go back to a point before the change occurred and introduce the change in a different way

You are responsible for announcing this change event to your staff. Using the format of SCQA to tell the story of why the change is required.

S (Situation)

Begin with the situation. What was the status quo before something happened that required the initiation of the change event. *Example: For three years, we have consistently captured 60 percent of the market for fast, convenient food.*

C (Complication)

Briefly explain what happened that complicated the situation and created the necessity for the change event. You want your audience to feel the impact of the complication. *Example: Even with this success, the consumer shift to healthier eating habits and locally sourced food has caused our revenue to decline by 31 percent per year.*

Q (Question)

Invite your audience to engage a solution by asking an open-ended, provocative, question. *Example: So, here is the question: How can we continue our dominance in the world of fast, convenient food and at the same time meet the shifting interests of the people we serve?*

A (Answer)

The answer is the actual introduction of the change initiative. In a visionary presentation, this answer could be suggested, or it could be facilitated. *Example 1: And that is why we are here today. To discuss our ideas and suggest changes moving forward. Example 2: And so that is why we are introducing our new initiative.*

Original material by Karl Mulle, © 2016 Association for Talent Development (ATD). Used with permission. EMOTIONAL INTELLIGENCE training 1

Handout 56: The Competency of Inspirational Leadership, *continued*

Activity: How to Tell a Good Story

Instructions: Now it's your turn to practice using the SCQA model to prepare a 2-minute presentation that communicates vision. Pick any simple topic that requires a change initiative.

S (Situation)

C (Complication)

Q (Question)

A (Answer)

Original material by Karl Mulle, © 2016 Association for Talent Development (ATD). Used with permission. EMOTIONAL INTELLIGENCE training 2

EMOTIONAL INTELLIGENCE training

Handout 57: The Fine Art of Asking Great Questions

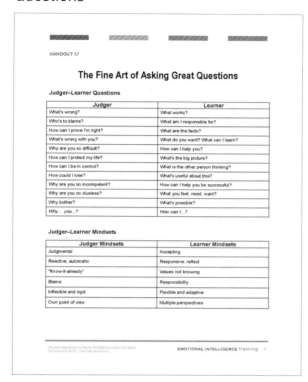

Handout 57: The Fine Art of Asking Great Questions, *continued*

Handout 58: GROW Coaching Model Questions

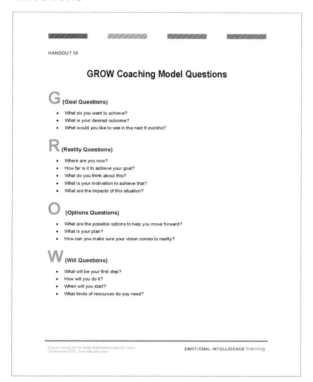

Handout 59: The Plus–Delta Model Questions

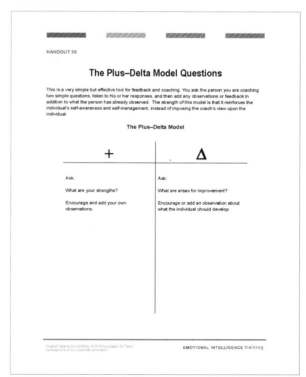

Handout 60: Coaching Dialogue Job Aid

Coaching Dialogue Job Aid

What Is a Coaching Dialogue?

A coaching dialogue is a problem solving and leadership development process that involves a small group working on real problems, taking action, and learning as individuals and as a team while doing so.

The Components of the Coaching Dialogue

- Project, challenge, task, or problem
- Group of 4-8 people with diverse perspectives
- Reflective questioning and listening
- Developing strategies and taking action
- Commitment to learning
- Facilitator

The Questioning/Problem Identifying Phase

1. One person briefly shares a problem or challenge (2-3 minutes).
2. Group members start asking questions.
3. Try to ask open-ended questions.
4. Answer yes/no questions with yes/no answers.
5. Keep all other answers as succinct as possible.
6. Statements allowed only in response to questions.
7. No solutions and no solutions couched as questions allowed: "Have you tried…?"
8. Really listen and respect the perceptions of others.
9. Build on each other's questions.
10. Draw others into the conversation.
11. Gain agreement on the problem.

Remember: The goal of this phase is to problem identify, not problem solve.

Handout 60: Coaching Dialogue Job Aid, *continued*

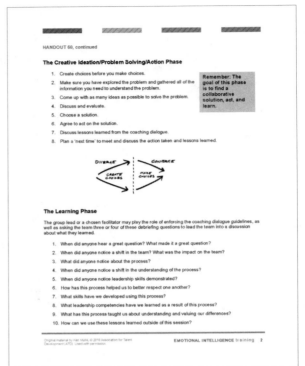

The Creative Ideation/Problem Solving/Action Phase

1. Create choices before you make choices.
2. Make sure you have explored the problem and gathered all of the information you need to understand the problem.
3. Come up with as many ideas as possible to solve the problem.
4. Discuss and evaluate.
5. Choose a solution.
6. Agree to act on the solution.
7. Discuss lessons learned from the coaching dialogue.
8. Plan a 'next time' to meet and discuss the action taken and lessons learned.

Remember: The goal of this phase is to find a collaborative solution, act, and learn.

The Learning Phase

The group lead or a chosen facilitator may play the role of enforcing the coaching dialogue guidelines, as well as asking the team three or four of these debriefing questions to lead the team into a discussion about what they learned.

1. When did anyone hear a great question? What made it a great question?
2. When did anyone notice a shift in the team? What was the impact on the team?
3. What did anyone notice about the process?
4. When did anyone notice a shift in the understanding of the process?
5. When did anyone notice leadership skills demonstrated?
6. How has this process helped us to better respect one another?
7. What skills have we developed using this process?
8. What leadership competencies have we learned as a result of this process?
9. What has this process taught us about understanding and valuing our differences?
10. How can we use these lessons learned outside of this session?

Handout 60: Coaching Dialogue Job Aid, *continued*

Problem Presenter

- Take 2-3 minutes to highlight the key elements of the problem:
  - Situation
  - Complication
  - Why is this issue important and urgent?
  - What do I want to get from this session?
- Answer the questions asked of you as concisely as you can: yes/no answers for yes/no questions
- Don't answer questions that you don't have the answer for ("I don't know") or which you have not yet formed an opinion ("I need to think about that question," or "I'm not sure")

Team Members

- Seek to gain a group-agreed understanding of the problem by asking questions
- Make statements only in response to questions directed specifically to you or to the group as a whole
- Feel free to ask questions of other group members as well
- Try to build on each other's questions rather than just on getting your questions answered

Facilitator

- Focus more on helping the group learn and improve and less on helping to solve the problem
- Provide instructions to the team about the process, ground rules, timing, etc.
- Only ask questions when intervening
- Maintain the attitude that learning and task are equally important
- Ensure objectivity and fairness
- Show confidence in the group

Handout 61: The Competency of Developing Others

The Competency of Developing Others

Discussion

1. Think of the best coaches you have ever partnered with. What was the essence of what they brought to your life?
2. Reflect on yourself as a coach to others, what word or phrase would you use to describe how you see yourself in this role?
3. Which coaching skill below do you feel you most need to improve?

- ☐ Setting clear expectations, goals, and accountabilities
- ☐ Clearly stating topic and positive intentions
- ☐ Confronting what needs to be confronted
- ☐ Sharing constructive, redirecting feedback
- ☐ Firming up action commitments and follow-through

Handout 62: Coaching Culture

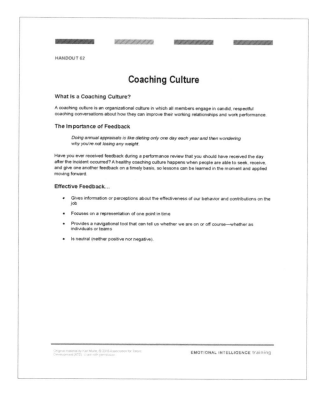

HANDOUT 62

Coaching Culture

What Is a Coaching Culture?

A coaching culture is an organizational culture in which all members engage in candid, respectful coaching conversations about how they can improve their working relationships and work performance.

The Importance of Feedback

Doing annual appraisals is like dieting only one day each year and then wondering why you're not losing any weight.

Have you ever received feedback during a performance review that you should have received the day after the incident occurred? A healthy coaching culture happens when people are able to seek, receive, and give one another feedback on a timely basis, so lessons can be learned in the moment and applied moving forward.

Effective Feedback...

- Gives information or perceptions about the effectiveness of our behavior and contributions on the job
- Focuses on a representation of one point in time
- Provides a navigational tool that can tell us whether we are on or off course—whether as individuals or teams
- Is neutral (neither positive nor negative).

EMOTIONAL INTELLIGENCE training

Handout 63: Two Types of Feedback

HANDOUT 63

Two Types of Feedback

There are two types of feedback:

- **Reinforcing Feedback:** Tells you what you are doing well and what you need to continue to do.
- **Redirecting Feedback:** Reveals behaviors that need to change or areas where you need more development.

Each type has its place in a coaching conversation, but reinforcing feedback is almost always more readily and accurately received by the recipient.

Redirecting feedback, by contrast, often meets resistance. If it is to be accepted, it is likely to be under these very specific conditions:

- It comes from a credible source.
- It is objective rather than subjective.
- It is specific rather than vague.
- It is descriptive rather than judgmental.
- It focuses on impact rather than intent.
- It is supported by hard data and specific examples.
- It concerns behaviors that are controllable by the recipient.
- It is job related.

EMOTIONAL INTELLIGENCE training

Handout 64: Guidelines for Effective Feedback

HANDOUT 64

Guidelines for Effective Feedback

Here are guidelines for effective feedback that you can use during your coaching dialogues:

- **Specific vs. General.** Focus on specific behaviors.

  Feedback is more readily accepted and valued when it is specific rather than general. Specific feedback tells the recipient why you are being critical or complimentary.

- **Descriptive vs. Evaluative.** Keep it impersonal.

  Remember, feedback should be descriptive, not judgmental or evaluative. Feedback should also be job related. When a people feel attacked or threatened, they stop listening and move to a defensive position.

- **Needs of the Receiver vs. Needs of the Sender.** Keep it goal oriented.

  Why are you providing feedback to someone? Hopefully, it's not just to dump or unload on someone, or to get something off your chest. The purpose of feedback is to improve performance or provide constructive information. Ask yourself whom the feedback is supposed to help. How is your feedback directed toward the goals of the recipient?

- **Timely vs. Out of Context.** Make it well timed.

  Feedback is most meaningful when there is a short time between the behavior and the receipt of feedback concerning the behavior. Delays in feedback lessen the likelihood that the feedback will be effective in bringing about the desired change.

- **Ensure understanding.**

  If feedback is to be effective, you must ensure that the recipient understands what you are saying. Use paraphrasing and clarification techniques to see if the recipient fully understands your feedback.

- **Applicable vs. Useless.**

  If redirecting, make sure the behavior is controllable by the recipient. Feedback loses its value when recipients receive redirecting feedback concerning behavior beyond their control. If recipients have no control over the behavior, it is pointless to criticize their behavior because there is nothing they can do to correct it.

EMOTIONAL INTELLIGENCE training   1

Handout 64: Guidelines for Effective Feedback, *continued*

HANDOUT 64, continued

The Situation Behavior Impact Model (SBI)

Situation	Provide the context and frequency of behavior.
Behavior	Describe the actual behavior that you see someone doing or not doing, without labeling or accusing.
Impact	Explain the impact of the behavior on you, the team, morale, productivity, the individual's career goals, and so on.

Keep in mind these helpful tips when coaching:

- **Explain what you think would be helpful.** This can be a recommendation, a request, or a requirement, depending on the nature of the relationship and the behavior.
- **Involve the receiver:** Listen, ask questions, brainstorm, and keep an open mind.
- **Agree on follow-up:** Both parties need to agree on monitoring, measuring progress, and follow-up.

EMOTIONAL INTELLIGENCE training   2

Handout 65: SBI Practice

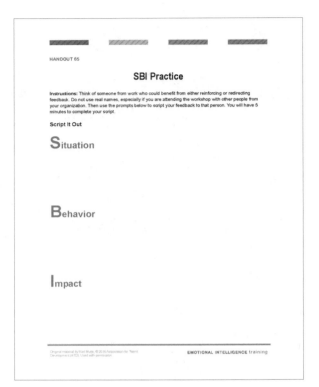

HANDOUT 65

SBI Practice

Instructions: Think of someone from work who could benefit from either reinforcing or redirecting feedback. Do not use real names, especially if you are attending the workshop with other people from your organization. Then use the prompts below to script your feedback to that person. You will have 5 minutes to complete your script.

Script It Out

Situation

Behavior

Impact

Original material by Karl Mulle, © 2016 Association for Talent Development (ATD). Used with permission.   EMOTIONAL INTELLIGENCE training

Handout 66: Coaching Action Plan

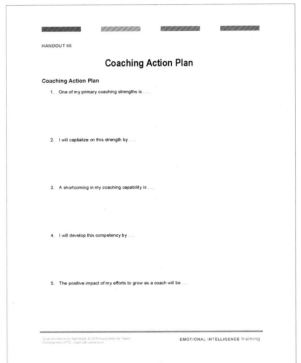

HANDOUT 66

Coaching Action Plan

Coaching Action Plan

1. One of my primary coaching strengths is . . .

2. I will capitalize on this strength by . . .

3. A shortcoming in my coaching capability is . . .

4. I will develop this competency by . . .

5. The positive impact of my efforts to grow as a coach will be . . .

Original material by Karl Mulle, © 2016 Association for Talent Development (ATD). Used with permission.   EMOTIONAL INTELLIGENCE training

Handout 67: Learning Objectives: Day Two

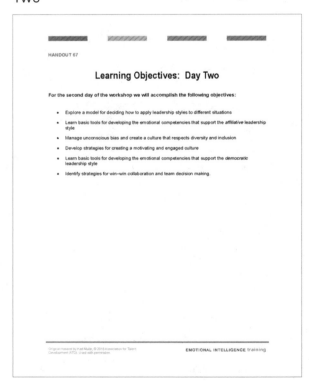

HANDOUT 67

Learning Objectives: Day Two

For the second day of the workshop we will accomplish the following objectives:

- Explore a model for deciding how to apply leadership styles to different situations
- Learn basic tools for developing the emotional competencies that support the *affiliative leadership* style
- Manage unconscious bias and create a culture that respects diversity and inclusion
- Develop strategies for creating a motivating and engaged culture
- Learn basic tools for developing the emotional competencies that support the *democratic* leadership style
- Identify strategies for win–win collaboration and team decision making.

Original material by Karl Mulle, © 2016 Association for Talent Development (ATD). Used with permission.   EMOTIONAL INTELLIGENCE training

Handout 68: Situational Leadership

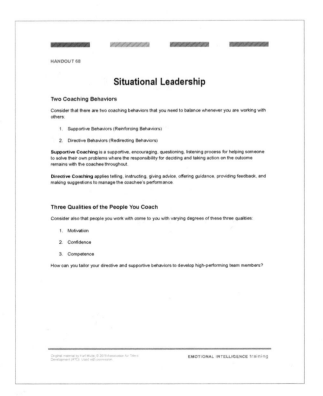

HANDOUT 68

Situational Leadership

Two Coaching Behaviors

Consider that there are two coaching behaviors that you need to balance whenever you are working with others.

1. Supportive Behaviors (Reinforcing Behaviors)

2. Directive Behaviors (Redirecting Behaviors)

Supportive Coaching is a supportive, encouraging, questioning, listening process for helping someone to solve their own problems where the responsibility for deciding and taking action on the outcome remains with the coachee throughout.

Directive Coaching applies telling, instructing, giving advice, offering guidance, providing feedback, and making suggestions to manage the coachee's performance.

Three Qualities of the People You Coach

Consider also that people you work with come to you with varying degrees of these three qualities:

1. Motivation

2. Confidence

3. Competence

How can you tailor your directive and supportive behaviors to develop high-performing team members?

Original material by Karl Mulle, © 2016 Association for Talent Development (ATD). Used with permission.   EMOTIONAL INTELLIGENCE training

Handout 69: A Meta-Model for Working Effectively With Others

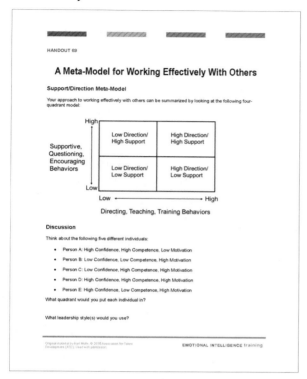

Handout 70: The Competency of Teamwork and Collaboration

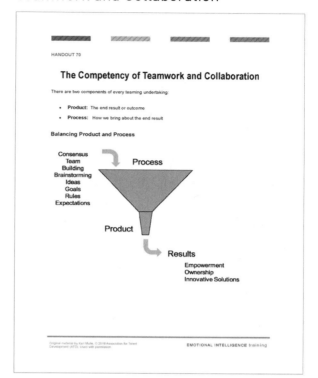

Handout 71: EQuip Yourself for Success: The Elements of Team Process

Handout 72: Affiliative Style and the Sense of Belonging

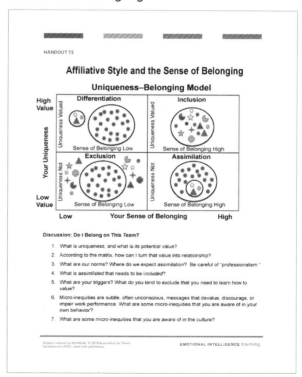

Handout 73: EQuip Yourself for Success: Tips for Creating an Inclusive Culture

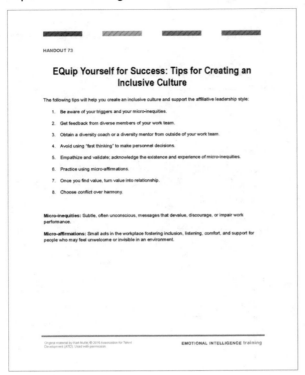

Handout 74: Affiliative Style and Aligning Strengths

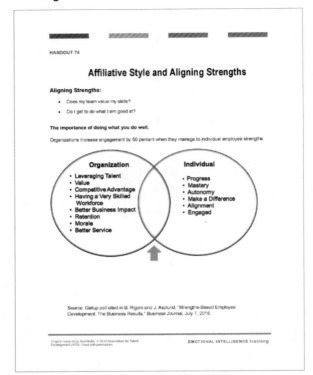

Handout 75: Affiliative Style and Motivation 3.0

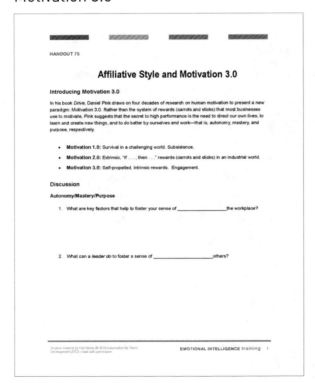

Handout 75: Affiliative Style and Motivation 3.0, *continued*

HANDOUT 75, continued

The Big Idea

Engagement and motivation are internally activated whenever your emotional needs for autonomy, mastery, and purpose are met.

This means that you can motivate yourself in any given situation by intentionally, mindfully choosing (autonomy) to connect your values, your competence, and your sense of noble purpose (mastery and purpose) to the requirements of situation.

Remember the visionary leadership style and relational thinking? This is the same thing. Once you discover that motivation is actually a skill, you can combine your visionary and affiliative styles and teach it to others.

This is good news for leaders who have a responsibility of motivating their teams. You do not actually motivate people, as much as you help people get their emotional needs met. People become optimally motivated when they discover how to fulfill their core emotional needs for autonomy, mastery, and purpose.

Source: D. H. Pink, *Drive: The Surprising Truth About What Motivates Us* (New York: Riverhead, 2011).

Handout 76: Using Employment Engagement Surveys

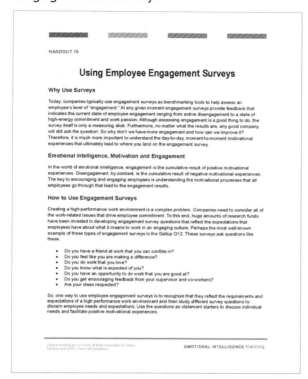

Handout 77: Democratic Style and the Competency of Influence

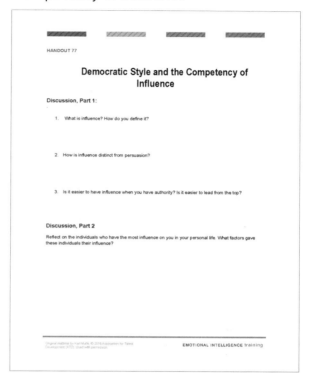

Handout 78: The Six Principles of Influence

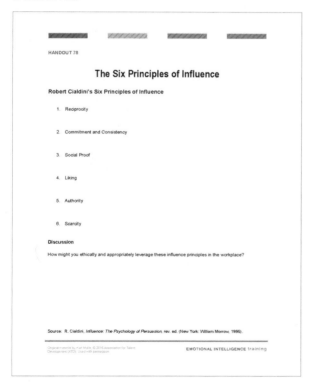

Handout 79: Democratic Style and the Competency of Conflict Management

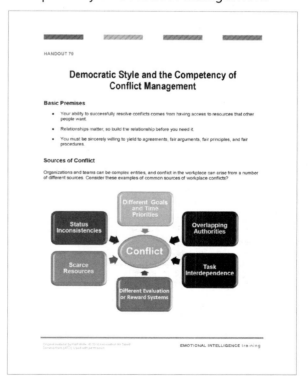

Handout 80: Examples of Conflict Worksheet

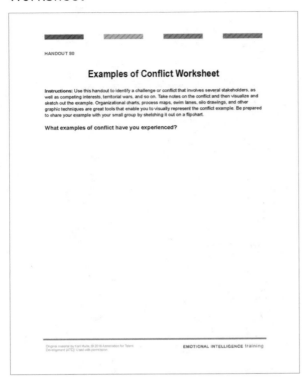

Handout 81: EQuip Yourself for Success: Four Steps of Conflict Management

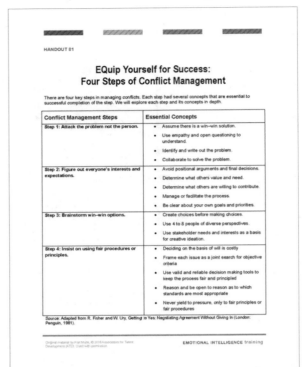

Handout 82: Step 1: Attack the Problem, Not the Person

Handout 83: Collaborate to Solve the Problem

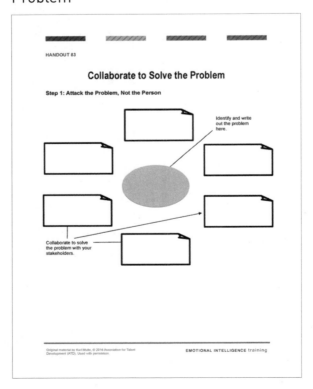

Handout 84: Step 2: Figure Out Everyone's Interests and Expectations

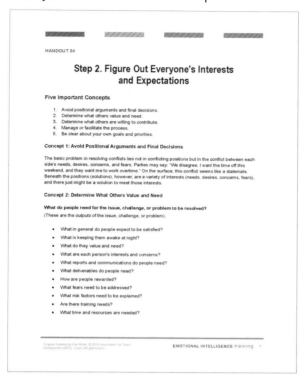

Handout 84: Step 2: Figure Out Everyone's Interests and Expectations, *continued*

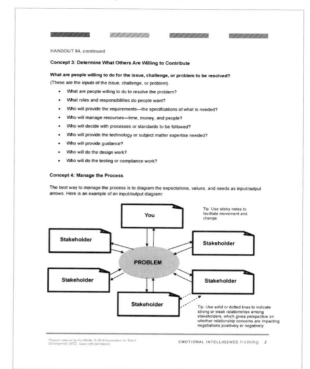

Handout 84: Step 2: Figure Out Everyone's Interests and Expectations, *continued*

Handout 85: Know Your BATNA

Handout 86: Step 3: Brainstorm Win–Win Options

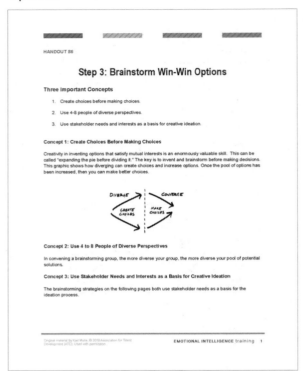

Handout 86: Step 3: Brainstorm Win–Win Options, *continued*

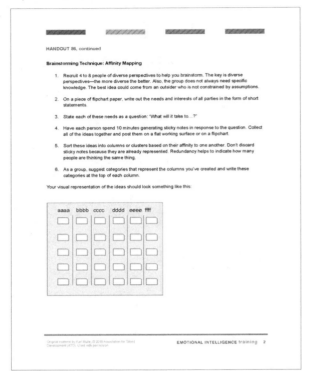

Handout 86: Step 3: Brainstorm Win–Win Options, *continued*

Handout 87: Step 4: Insist on Using Fair Procedures and Principles

Handout 88: Decision Matrix Tool

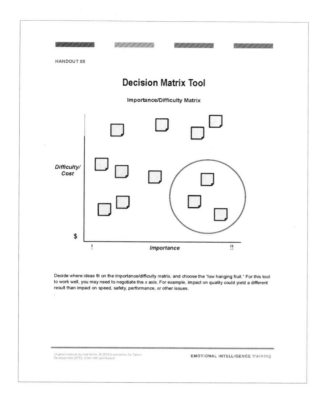

Handout 89: EQuip Yourself for Success: Action Plan

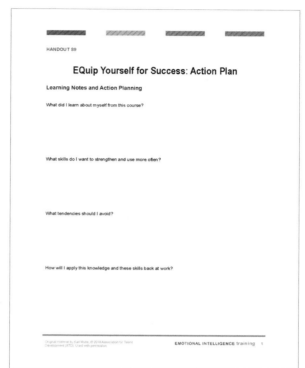

Handout 89: EQuip Yourself for Success: Action Plan, *continued*

What do I want to develop or improve?	Why is it important?

How will I do it?	What values will motivate me to do it?

Dates Applied	I did...	Discoveries

Chapter 14

Online Supporting Documents and Downloads

What's in This Chapter

- Instructions to access supporting materials
- Options for using tools and downloads
- Licensing and copyright information for workshop programs
- Tips for working with the downloaded files

The ATD Workshop Series is designed to give you flexible options for many levels of training facilitation and topic expertise. As you prepare your program, you will want to incorporate many of the handouts, assessments, presentation slides, and other training tools provided as supplementary materials with this volume. We wish you the best of luck in delivering your training workshops. It is exciting work that ultimately can change lives.

Access to Free Supporting Materials

To get started, visit the ATD Workshop Series page: www.td.org/workshopbooks. This page includes links to download all the free supporting materials that accompany this book, as well as up-to-date information about additions to the series and new program offerings.

These downloads, which are included in the price of the book, feature ready-to-use learning activities, handouts, assessments, and presentation slide files in PDF format. Use these files to deliver your workshop program and as a resource to help you prepare your own materials. You may download and use any of these files as part of your training delivery for the workshops, provided no changes are made to the original materials. To access this material, you will be asked to log into the ATD website. If you are not an ATD member, you will have to create an ATD account.

If you choose to re-create these documents, they can only be used within your organization; they cannot be presented or sold as your original work. Please note that all materials included in the book are copyrighted and you are using them with permission of ATD. If you choose to re-create the materials, per copyright usage requirements, you must provide attribution to the original source of the content and display a copyright notice as follows:

© 2016 ATD. Adapted and used with permission.

Customizable Materials

You can also choose to customize this supporting content for an additional licensing fee. This option gives you access to a downloadable zip file with the entire collection of supporting materials in Microsoft Word and PowerPoint file formats. Once purchased, you will have indefinite and unlimited access to these materials through the My Downloads section of your ATD account. Then, you will be able to customize and personalize all the documents and presentations using Microsoft Word and PowerPoint. You can add your own content, change the order or format, include your company logo, or make any other customization.

Please note that all the original documents contain attribution to ATD and this book as the original source for the material. As you customize the documents, remember to keep these attributions intact (see the copyright notice above). By doing so, you are practicing professional courtesy by respecting the intellectual property rights of another trainer (the author) and modeling respect for copyright and intellectual property laws for your program participants.

ATD offers two custom material license options: *Internal Use* and *Client Use*. To determine which license option you need to purchase, ask yourself the following question:

Will I or my employer be charging a person or outside organization a fee for providing services or for delivering training that includes any ATD Workshop content that I wish to customize?

If the answer is yes, then you need to purchase a *Client Use* license.

If the answer is no, and you plan to customize ATD Workshop content to deliver training at no cost to employees within your own department or company only, you need to purchase the *Internal Use* license.

Working With the Files

PDF Documents

To read or print the PDF files you download, you must have PDF reader software such as Adobe Acrobat Reader installed on your system. The program can be downloaded free of cost from the Adobe website: www.adobe.com. To print documents, simply use the PDF reader to open the downloaded files and print as many copies as you need.

PowerPoint Slides

To use or adapt the contents of the PowerPoint presentation files (available with the Internal Use and Client Use licenses), you must have Microsoft PowerPoint software installed on your system. If you simply want to view the PowerPoint documents, you only need an appropriate viewer on your system. Microsoft provides various viewers at www.microsoft.com for free download.

Once you have downloaded the files to your computer system, use Microsoft PowerPoint (or free viewer) to print as many copies of the presentation slides as you need. You can also make handouts of the presentations by choosing the "print three slides per page" option on the print menu.

You can modify or otherwise customize the slides by opening and editing them in Microsoft PowerPoint. However, you must retain the credit line denoting the original source of the material, as noted earlier in this chapter. It is illegal to present this content as your own work. The files will open as read-only files, so before you adapt them you will need to save them onto your hard drive. Further use of the images in the slides for any purpose other than presentation for these workshops is strictly prohibited by law.

The PowerPoint slides included in this volume support the three workshop agendas:

- Two-Day Workshop
- One-Day Workshop
- Half-Day Workshop.

For PowerPoint slides to successfully support and augment your learning program, it is essential that you practice giving presentations with the slides *before* using them in live training situations. You should be confident that you can logically expand on the points featured in the presentations and discuss the methods for working through them. If you want to fully engage your participants, become familiar with this technology before you use it. See the sidebar that follows for a cheat sheet to help you navigate through the presentation. A good practice is to insert comments into PowerPoint's notes feature, which you can print out and use when you present the slides. The workshop agendas in this book show thumbnails of each slide to help you keep your place as you deliver the workshop.

NAVIGATING THROUGH A POWERPOINT PRESENTATION	
Key	**PowerPoint "Show" Action**
Space bar or Enter or Mouse click	Advance through custom animations embedded in the presentation
Backspace	Back up to the last projected element of the presentation
Escape	Abort the presentation
B or b	Blank the screen to black
B or b (repeat)	Resume the presentation
W or w	Blank the screen to white
W or w (repeat)	Resume the presentation

Acknowledgments

I am blessed by a tremendous cadre of trainers and workshop designers with whom I have had the privilege of working. I am always amazed that I can send out an email at 2:30 in the afternoon asking for a learning activity or an illustration to make a concept more accessible and to make the learning experience more fun, and by 3:00 I have seven replies and 10 great ideas. I know enough about time management to know that I did absolutely nothing to deserve to go that quickly to the top of so many next action lists, but such is the discretionary energy my amazing colleagues so generously give. So, thank you, Dick, Carol Ann, Stephan, Jeff, Bruce, Lou, Tom, Don, Gina, John, Rich, Trish, Leslie, Jim, Elaine, Christie, Ruby, Gwen, Kathleen, Rick, Dave, Bonnie, Susan, Dana, Larry, Jeanne, Harold, Beth, Lisa, and, of course, my brother Mark.

I am thankful to Bruce Christopher and Jeff Feldman. I still remember fondly the process of storyboarding our original EI workshop on Bruce's living room floor. Thank you Jeff for being with me every step of the way, as we converted that original workshop into a book. Jeff has contributed greatly to the many learning activities that are part of this series. Thank you, Cat Russo, for convincing us to turn that book into this workshop series. I am truly sorry that I missed so many deadlines. Also, thank you to Jacki Edlund-Braun for making me look so good. Your editing skills are remarkable. If I could turn you into an app and carry you everywhere I go, I would.

I am grateful to Tom Dearth who has contributed so much to my understanding of how to set up a good learning activity. Tom's wisdom and design genius is particularly present in the listening activities in this series. Thank you to Lou Russell who has taught me so much about accelerated learning and also about how to use project management tools in soft skill courses.

I am especially grateful to my wife, Jessica, and to my sweet little 5-year-old, Kaitlyn, who both put up with about four months of my traveling and writing. Thank you my two loves for your patience and your support.

About the Author

Karl Mulle is a corporate trainer, coach, and a popular keynote speaker, as well as a psychotherapist in private practice. He has more than 33 years of experience in the design and delivery of energizing and fun programs on human effectiveness. He specializes in developing leaders, building healthy relationships, increasing emotional intelligence, managing diversity, developing communication and presentation skills, managing change, and building effective teams. Karl applies an experiential approach to learning, creatively designing sessions to maximize interaction and self-discovery for businesses, organizations, and associations worldwide. His clients include General Electric, Chevron, Johnson & Johnson, 3M, Citibank, Nielsen, Cigna, the U.S. Food and Drug Administration, and the U.S. Office of Personnel Management.

Karl coauthored *Put Emotional Intelligence to Work: EQuip Yourself for Success* (ASTD 2008, with Jeff Feldman).

Karl holds a bachelor of arts from Cornell University, a master of divinity from Trinity International University, and a master of arts in counseling psychology from Trinity International University.

He has traveled extensively throughout the United States (46 states) and European/Asian countries (31 countries) and resides in Bloomington, Minnesota.

About ATD

The Association for Talent Development (ATD), formerly ASTD, is the world's largest association dedicated to those who develop talent in organizations. These professionals help others achieve their full potential by improving their knowledge, skills, and abilities.

ATD's members come from more than 120 countries and work in public and private organizations in every industry sector.

ATD supports the work of professionals locally in more than 125 chapters, international strategic partners, and global member networks.

1640 King Street
Alexandria, VA 22314
www.td.org
800.628.2783
703.683.8100

HOW TO PURCHASE ATD PRESS PUBLICATIONS

ATD Press publications are available worldwide in print and electronic format.

To place an order, please visit our online store: www.td.org/books.

Our publications are also available at select online and brick-and-mortar retailers.

Outside the United States, English-language ATD Press titles may be purchased through the following distributors:

United Kingdom, Continental Europe, the Middle East, North Africa, Central Asia, Australia, New Zealand, and Latin America
Eurospan Group
Phone: 44.1767.604.972
Fax: 44.1767.601.640
Email: eurospan@turpin-distribution.com
Website: www.eurospanbookstore.com

Asia
Cengage Learning Asia Pte. Ltd.
Phone: (65)6410-1200
Email: asia.info@cengage.com
Website: www.cengageasia.com

Nigeria
Paradise Bookshops
Phone: 08033075133
Email: paradisebookshops@gmail.com
Website: www.paradisebookshops.com

South Africa
Knowledge Resources
Phone: +27 (11) 706.6009
Fax: +27 (11) 706.1127
Email: sharon@knowres.co.za
Web: www.kr.co.za

For all other territories, customers may place their orders at the ATD online store: **www.td.org/books**.

021514562220